Stone, Ronald
Reinhold Niebuhr

WITHDRAWN

REINHOLD NIEBUHR
prophet to politicians

REINHOLD NIEBUHR
prophet to politicians

RONALD H. STONE

NASHVILLE / ABINGDON PRESS / NEW YORK

REINHOLD NIEBUHR: PROPHET TO POLITICIANS

Copyright © 1972 by Abingdon Press

ISBN 0-687-36272-5

Library of Congress Catalog Card Number: 71-172813

Scripture quotations unless otherwise noted are from the Revised Standard Version of the Bible, copyrighted 1946 and 1952 by the Division of Christian Education, National Council of Churches, and are used by permission.

Quotations from the following books by Reinhold Niebuhr, published and copyrighted by Charles Scribner's Sons, are used by permission of the publishers:
Reflections on the End of an Era;
Christian Realism and Political Problems;
The Nature and Destiny of Man;
The Irony of American History.

Quotations from *Leaves from the Notebook of a Tamed Cynic* by Reinhold Niebuhr and published by Willet, Clark & Colby, copyright © 1929 by Reinhold Niebuhr, are used by permission of The World Publishing Company.

Quotations from the article "The Religion of Communism" by Reinhold Niebuhr in the *Atlantic Monthly*, CXLVII (April, 1931), copyright © 1931, by The Atlantic Monthly Company, Boston, Mass., are reprinted with permission.

Quotations from the following articles are reprinted by permission of *Christianity and Crisis* and Reinhold Niebuhr:
"The Blindness of Liberalism" by Reinhold Niebuhr, published in *Radical Religion*, I (Autumn 1936);
"Repeal the Neutrality Act" by Reinhold Niebuhr, published in *Christianity and Crisis*, I (Oct. 20, 1941);
"The Limits of American Power" by Reinhold Niebuhr, published in *Christianity and Society*, XVI (Autumn 1952);
"An interview with Reinhold Niebuhr" by Ronald H. Stone, published in *Christianity and Crisis*, XXIX (March 17, 1969).

SET UP, PRINTED, AND BOUND BY THE
PARTHENON PRESS, AT NASHVILLE,
TENNESSEE, UNITED STATES OF AMERICA

to joann and randall
with love

PREFACE

The agonies of twentieth-century American religious and political life found an interpretor in Reinhold Niebuhr. For over half a century he criticized the illusions of a deceived country and shouldered the burdens of responsible statesmanship. The importance of Reinhold Niebuhr to American religious and political thought and life is generally recognized. This book is an interpretation of his work. It presents an understanding of his thought through examining the sources of his philosophy, the context of his times, and the characteristic way he handled problems. The intellectual biography presented here spans the years 1915-1971, from his graduation from Yale to his death in his home in Stockbridge, Massachusetts. The book touches on many subjects and on many twentieth-century problems. The emphases of the book are on his understanding of American foreign policy and his perspective on religious faith.

The book is not an apology for Reinhold Niebuhr. He needs none, and there are many points of critique in the volume. However, I have not hesitated to counterattack what I have regarded as misplaced criticisms of Niebuhr's thought. Five years of study of his writings have left me more persuaded of the strength and relevance of his thought than I was when I undertook the task.

Various aspects of Niebuhr's thought have been the subjects of many studies. Most of the previous studies have been consulted for this book, and many of them are referred to or criticized in this work. Niebuhr's thought on politics, particularly on foreign policy, has been studied less thoroughly than his contribution to theology. Earlier studies of Niebuhr's thought on international politics have contained certain deficiencies. Most of them were conducted before the evolution of Niebuhr's political philosophy had reached its fullest development. The earlier studies met a need to interpret Niebuhr to the political or theological worlds, but their interpretations have been dated by the continued evolution of his thought. Many studies have erred by oversystematizing

Niebuhr's thought. Authors repeatedly understood well one aspect of Niebuhr (perhaps his Christology, his doctrine of sin, or his doctrine of man) and tried to derive the remainder of his thought from one central doctrine. There is no central principle on which his thought in other areas depends. Too often the chronological development of his thought has not been taken seriously enough. Niebuhr's thought altered significantly through more than half a century of writing, and no interpretation of his thought can neglect the chronology and remain accurate. The inadequacies of existing interpretations of Niebuhr's thought were a major motivation for undertaking this study.

Resources for the study included all of Niebuhr's books; an estimated six hundred occasional pieces (including major articles, forewords, reviews, and editorials); most of the secondary material in books, articles, and reviews; five thousand six hundred pieces of the Niebuhr Papers in the Library of Congress (including correspondence, class notes, manuscripts of speeches, manuscripts for articles, records of meetings, business papers, etc.); taped class lectures and sermons at Union Theological Seminary; the Oral History Research Project manuscript at Columbia University; the recollections of numerous of his colleagues; and many conversations with Reinhold Niebuhr.

Reinhold Niebuhr contributed to the analysis of American foreign policy for over half a century as a Protestant churchman. His thought shows the characteristics of American Protestantism during this period. Though involved in various political parties, with the German underground, and in fulfilling various roles in international politics for the United States government, his vocation was that of a churchman—first a pastor, and then a teacher of theological students.

Niebuhr's drive to comprehend man in all his glory and agony led him into the social sciences, philosophy, and theology, and he contributed significantly to all three fields. His admirers applauded him as the leading American political philosopher, moralist, and theologian of his day. The titles of philosopher and theologian were rejected by him, and he abhorred the title of moralist. The traditional academic disciplines would not contain his energies. When he defined his role in 1965,[1] he chose to regard himself as a social philosopher who taught ethics in Union Theological Seminary. This definition brought together his three central tasks and hinted at a preference for political and social philosophy.[2]

Niebuhr can legitimately be studied from the perspective of theology, ethics, or political philosophy. The three disciplines are woven together in his writing, and no single one can be regarded as fundamental in a sense which would make the other two derivative. This study emphasizes Reinhold Niebuhr as a political philosopher with a specific focus on his thought on American foreign policy. His thought on American foreign policy depended upon and also shaped his broader philosophical treatment of politics. Consideration of his thought on foreign policy involves theological and moral reflection as well as empirical observation, for the most striking feature of Niebuhr's writing on political problems is his custom of examining a given policy problem in the light of the sweep of political philosophy and in the perspective of assumptions about man's purpose and his destiny. This study attempts to correct one-sided theological interpretations of Niebuhr's thought without committing the error of reducing his theology to the level of politics.

The many tributes to Niebuhr's influence as a political philosopher, from both politicians and scholars, leave no doubt of the significance of his contribution in this field. Hans J. Morgenthau has said, estimating Niebuhr's importance, "I have always considered Reinhold Niebuhr the greatest living political philosopher of America, perhaps the only creative political philosopher since Calhoun."[3] Hubert H. Humphrey joined the chorus acclaiming him as a great political philosopher: "No preacher or teacher at least in my time has had a greater impact on the secular world. No American has made a greater contribution to political wisdom and moral responsibility."[4] George Kennan has said of the group

9

tagged by Kenneth Thompson as liberal realists, "Niebuhr is the father of us all." [5]

Particular features of Niebuhr's philosophy require that his thought be approached historically. His writing reflects a tension between immediate political situations and philosophical reflection. For half a century he commented publicly on political problems in journals. Much of his writing was as a political essayist, subject to the exigencies of editorial deadlines. His theoretical works also reflect the current political situation and his own political activities. His epistemology, as well as his avocation as a journalist, required that he continually check general comments against particular events. An understanding of his thought is based upon grasping both the historical situation and his philosophical generalizations. Over the half century of his active political comment, the American political scene, as well as Niebuhr's political philosophy, underwent radical alterations.

In addition to the changes in the political phenomena which Niebuhr studied, the evolution in his thought renders it impossible to present his thought in the shape of a formalized system. The structure of his thought at particular times can be analyzed, but change is so central a feature of his thought that the structure at any one point cannot be regarded as definitive. This study avoids oversystematization by allowing chronology to bear a major part of the burden of organization. The career of Niebuhr, the political philosopher, divides itself chronologically into four periods: the liberal, the socialist, the Christian realist, and the pragmatic-liberal. In each period Niebuhr imposes his own perspective upon the school of thought in which he is most interested. These phases of his thought are not regarded as mutually exclusive. There are elements of Christian realism in his early liberal writings and elements of liberal political philosophy in his most socialist period. Each phase is characterized by the movement of certain concepts of political philosophy from the periphery of his thought to the center, by a solution to the ideal-real issue which differs from the solution of the preceding period, and by

Niebuhr's recognition that his thought in this phase is significantly different from his thought in the preceding period.

The organizing principle underlying the divisions of the study is Niebuhr's definition of and judgment about liberalism in each period. His public career can best be organized around his disillusionment with liberalism, the Marxist critique of liberalism, the most severe theological critique of liberalism, and the rediscovery of liberalism by the pragmatist. His wrestling with his liberal heritage is the most obvious continual thread in Niebuhr's political thought.

A second major thread of continuity is his handling of the relationship of the ideal and the real. It is the issue which continually confuses American policy, and this problem appears in each phase of Niebuhr's political development. He has himself recognized that the central problem of political philosophy is the relationship of man's imaginary communities to the communities in which he lives.[6] The problem appears as a moral and a metaphysical issue in his first book.[7] It is the major concern of his early Christology and a submerged issue in his later christological writing. The relationship of the ideal to the real is apparent: in the perfectionist theme which runs through the ascetic criticism of bourgeois civilization in *Does Civilization Need Religion?* in the radical criticism of parliamentary socialism in *Moral Man and Immoral Society,* in the dialectical criticism of justice and love in *An Interpretation of Christian Ethics,* and in the polarization and interaction of love and prudence which characterize *The Children of Light and the Children of Darkness.* It is seen both in the opposition of communal interests versus personal interests in a 1916 article,[8] and in the major essay of his 1965 book which discusses idealist and realist political theories. Again and again the volumes between his first article and his most recent work return to this problem which reveals the dynamics of Niebuhr's own mind as well as a perennial problem of mankind. This tension within his own thought and his willingness to examine political issues in the context of this puzzling issue have given power and appeal to his

11

political writing. The presence of this problem gives a degree of unity to the shifting perspectives of Niebuhr's political thought, and reference to it provides a link between various stages of his thought.

Niebuhr analyzed problems of American foreign policy for more than fifty years in the light of the tension in his own person between Christian perfectionism and political cynicism. The relationship between these two poles of his thought varies throughout his career. The discovery of these two poles should not obscure the fact that they are submerged in the pressing demands of the contemporary political scene. Niebuhr's mind reveals a passion for the immediate, even though it examines the immediate in a broad perspective. Cynicism and perfectionism, though both present and extremely important, are qualified by empiricism, common sense, and charity.

The first chapter describes the background from which the young Niebuhr came. Chapters two through five discuss the chronological development of his thought. Chapters six and seven discuss his perspective on American foreign policy and the relevance of his understanding of faith.

Thanks for gifts of which I am every day becoming more aware are due to the faculties of Union Theological Seminary and Columbia University's Departments of Religion and Public Law and Government, 1960-1968. John C. Bennett and Roger L. Shinn nurtured me through the ordeal of writing a dissertation and proved to be all a student could hope for in professors. A word of gratitude to W. T. R. Fox for his counsel and rigorous questioning at the time of dissertation defense is in order. James A. Martin, teacher and colleague, encouraged me in my plans to write this book.

My deepest feelings of gratitude are, of course, to my wife, Joann, who translated my rough handwritten manuscript into usable first and second drafts. She also prepared the index. The completion of the project means more time together, farther away from the typewriter. I hope now to make reparations for the neglect of years of graduate education.

Miss Doris S. Liles, a Union Seminary graduate student, was of immense help in preparing the manuscript. She has my best wishes for her thesis on Reinhold Niebuhr and John Dewey. Two secretaries from Pittsburgh Theological Seminary, Mrs. Elizabeth Eakin and Mrs. Clare M. Cashdollar, rushed the manuscript through to its final form, and I am in their debt.

Mrs. June Bingham assisted my research by granting permission for the use of the papers and letters she collected for *The Courage to Change*.

Reinhold Niebuhr, who is the inspiration and the subject of the study, never asked to be spared criticism. He only reminded me that he himself was pleased because as much as he disagreed with his professor, D. C. Macintosh of Yale, he never misrepresented him. I hope I have not misrepresented Niebuhr's thought; it obviously is his thought as understood by me and not by him. He was generous enough to grant permission to be quoted without checking the quotes. Mrs. Ursula Niebuhr has given her life to Reinhold and their common interests in religion, culture, and politics. She has informed Reinhold, edited his work, inspired him, in his sickness nursed and protected him, and most of all loved him. I would have said more about her in the book except for the fact that they have grown together so that her additions or corrections to his work are indistinguishable from his. Decades of a happy marriage and joint intellectual endeavors necessarily obscure their distinctive features. Her interest in the book encouraged me to proceed.

RONALD H. STONE
Pittsburgh

CONTENTS

I. THE EARLY YEARS

The Family Setting

The origins of Reinhold Niebuhr's wisdom lie in the combination of German-Lutheran ancestry and the values of the American heartland. His intellectual saga, to be sure, encompasses the vast range of the Western world's intellectual history and in many ways owes more to the Anglo-Saxon world than to the German. His faith, however, was carefully nurtured in the cradle of German-Lutheran piety. His early attitudes toward politics were set by his father's reaction against German authoritarianism and his appropriation of midwestern egalitarianism and patriotism.

Reinhold Niebuhr's father immigrated to the United States in 1878. Gustav Niebuhr had left his father's farm in Hardissen bei Lage in the northwestern part of Germany. His father had been a substantial landowner, and the son's leaving was not so much the need to seek opportunity elsewhere as to express the seventeen-year-old's reaction against the authoritarianism of his father.

Gustav Niebuhr worked as a hand on the farm of Hummermeyer near Freeport, Illinois, until the farmer, recognizing his religious sensitivities and intellectual abilities, sent him to the denominational school, Eden Theological Seminary, now located in Webster Groves, Missouri.

The Evangelical Synod [1] assigned Gustav Niebuhr to San Francisco. There he met and married the daughter of his senior pastor, Miss Lydia Hosto, a second-generation German-American. Three children were born to the couple in San Francisco. Hulda, the first, though not encouraged by her father in her academic interests, eventually became professor of Christian education at McCormick Theological Seminary of the United Presbyterian Church in the U.S.A. in Chicago. She is particularly remembered as the author of numerous stories for children and as an important leader in the field of Christian education.[2] The second child, Walter, was the only one of the family who did not choose to enter the professional work of the church. He died in 1946 after having made and lost several fortunes in the newspaper and film industries. A third child, Herbert, died in infancy.

The two children born after the couple had moved to Wright City, Missouri, were to dominate the thought of American Christain ethics for four decades. Reinhold arrived shortly after the Niebuhr family moved to Wright City on June 21, 1892. Within two years the family was completed with the birth of Helmut Richard. As professor of Christian ethics at Yale Divinity School, H. Richard Niebuhr was for years regarded by others, particularly the students at Yale and Union Theological Seminary, as his brother's most serious rival for acknowledgment as the leading ethicist in contemporary Christian theology.[3]

Gustav Niebuhr inspired in his son deep admiration and the conviction that the vocation of the pastorate was the most interesting position in town. Reinhold's father read from the Bible every morning in both Hebrew and Greek and conducted a learned ministry which inclined his denominational seminary to offer him a post as a professor.

His father held together his religious and social interests in a harmony which Reinhold always remembered fondly. He has commented to the effect that the sons of pastors live in an atypical religious situation. If the father comes into sharp conflict with the sons, particularly by being overly strict and dogmatic, the sons are likely not to enter the ministry. The reverse is also true however, he claimed, and if a father-pastor exhibits "real grace" in the religious life of the family the son is very likely to enter the ministry.

Reinhold's relationship with his father was warm and trusting. The father sacrificed to provide out of his condition of genteel poverty that characterized the pastorate in the 1890s for some of the boy's whims as well as his necessities. Gustav planned with Reinhold for his moving beyond the confines of midwestern culture by helping him to decide to attend Yale University after Elmhurst College and Eden Theological Seminary. His father died from a diabetes attack in April, 1913, just before he could see Reinhold leave for Yale.

Mrs. Lydia Niebuhr lived to see her son's career fulfilled and the seeds of faith which she had planted grow into volumes of eagerly read theology. Reinhold substituted in his father's final pulpit in Lincoln, Illinois, the summer before leaving for Yale, after his father's death. Lydia moved to Detroit with Reinhold after his graduation from Yale in 1915 and managed the affairs of the parsonage. According to his recollections, she also ran the women's meetings of the parish in Detroit for which he had no taste and became in effect almost an assistant pastor. Lydia lived with Reinhold Niebuhr in New York until his marriage in 1931 to Miss Ursula Keppel-Compton made that arrangement, particularly with the arrival of children, difficult. Eventually Mrs. Lydia Niebuhr returned to the Midwest to live with her daughter, Hulda, at McCormick Theological Seminary in Chicago.

The Niebuhr family provided a secure setting which gave deep religious foundations to all the children. It also imbued them with a fervor for the values of freedom and equality and a high priority to the values of the academic life.[4]

A Yale Liberal

Reinhold Niebuhr's preparation for the ministry began as his father tutored him in Greek. It continued in the little college of the Evangelical Synod. Elmhurst College in Chicago was at the time patterned after the German gymnasium and was designed to serve only pretheological students. It had an excellent program in classical studies but offered very little else. Upon graduation from Elmhurst in 1910, Niebuhr still lacked training in the physical and social sciences. He then attended Eden Theological Seminary, at that time located in St. Louis. He graduated from Eden in 1913 after impressing both teachers and fellow students with unusual intellectual and oral gifts.

Eden Seminary, like Elmhurst College,[5] had rather undiscriminating standards during the years that Reinhold and H. Richard attended it. Reinhold always remembered one professor of New Testament, Dr. Samuel Press, as his Mark Hopkins. Reinhold continued to correspond with Professor Press after leaving Eden, and the letters from Reinhold that Press saved are the best record of his years at Yale.[6] The influence of Dr. Press upon Niebuhr is seen in his continuing deep interest in New Testament studies at Yale. Reflecting upon his intellectual development, he wrote:

> The seminary was influential in my life primarily because of the creative effect upon me of the life of a very remarkable man, Dr. S. D. Press, who combined a childlike innocency with a rigorous scholarship in Biblical and systematic subjects. This proved the point that an educational institution needs only to have Mark Hopkins on one end of a log and a student on the other.[7]

Though Niebuhr had earned a Bachelor of Divinity (B.D.) degree at Eden, he entered Yale in 1913 as a B.D. candidate. Yale had a policy during the years in which it was strengthening its divinity school of admitting candidates who had B.D. degrees from nonaccredited seminaries to another year of study for a Yale B.D. degree. Niebuhr has often humorously remarked that he could not have been admitted to Union Theological Seminary because of its higher standards. The accuracy of such a judgment remains unverifiable, as he never applied.

His arrival at Yale was characterized by the usual fears a young man from the Midwest brings to a prestigious eastern university. He was conscious of his midwestern accent and of his poverty amidst the wealth and sophistication of Yale. He had doubts about the quality of his preparation for Yale. There was, finally, the uneasiness of being a theological student in the midst of a secular university. New Haven itself was rather disillusioning; the campus bore the usual signs of academic leisure and restfulness, but the town was a rather dingy industrial city. The transition from Eden to Yale was marked also by his descent as probably the best student at Eden to that of a graduate of an unknown seminary competing with the graduates of well-known schools at Yale.

Yale's academic life thrilled him; he rejoiced in the written assignments and in the quality of instruction he received. Professors Douglas C. Macintosh in philosophical theology and Frank C. Porter and Benjamin Bacon in New Testament studies particularly impressed him. His B.D. thesis was written on "The Validity of Religious Experience and the Certainty of Religious Knowledge." [8] After completing the year required for the B.D., he applied to the graduate school. The dean rebuffed his inquiries concerning graduate work, but the dean, a German scholar, went back to Germany in the summer of 1914 and got caught up in the events of World War I. A second interview, now with the new dean, Wilbur Cross (to become governor of Connecticut), was more fruitful. Cross admitted Niebuhr as a special student with the stipulation that he would admit him to degree status after he had maintained a straight A average.

He maintained the necessary standards while serving a small congregation in Derby, Connecticut. His work was mainly under the supervision of Douglas C. Macintosh, and he threw himself into philosophical studies with a purpose that was new to him. Professor Macintosh loaned him books from his study and encouraged him to pursue doctoral studies.

He received the M.A. degree in 1915. Several issues inclined him not to pursue the Ph.D. at Yale University. One was a growing dissatisfaction with what seemed to him the unimportant or trivial classification of epistemologies which was the central concern of Professor Macintosh at that time. The other was that for the two years at Yale he had postponed the fulfillment of a pledge to his church to serve in a church after the completion of his studies at Eden. The churches pressured young divinity students then as they do now to involve themselves in the pastorate. The churches feared their best young candidates for the ministry would be diverted into higher education by too many years spent in graduate school. A certain uneasiness with studies at Yale, a sense that he already had two years of training beyond the average minister of the Evangelical Synod, the need to meet the obligation to his church, and finally a sense that he should provide a home for his widowed mother led him to turn his back on higher education and take a pastorate in Detroit.

Two other incidents while at Yale throw light on his future career and development. He won the Church Peace Union's essay contest on the subject of needed developments or initiatives toward world peace.[9] The prize of one hundred dollars was quite welcome to the student with growing debts. While visiting in Lincoln, Illinois, between his two years at Yale, Carl Vrooman, an Assistant Secretary of Agriculture under Woodrow Wilson, offered him a job as secretary. The young student, whose political leanings had been recognized, was also tempted by the salary which was more than he had any chance of attaining through advancement within the Evangelical ministry; but he returned to Yale. At quite an early date Niebuhr found his commitment to religion complemented by a strong political interest.

Niebuhr was deeply influenced by the liberal social thought and theology of Yale University. Though the impact of teachers upon most graduate students is immense, it may be more directly noticed among divinity students and students in the humanities who are explicitly dealing with questions of personality and human value. Niebuhr came to have deep disagreements[10] with Professor Macintosh, but he was never ungrateful, and he was proud even as an elderly gentleman that he had not in his writing misrepresented Douglas Macintosh's thought.

The major extant work of Niebuhr from two years at Yale is "The Contribution of Christianity to the Doctrine of Immortality," his 1915 Master of Arts thesis.[11] It revealed the extent to which the young Niebuhr was a product of the early twentieth-century liberal theology. The purpose of the thesis was to argue that the idea of the immortality of the soul was enriched by Christianity, and that the idea of immortality could be maintained after the Christian claims for the physical resurrection of Jesus were abandoned. The thesis does not fall neatly into either New Testament studies or philosophy of religion, but as a borderline study illustrates the influence of Professors Bacon and Porter in New Testament as well as Macintosh in philosophy of religion.

The thesis gives no hint of its author's future contribution as a social philosopher. It is important in understanding Niebuhr because it establishes his early complete acceptance of the historical-critical method. It also shows that he did not follow the more conservative biblical critics. It makes clear beyond any reasonable doubt that, as a young man, he shared the liberal temper of his time and rejected traditional Christian claims on the basis of their incredibility to the sophisticated mind of his day. It reveals his own positive evaluation of religious optimism. Individualism was stressed in the thesis; the themes of social solidarity, later to become very important in his understanding of the resurrection, were of relatively minor importance in the thesis.

The thesis also indicates Niebuhr's awareness of the threat of death which was later to become a major source of his emphasis upon the finitude of man and the contrast between man's finitude and his claims for himself. In his short thesis he answered affirmatively the query, "Can we still hold to the 'sublime idea' though we are forced to give up the 'sublime event'?" [12] Fifty years later he was still answering the query positively, though many suspected him of betraying his "orthodox" theology by admitting the contingent character of religious symbols.

A Detroit Pastor

The young Yale graduate arrived in 1915 in a city in which the automobile industry was maturing. Henry Ford had displayed the process of mass production at the Panama-Pacific Exposition in San Francisco on February 20, 1915. The process of focusing on Ford's seven principles of power, accuracy, economy, continuity, system, speed, and repetition in the manufacturing process was changing the industrial landscape. Ford was the dominant company with 46.6 percent of the total automobile production in the industry which was rapidly altering Detroit and promising to revolutionize transportation in the country.

Europe was at war in 1915. The United States was piling technological-industrial advance upon advance. The Panama Canal was opened in 1914; the transcontinental telephone lines were connected in January, 1915; by 1915 the country's industrial production equaled the combined product of Germany and Britain.[13]

If culturally the United States was still immature and most of the trend-setters were European, industrially the country had come into the strength of early adulthood and its material accomplishments were impressive. The strengths of the country: vast resources, adaptable and skillful workers, brilliant engineers, the world's leading tool producing plants, and bold resourceful entrepreneurs were concentrated in Detroit and other growing industrial cities.

Detroit was in flux. The pressures of urban life combined with the new pressures of mass production to strain all who participated in the city's life. The city itself is best caught metaphorically in Allan Nevins' description of a Ford manufacturing plant:

> A kinetic plant!—moving, moving, moving; every segment—presses, furnaces, welders, stamps, drills, paint-baths, lathes—in use every minute; not an ounce of metal or a degree of heat avoidably wasted; and the economy in time and labor matching the economy in materials. Fascinating in its intricate intermeshing of activities, it meant a new era.[14]

Reinhold Niebuhr's years in Detroit (1915-1928) were full of the social activism and wrestling with issues of theology which were to characterize his later life. However, in Detroit he was first a pastor. He had left Yale University to come to the Bethel Evangelical Church with some reluctance, under the prodding of his ecclesiastical superiors. Thirteen years in Detroit made him fond of the pastorate and, when he left in 1928 to join the faculty of Union Theological Seminary in New York, he regretted leaving the people of his congregation.

He criticized the failures of both the churches and the ministry but, upon leaving the parish ministry in 1928, he wrote glowingly of the opportunities available to the minister. He saw no other profession which had as many opportunities to serve in different areas as the ministry. He enumerated particularly the chance to influence the lives of children and young people, the opportunity to engage in significant social action, the challenges of race relations in a polyglot city, and the provision of a message of hope to men and women who needed guidance in finding goals worthy of devotion. He took up the task of helping men to separate hope from illusions so that religious faith would not perish with the shattering of illusions. It was a responsibility which no one could completely fulfill, but which required the talents of a social scientist, poet, businessman, and philosopher in one person.[15]

Pages from his diary for the years 1915-1928 were edited and published in 1929 under the title, *Leaves from the Notebook of a Tamed Cynic*. The pages testify to the happiness Niebuhr knew as a pastor and point toward the problems he would wrestle with at a later date. The slender volume, which reveals the young student turned pastor finding his Christian liberalism and innocence challenged by Detroit in the period of its predepression expansion, deserves to be read by all young men contemplating a career in the Christian ministry.

The young minister was surprised to find on his first Sunday in the pulpit that his small chapel was filled. He thought to himself: "Well this isn't a bad congregation, except that the composition is a little curious." His thoughts about the composition of the congregation, which was almost entirely made up of the very elderly and the very young, were clarified after the church service. It was explained to him that only twenty members of the congregation actually belonged to the church while the others, representing the extreme age groups, were guests from a local orphanage and a nearby rest home for elderly people.

The church, which was originally supported financially from the central denominational offices, soon began to revive under the leadership of its young pastor. By the end of Niebuhr's pastorate the membership had increased tenfold from 65 to 656, and its benevolence budget from $75 to $3,889.[16] As the congregation grew, a new church was built. Though the minister was very active in Detroit industrial conflicts and race relations, the church was largely middle class with some workers, a few very wealthy patrons, and a few blacks.

In reflecting upon his preaching, Niebuhr contrasted the temper of his preaching with his work in the study. He asked: "Why is it that when I arise in the pulpit I try to be imaginative and am sometimes possessed by a kind of madness which makes my utterances extravagant and dogmatic?"[17] In his preaching he desired to proclaim a message and to move his audience. He was not averse to exaggerating a point to reach an essential truth. As he preached twice a week, once on Sunday morning and again on Sunday evening, he tried to maintain a balance by seeking to provide inspiration in the morning and education in the evening.[18] His preaching attracted attention, and increasingly he was asked to address college audiences and conferences across the country. His mother, who had moved from Lincoln to Detroit, assumed some of the chores of administration that normally fall upon the minister. Toward the end of his pastorate he was able to obtain assistant pastors who carried part of the ministerial responsibilities as he became more and more in demand as a lecturer.

Niebuhr discovered in Detroit, as have many pastors, that the nuances of doctrine are not so important in the pastor's relationship to his congregation as the attitudes of the pastor toward the people of his church. Though his theology was liberal and his people, particularly the older members at the beginning of his pastorate, were quite conservative, they did not attempt to make life difficult for him. The notes in his diary reveal again and again his deep affection for the persons of his congregation. Niebuhr had a tendency to announce his affirmations boldly and to leave it to his detractors to find the weaknesses of his position if they could. This tendency, which reflects his training as a preacher, was articulated in his diary:

> If preachers get into trouble in pursuance of their task of reinterpreting religious affirmations in the light of modern knowledge I think it must be partly because they beat their drums too loudly when they make their retreats from untenable positions of ancient orthodoxy. The correct strategy is to advance at the center with beating drums and let your retreats at the wings follow as a matter of course and in the interest of the central strategy. You must be honest, of course, but you might just as well straighten and shorten your lines without mock heroics and a fanfare of trumpets.[19]

The tendency to preach boldly his affirmations sometimes confused both his admirers and critics who regarded him as more conservative in theology than he actually was. Most of the sharp conflicts in which he found himself in Detroit were due to his social liberalism rather than theological liberalism. Because he held that religion was in large part a matter of poetic vision and theology was the attempt to organize symbols so that they would express the religious needs of humanity, he could preach creatively to his congregation even without sharing many of the more outdated aspects of their world view.

Henry Ford and His Workers

The experiences of Detroit [20] raised questions in Niebuhr's mind about the adequacy of his liberal theology and social philosophy. The rest of his career was, in a sense, the elaboration of issues raised in Detroit as he saw piety and moral idealism cloak the brutalities of an expanding industrial order. Though the problems were far broader, Niebuhr in his writing focused primarily on Henry Ford's relationship to his workers. Ford became a symbol to Niebuhr of America's technical genius and social ineptitude.

Niebuhr's pastorate occurred during the years (1915-1928) in which Detroit and the Ford Motor Company were both growing rapidly. There had been a period in which Henry Ford's $5/day minimum wage had been an improvement in the salaries paid to industrial workers. By the time Niebuhr left Detroit the relative income of the Ford worker had declined vis à vis General Motor workers and also in relationship to the earlier period in which the $5/day minimum wage was an innovation.

Ford's reputation as a fair employer and a great benefactor of the working man had outlived the facts, and Niebuhr set out to confront the myth of Ford with financial data.[21] Other clergy, writers, and journalists undertook the same task. It was not an easy cause to join if one wished to continue in Detroit in any capacity related to the automobile industry. One of Henry Ford's most ardent critics was Samuel S. Marquis, an Episcopalian clergyman who had been dean of the Cathedral before being asked to head up Ford Motor Company's Sociological Department. Marquis accepted the position as head of the department in 1915 and held it for five years, when the department was phased out by Henry Ford for unknown reasons. The Sociological Department was itself a result of Ford's paternalistic humanitarian side. It was designed to help workers find homes and to provide them with minimal welfare services. It also collected data on the personal lives of the workers and attempted to reinforce middle-class mores upon the laboring class. Marquis himself regarded the demise of the department as a sign of the lessening in importance of humanitarian motives in the company. Niebuhr met Marquis in 1917 and knew him very well for years. After his retirement Marquis published a volume which focused on the ambivalence of Ford's character, detailing both the humanitarian motivations and the brutal side to his personality. He accused Ford of a series of brutal actions and his lieutenants in the industry of worse. The Marquis book was taken out of the Detroit libraries and disappeared from book stores soon after its publication.[22]

Niebuhr's sharpest polemic against the pretensions of Henry Ford appeared in *The Christian Century* in 1926. His name had appeared as an editor on the February 12, 1925 issue, and the magazine had won a reputation in Detroit Motor Company circles for being anti-Ford.

Niebuhr first accused Henry Ford of not supporting the various philanthropic organizations which met the needs of Ford workers. He said that Ford's pretensions of serving justice rather than charity by paying an adequate wage would have earned him the reputation of humanitarian which his public-relations men fostered, if the claims had been true. Niebuhr had done his research, and he documented his charges that in 1926 the actual wage was considerably lower for the average Ford worker than it had been in 1913.[23] He criticized the company for providing no unemployment insurance and for policies of frequent, erratic short-work shifts.

The practice of speeding up the production lines also came under criticism for its tendency to work men so hard that they were physical wrecks before they were fifty years old. Ford's pretensions about relieving delinquency by hiring youth were countered by the argument that the Ford plants had no place for the older men they had worn out.

Niebuhr joined in the speculation which characterized Detroit about Henry Ford's motives.

It is difficult to determine whether Mr. Ford is simply a shrewd exploiter of a gullible public in his humanitarian pretensions or whether he suffers from self-deception. My own guess is that he is at least as naïve as he is shrewd, that he does not think profoundly on the social implications of his industrial policies, and that in some of his avowed humanitarian motives he is actually deceived.[24]

Even though Ford might in some cases have innocent intentions, his policies wreaked havoc among the workers, and many of his personnel policies among the higher executives of the corporation revealed a stark delight in destroying men's careers.

Ernest Liebold, Henry Ford's private secretary, wrote to one of the millionaires in Niebuhr's congregation who had, in the past, manufactured parts as a subcontractor for Ford automobiles. Liebold pressed the retired manufacturer to obtain a retraction from the young, well-intentioned, but of course misguided minister. Years later, Niebuhr was amused that Liebold apparently suffered under the impression that the traditionally anti-Ford *Christian Century* had beguiled the young minister into deep water. The fact was that Niebuhr's earlier, unsigned editorials were in large part responsible for the reputation of the journal which was now represented as ensnaring the young minister. Reflecting on the incident decades later, Niebuhr mused:

> The letter, as I remember it, said: "We want to protest against the wholly untrue article on Ford wage policy, written by the pastor of your church. He is no doubt an honest person, but he has fallen in the clutches of the worst anti-Ford journal in the country, *The Christian Century*." Since the charge involved, in part at least, the similarity between the anonymous *Century* correspondence and my article, he was, in effect, accusing me of corrupting myself.[25]

The manufacturer, William J. Hartwig, stood firmly behind his minister, as many other laymen had been unable to do when Ford Motor Company attacked their ministers, and replied that he was sure the minister of his church would retract any item in the article that could be proven untrue.

The membership of the Bethel Church also stood behind its minister when he was one of two ministers in the city who resisted Chamber of Commerce pressure to deny the Sunday evening pulpit to a representative of the American Federation of Labor in 1926. The pressure brought on the ministers of Detroit drew the attention of the *New York World*, and Walter Lippmann gave the incident national attention in his column. Members of the Chamber of Commerce in Niebuhr's church respected the freedom of the pulpit even when they disagreed with the A. F. of L., and they did not really believe their minister would surrender to pressure from the Chamber of Commerce in any case. The A. F. of L. did not prove able to organize the auto workers, and Niebuhr's hopes for the organization of the workers and an annual wage were years from fulfillment when he left Detroit.

Niebuhr had seen severe economic distress in Detroit in 1921 when the Ford plants were shut down for months of retooling after the Model T was no longer competitive. His identification with the workers' plight drove him into the mild socialism of the Social Gospel, but his deep involvement with Marxist theory did not occur or at least appear in his writing until after his move to New York in 1928. A small group including Bishop Charles Williams, the Jewish lawyer Fred M. Butzel, and Niebuhr pushed for an annual guaranteed wage and protection against the whims of Detroit management. In 1926, in a debate with an English preacher named Studdert Kennedy at a student conference, Niebuhr advocated socialistic answers to the problems of modern industry and argued that property the size of Ford Motor Company was in fact a public corporation and should no longer be privately owned. His writing dealt both with the structural aspects of industrial society and with the individual decision-makers, which were inadequate to regulate society in the 1920s. By the time of the 1929 crash, he had moved to an academic environment in New York, and his reaction to the deepening industrial crisis is part of the story of his attraction to Marxism discussed in Chapter III.

Race Relations in Detroit

Racial conflict broke out in the streets of Detroit in 1925. Black immigration from the South had increased the population from 10,000 at the end of World War I to 80,000 in 1925, and the massive migrations still lay ahead.

Niebuhr accepted the chairmanship of the Mayor's Race Committee despite the complaint from some of his fellow pastors that a Christian minister should not cooperate with a mayor with such a shady political record. The vice-chairman of the group was Bishop William T. Vernon of the African Methodist Episcopal Church. Other members of the committee included lawyers, representatives from Ford Motor Company, physicians, and other leaders in Detroit. Fred M. Butzel provided much of the leadership of the committee and became a lifelong friend of Niebuhr. Niebuhr often used Butzel as an example of the vitalities of prophetic Judaism.

The work of the committee was not crowned with success. It will be remembered in the history of Detroit as one of many twentieth-century race relations committees which failed to translate its findings into the needed reforms. The committee did, however, base its recommendations on a study by the Detroit Bureau of Governmental Research, and its findings in 1926 seem quite farsighted given the situation in 1970. The study of Detroit was undertaken in the summer of 1926, and in its report it called for the creation of a permanent race commission to combat prejudice through education and through the exercise of control over public agencies whose practices were relevant to racial discrimination. The report also called for several immediate changes in practice in the municipal government, business, education, welfare agencies, recreational opportunities, and in real estate practice.

The committee found a drop in real estate values in integrating neighborhoods to be a result of fear and not a necessary consequence of integration. Recommendations were made to encourage integrative tendencies in the real estate business and in the financing of house purchases. The need for city agencies to provide equitable services in Negro neighborhoods was recognized. The report of the committee reveals at places a note of paternalism toward blacks; it recommends a plan of education to help them keep their neighborhoods in attractive condition. Someone on the committee even got that recommendation followed by a sentence that violates the organization of the paragraph: "A similar emphasis upon the personal appearance and demeanor of colored people and their children is equally desirable." [26] Probably some conservative housewife on the committee insisted on that sentence, but it is strange to see it in a report of a committee Niebuhr chaired. On the other hand, attitudes toward race have changed abruptly in the last few years, and some of Niebuhr's own writing on race is almost as badly dated. In a 1944 book he suggested the need to give blacks full credit for their native abilities and specifically mentioned only "artistic gifts." [27] The report also put much of the blame for the failure to maintain Negro areas upon Negro groups who were supposedly neglecting the upkeep of their property; it failed to wrestle significantly with white ownership of black-slum housing.

The committee faced forthrightly the racism in the police department and called for the immediate transfer from black[28] neighborhoods of prejudiced police and for intensive efforts to hire more Negro police. The inequity in the administration of justice was noted, but the committee felt it impossible to agree as to the causes of the unfairness. Most of the public services to the Negroes were found to be inadequate and recommendations for changes were made.[29]

In industry, discrimination on the part of both employers and unions was reported, but the committee trusted to the example of the success of nondiscriminatory employers and unions for the promotion of change. Employers were urged to hire more blacks and to promote them, but the lead sentence of that section of the report set the tone: "The progress of the Negro in the industrial life of the city, following the large migrations since the war, has been most creditable." [30] The possibility of the committee saying anything very critical was probably greatly reduced by the presence of the employment officer of Ford Motor Company and the president of Vulcan Manufacturing Company on the committee.

In both education and medical services the committee reported some discrimination and no blacks in important posts in the institutions. Mild recommendations for change were recorded.

The committee studied the churches and recommended several actions. The changes recommended were: (1) the Negro churches should organize an interdenominational organization; (2) the interdenominational agency should combat "irresponsible religious organizations which enjoy a mushroom growth in the city"; [31]

(3) white churches should help Negro churches financially. The report seemed to accept, or at least did not question, the division of the churches into black and white organizations. This section of the report bears the unmistakable marks of having been written by a Negro whose interests resided in the ecclesiastical structure of the black churches. The report gave no hint of the churches' role in combating segregation. The recommendations of the report on the churches were confined to bureaucratic intramural details of only incidental significance to Detroit.

The report by 1970 standards was very mild and innocuous. It did, however, put an official voice of criticism against most of the structures of Detroit. Its proposals for reform, though perhaps inadequate, were stronger than Detroit in 1926 was willing to put into effect. The report was a composite of recommendations of many individuals, and it reveals the mind of a representative group of the establishment of Detroit more clearly than the particular convictions of its chairman.

Detroit brought to consciousness the outlines of the broad problems with which Niebuhr would wrestle for the rest of his career. He worked on the problems of racial strife, economic injustice, and international disorder which are discussed further in the next chapter. He ministered to the personal problems of troubled individuals who sought his counsel. In his own mind he questioned the relevance of Christian faith to the turmoil of society. By the time he left Detroit for New York City in 1928, it was clear to him that somewhere between cynicism and hypocrisy there was a way to articulate the relevance of faith to social man. He set himself the task of seeking to reinterpret the Christian faith so that it could serve man's needs in a technological society.

II. THE DISILLUSIONING OF A LIBERAL

Reinhold Niebuhr's relationship to the broad cultural movement known as liberalism is one of the most interesting and complex aspects of his intellectual development. He became known as one of its most ardent critics, and yet he began and concluded his career as a liberal. His relationship to the philosophy spanned half a century of American intellectual development, and over that period changes took place in Niebuhr, in the phenomenon, and in Niebuhr's definitions of it. Niebuhr encountered various forms of liberalism, sometimes rejecting, sometimes utilizing, sometimes alternately using and rejecting them.

Four major expressions of liberalism are relevant to Niebuhr's thought: political, theological, economic, and trust in moral progress in history. Niebuhr's polemics against liberalism were directed at trust in the evolutionary advance of man over moral problems. Economic liberalism is considered in the next chapter, which analyzes Niebuhr's Marxism. Theological and political liberalism were alternately affirmed and criticized by Niebuhr.

The Shape of Liberalism

Various factors in the cultural milieu and intellectual climate of the century combined to discredit Protestant orthodoxy and to encourage the rise of liberal theology, which dominated the American Protestant theological scene for the first three decades of the twentieth century. Liberal theology was supported by cultural factors which emphasized continuity rather than discontinuity, elevated human reason and discredited revelation, and encouraged the replacement of static categories of life with evolutionary categories.[1] Though there were many types of theological liberalism, it is possible to identify characteristics which applied to the movement in general. Several of these broad themes which were important to Niebuhr include: (1) an emphasis upon the authority of experience; (2) an emphasis on ethics; (3) a recognition of the importance of man's social environment; (4) a confidence in reason; (5) the devaluation of the authority of scripture; (6) the acceptance of the historical investigation of the Christian faith; (7) a regard for a dynamic view of history; (8) an emphasis upon the humanity of Jesus; and (9) a recognition of the importance of toleration.[2] The motifs of the evolutionary view of nature and history, the immanence of God, and the importance of religious experience shaped theological liberalism.

The themes of political liberalism have their roots in the seventeenth century. A body of ideas about freedom and the conditions for securing human freedom were enunciated in the revolt against political and ecclesiastical absolutisms. The Declaration of Independence enshrines the creed of liberalism as it was defined for the revolting colonies. The demands of the Declaration of Independence represent John Locke's expression of man's obligation to struggle for fundamental rights which are his as man. The Bill of Rights expresses another of its themes, that freedom is guaranteed only when the powers of government are restricted. Leading representatives of liberalism, understood as the attempt to secure and guarantee the widest possible degree of human freedom, include figures as different as John Locke, John Milton, John Stuart Mill, Edmund Burke, Tocqueville, Benjamin Constant, Voltaire, Montesquieu, Thomas Jefferson, and James Madison.

The term *liberal*, used in this sense, gained currency only in the early part of the nineteenth century. It is an older term than *socialist*, but of about the same vintage as *radical*.[3] The idea of liberty, as known in the West and given classical expression in Locke, is connected with the emergence of the nation-state, the rise of the bourgeoisie, and the proliferation of religious sects. The Old World produced the philosophical expressions of liberty as a protest against traditional institutions, but the ideas were more nearly fulfilled in the New World where the traditional institutions were not so prestigious.

Prior to World War I, liberalism became identified in American political life with the New Freedom of Woodrow Wilson's first term in office. The conceptions of the 1912 campaign were turned into a legislative program designed to encourage the rising bourgeois American. With his nearly complete dominance of Congress, Wilson was able to revise tariffs downward, to revamp the banking and credit system, to pass a farm act, to pass the Clayton Act to regulate trusts, to create the Federal Trade Commission, to exempt labor unions from antitrust suits, to reform the working conditions on the railways, and to pass a compensation law for the Civil Service. Wilson's domestic reforms, though substantial, were not radical; they were rooted in a movement to preserve American institutions. With liberalism enshrined in the Constitution, its American forms had an inevitably conservative tone.

Wilson's domestic reforms were frustrated by the entry of the United States into the war. Wilson tried valiantly but unsuccessfully to avoid entrance into the war, but having entered reluctantly he justified it to the American people and to himself. Wilson's Fourteen Points reflected the long-standing liberal principles of consent of the governed and respect for the organized opinion of mankind. The discontinuity between the liberal rhetoric of the war and its realities made a profound and lasting impression upon the young Reinhold Niebuhr.

Niebuhr's style has obscured his debt to liberalism. His writing reveals a homiletic predilection for exaggeration and simplification. The very vigor of his polemic often leaves the impression that he is rejecting a whole school of thought when his concern is to correct distortions within the school. Further, he concentrates his polemic on positions which he regards as possible alternatives to his own position. In reflecting upon the publication of pages from his diary, he wrote: "The author is not unconscious of what the critical reader will himself divine, a tendency to be most critical of that in other men to which he is most tempted himself." [4]

Niebuhr characteristically isolates cultural traits which he regards as central to complex movements. He refuses to be deterred by trivia or to worry about the complex development of a particular historical idea. Rather, he sees various cultures as possessing certain unifying ideas which can be isolated, abstracted, and compared with the unifying ideas of other cultures. The unifying idea, or "principle of ultimate meaning," in modern civilization is historical optimism. The historical optimism of the liberal, bourgeois, democratic culture contrasts both with classical and Christian concepts of history. According to Niebuhr, the classical view consigned history to nature's cycles of rebirth, growth, and death and found meaning only in a postulated realm of eternal ideas or a Stoic escape from the vicissitudes of history. The Christian view regarded history rather statically, not recognizing adequately the phenomenon of social change, and taught that history could be fulfilled only eschatologically. The modern liberal view recognizes growth and social evolution, but dismisses the Christian hope of eschatological fulfillment as illusion and declares that the meaning of history is found within history itself. History, or the evolutionary process, will usher in a new world of the mature man living in a world of nature which he has adapted to serve his ends.

Niebuhr's method of isolating a central trait of a movement has enabled him to criticize liberalism at one of its weakest points, its confidence in moral progress in history. On the other hand, his exposure of the optimism of modern man often led him to equate liberalism and optimism and to attack liberalism when the illusion he wanted to criticize was sentimental optimism. Niebuhr has recognized this tendency to over-generalize in a reply to criticism from Daniel D. Williams.[5] The liberalism against which Niebuhr directed his polemics consisted of the illusion of moral progress, which he found in very diverse forms in Leibnitz, Herder, Kant, Hegel, Mill, Spencer, Darwin, Marx, Comte, Condorcet, McConnell, and Dewey. Liberalism for Niebuhr necessarily included an illusion of optimism, and the illusion became

38

the central theme in Niebuhr's attacks upon it. A passage from Niebuhr's first book attacking liberalism reveals optimism to have been the real object of his polemic. "Modern liberalism is steeped in a religious optimism which is true to the facts of neither the world of nature nor the world of history." [6]

What Niebuhr means by liberalism has been obscured by his polemics against historical optimism. Nevertheless, he has recognized many meanings of liberalism. In its broadest sense it is synonymous for Niebuhr with the democratic protest against feudal society. Its purpose is to remove the traditional forms of restraint and to stress individual liberty. It came to be identified with the opposing doctrines of laissez-faire economics and state regulation of capital. It is not the social policy of the French Enlightenment which Niebuhr castigates when he attacks liberalism so much as it is the optimistic philosophy of life which supported these policies in their battle against traditional restraints.

The French Enlightenment was "liberal" in its social policy in the sense that it championed all the extensions of political power and freedom from political control of economic interprise which characterized the whole middle-class movement in its struggle with the feudal past. But it also had a total philosophy of life based on confidence in the perfectibility of man and on the idea of historical progress.[7]

Though he often granted that there were variations in the philosophy of liberalism (particularly between the secular and religious liberals), Niebuhr stressed their common features. He once posited a liberal creed, the six articles of which he contended represented liberalism, in the special sense of a total optimistic philosophy of life.

Some of the articles in the credo are:
a. That injustice is caused by ignorance and will yield to education and greater intelligence.
b. That civilization is becoming gradually more moral and that it is a sin to challenge either the inevitability or the efficacy of gradualness.
c. That the character of individuals rather than social systems and arrangements is the guarantee of justice in society.

39

d. That appeals to love, justice, good-will and brotherhood are bound to be efficacious in the end. If they have not been so to date we must have more appeals to love, justice, good-will and brotherhood.

e. That goodness makes for happiness and that the increasing knowledge of this fact will overcome human selfishness and greed.

f. That wars are stupid and can therefore only be caused by people who are more stupid than those who recognize the stupidity of war.[8]

This creed is a caricature of liberalism, but it represents six errors Niebuhr has ascribed to it, against which he set his new publication, *Radical Religion,* in 1936. Niebuhr heaped scorn upon this version of liberalism, even defining it as a form of blindness.

Liberalism is in short a kind of blindness. . . . It is a blindness which does not see the perennial difference between human actions and aspirations, the perennial source of conflict between life and life, . . . the torturous character of human history.[9]

The Great War, Disillusionment, and Pacifism

The importance of World War I to Reinhold Niebuhr's thought can hardly be overestimated. It is the first and most important example of Niebuhr's thought being adjusted so that it could more adequately interpret current events in international politics.

Before the entry of the United States, Niebuhr regarded the war as a result of the economic egoism of the European nations. It revealed their political blindness and contained no promise of renewal for the European political situation.[10] The Great War was being fought over petty issues, requiring disproportionate sacrifices from ill-led peoples.

Niebuhr's position changed with the entry of the United States into the conflict. His political liberalism and his American nationalism combined to elicit his somewhat reluctant support for the war. He was alternately drawn toward and repelled by the pacifist opponents of the war, and consistently repelled by clergy who were eager to make the war a holy cause.

The young Niebuhr was enthusiastically in favor of Wilson's liberal foreign policy. Wilson had entered the war reluctantly, but once in the conflict he interpreted it in terms of a crusade for a new political order. His Fourteen Points, and particularly the emphases upon freedom of the seas, League of Nations, disarmament, abolition of secret diplomacy, and respect for the consent of the governed, appealed to Niebuhr and helped him shed his reservations about the war. Given the fact of United States participation in the war, Niebuhr fixed his attention upon the proclaimed goals of the war and repressed earlier insights concerning the petty economic and political motivations behind the struggle.

Nationalism was the second major factor which prompted Niebuhr's support of the war. Self-consciously regarding himself as a member of an immigrant minority, he judged that the United States as a young nation was entitled to protect its unity. He saw many Germans harboring sentiments of resentment toward the United States and romanticizing the Kaiser; Niebuhr sharply attacked what he regarded as reluctant citizenship on the part of the German-American community. He deplored the conservatism of most German-Americans, attributing it partially to their peasant-class origins which had excluded them from the German universities and partially to the fact that they had emigrated prior to the rise of progressive Germany. He argued that the German-American had served America well only where the interests of the country coincided with his own personal interest, particularly in business. The great moral, political, and religious questions had aroused no great interest on the part of the German-Americans.[11] Niebuhr contrasted the Jewish contribution to progressive social reform with the failure of the German-Americans. The one activity which the German-Americans had undertaken as a community was opposing prohibition.[12] His strong resentment of the provincialisms of his immigrant group, coupled with his deep sense of patriotism, made it impossible for him with his German background to define himself in opposition to the United States. He felt that opposition to a country's war efforts should

41

be expressed only on the "basis of an unmistakably higher loyalty." He regarded most German dissent as showing baser motives, and he could not associate himself with the dissenters. His attack upon those German-Americans who hid their German nationalism under the cloak of pietistic pacifism gave indications of his later polemics against using religious beliefs to cover political programs. The tension between his hatred of war and the peculiar position in which he found himself was expressed poignantly in his diary.

> Out at Funston I watched a bayonet practice. It was enough to make me feel like a brazen hypocrite for being in this thing, even in a rather indirect way. Yet I cannot bring myself to associate with the pacifists. Perhaps if I were not of German blood I could.[13]

The Versailles conference shook Niebuhr's liberal hopes for a better order, and he came to regard Wilson as the typical product of the manse who trusted too much in the power of words. In 1919 it appeared to him that Lloyd George and Clemenceau were determining the peace settlement, restricting Wilson's contribution to an ideological one.[14] Still he hoped that the ideals being announced would eventually mold reality even if at present they were being used cynically as ideology.

The hopes of 1919 went unfulfilled, and by 1923 Niebuhr was disillusioned with Wilsonian diplomacy. He regarded the war as a contest for power dependent upon economic interest and the caprice of the statesmen.[15] He regretted his defense of the war effort on the basis of Wilson's reforming principles. His cynicism about the lofty ideals with which he had justified World War I was completed by observations in 1923 of the French vengeance on the Germans. While in Germany that year he resolved to have nothing to do with "the war business" and associated himself with the pacifists. His position is not surprising in view of the fact that, once hostilities ceased, the major factors which had evoked his support of the war dissolved. After the war even a German-American could be a pacifist without seeming disloyal to the

United States. Niebuhr's disillusionment with Wilsonian idealism deprived military policies of their moral supports. These two developments facilitated Niebuhr's return to pacifism.

Niebuhr's declaration of pacifism reflected his growing interest in emphasizing the conflict between the gospel and the world. Loyalty to the gospel meant a break with the world's values. In his view, the "easy optimism" of his youth and of the nineteenth century was discredited.[16] In 1923, the perfectionist Christian and the cynical observer of the political scene were united in Niebuhr, the pacifist. One of the great evils of the moral obfuscation of World War I was the enthusiasm with which the church supported the slaughter. Niebuhr resolved not to find himself in that position again, and he turned his investigations upon the church's social teaching.

Does Civilization Need Religion?

Niebuhr's growing awareness in the 1920s of a gulf separating Christianity and civilization was not shared by all social reforming Christians. The mood of the liberal-Protestant churches in the years following the war was generally one of confidence in the union of righteousness and power.[17] Churchmen had urged the war in moral terms, and successful prosecution of the war seemed to vindicate their preaching. A sense of victory at the armistice, a victory in the struggle for prohibition, and the great success of Protestant fund-raising programs patterned on the wartime bond drives buoyed the Christian reformers' hopes for the appearance of a new social order.

The irrelevance of the church to the industrial order of Detroit [18] combined in his thinking with the vindictive peace of Versailles to encourage the apprehension of a disjuncture between Christianity and civilization. Power and righteousness were not simply united. Niebuhr's 1927 volume, *Does Civilization Need Religion?* reflected this developing polarization of might and right in his thought.

Does Civilization Need Religion? represents an intermediate stage in the development of Niebuhr's political philosophy. It is not as thoroughly realistic as his mature writings, nor does it reflect the mastery of political theory which occurred later. It represents the thought of Niebuhr in his pre-Augustinian and pre-Marxist periods. *Does Civilization Need Religion?* attacked "sentimental optimism" but avoided a decisive break with liberalism.[19]

The disillusionment derived from postwar developments in international politics and industry was reinforced by a sense of the inevitable failure of man's hopes and aspirations which Niebuhr had drawn from Unamuno and Spengler. He combined Unamuno's focus on the mortality of all men with Spengler's critique of the hopes of liberal culture. He attempted to resist Spengler's conclusion that only a defiant courage in the face of the decline of Western civilization was possible. The cynicism which grew easily out of Spengler's analysis was inadequate. There still were resources for renewal. Religion[20] contained resources for the renewal of Western civilization, but tapping these resources was more difficult than the liberals had realized. He assumed with Ernst Troeltsch that Christianity was fated to be the chief source of spiritual idealism for Western culture.

Niebuhr's hopes that religion could become a source of social renewal did not depend on an optimistic evaluation of the strength of religion. He saw religion beset by many problems and interpreted the cultural drift toward secularization as a threat to the existence of religion. Yet Niebuhr could not imagine religion disappearing; for him it was an essential defense of personality against the attacks of a seemingly hostile world. Religion, according to Niebuhr, defended personality in the realms of metaphysics and ethics. Properly equipped for its task, religion could provide man with an assurance that his world is not ultimately hostile to his best purposes. and it could also help him to make the social world more amenable to the pursuit of his best purposes. Niebuhr's first book assumes a Social Gospel standpoint, examines the malaise of contemporary society, and asks what resources in religion are relevant to the reconstruction of that society. The volume is full of unresolved tensions; its author, though aware of disjuncture between the values of an increasingly secular civilization and traditional religion, had not yet reached a position which could free him from his liberalism, which presupposed a great deal of continuity between religion and politics. His doubts about the metaphysical and ethical adequacy of traditional religion were recorded in the most explicitly metaphysical writing of Niebuhr's career.

The impetus behind the chapter entitled "A Philosophy for an Ethical Religion" in *Does Civilization Need Religion?* was Niebuhr's concern to develop an ethic which would encourage action while avoiding illusion. The metaphysical reflection in the chapter was subservient to the concern for ethics. The contrast between the ideal and the real was, in its origins, an ethical problem for Niebuhr.[21] This contrast, stemming from man's visions of brotherhood as opposed to the squalid communities he builds, became a model for Niebuhr's Christology, political theory, and metaphysics. Niebuhr revealed no distaste for metaphysics in this work and argued specifically that the development of an adequate metaphysics was next in importance to the development of an adequate ethic for the apologetic task of the church. Metaphysics and ethics depended on each other. The metaphysical assumption that the universe was not destructive of all the values of personality encouraged ethical action. The achievement of moral man in turn prompted men to consider that the universe was not foreign to personality. Niebuhr did not carefully refine his understanding of metaphysical dualism. He did not mean to advocate total opposition between God and the universe, spirit and matter, good and evil, or man and nature. What he was concerned to establish was that the creative purpose met resistance in the universe and that, though the ideal was present in the real, it was also contrasted with it.[22]

Drawing upon Whitehead, Niebuhr regarded Christianity's metaphysical untidiness and tendencies toward pluralism as more inclusive of the facts of existence than monism. Niebuhr did not enter into exhaustive metaphysical analysis, but he identified himself with William James's pluralism and Whitehead's doctrine of continual creation. He regarded the latter's discussion of God as the principle of concretion as a justification for religious belief: "In other words the faith of religion in both the transcendence and immanence of God is given a new metaphysical validation." [23]

Niebuhr found little affinity between the God of a robust theism and the all-knowing Absolute of monistic philosophers which he regarded as primarily an attempt to solve the epistemological problem. God was active in the structures of the world and suffered at the hands of the world. Niebuhr regarded his dualism as metaphysically sound and close to the naïve religious faith in the Bible. With William James he regarded the Absolute as destructive of practical effort to reform the world.

The Hebrew prophets drew much of their religious genius, Niebuhr believed, from a sense of the struggle between good and evil, as did Jesus. Though the capitulation of the church to Greek philosophy accentuated the countertendency to monism, the dualistic elements were preserved. Dualism helped religion in the fulfillment of its two great functions by recognizing the seriousness of the moral struggle while preserving hope for a victory over the struggle. Dualism as used by the prophets and Jesus prompted men to repent of their sins, but it also encouraged men to hope for redemption from them.[24]

Early Christology and Dualism

Does Civilization Need Religion? reveals the transmutation of the metaphysical dualism into christological symbols. In later writings, Niebuhr often connected his ethics with theological symbols, but nowhere else is the metaphysical basis for these symbols so clear.

The interpreter who regards Niebuhr's Christology as central to his thought must explain the lack of a developed Christology in the early writings, Niebuhr's own claim that Christology was elaborated only in connection with an analysis of the human situation,[25] and many omissions and obvious shortcomings quickly apparent to theologians. Paul Lehmann has traced the development of Niebuhr's Christology and concluded that it is the key to understanding Niebuhr.[26] Still, Lehmann has described the early Christology as elusive and noted that Niebuhr's contemporaries did not recognize Christology as the center of his thought. This failure on the part of Niebuhr's contemporaries, Lehmann argued, was due to an "oversight" of Niebuhr's. This "oversight," which is Lehmann's principal objection to Niebuhr's Christology, is that it is not adequately trinitarian; ". . . it is in the last analysis binitarian," resulting in the cross being "not adequately apprehended and interpreted as *operative* wisdom and power."[27] Niebuhr's writing as a whole displays little interest in the two-nature, trinitarian, or filioque controversies which have been the classical problems of Christology.

The tendency toward binitarianism which Lehmann discovered is not an "oversight"; rather it is a deliberate tendency in Niebuhr's work. Consideration of this tendency as it first appeared will reveal that Niebuhr was more concerned with the conflict between good and evil than with elaborating Christology. Rather than being a thinker who ignored serious issues at the heart of his thought, as Lehmann portrayed him, he is a thinker who used christological symbols to express the dualism which he considered essential to a vigorous ethic. Reference to *Does Civilization Need Religion?* indicates that Niebuhr regarded the doctrines of the trinity, incarnation, and atonement as expressions of the fundamental dualism which an adequate morality required:

In the early Christian church the naïve dualism of Jesus was given dramatic and dynamic force through his deification, so that he became, in a sense, the God of the ideal, the symbol of the redemptive force in life which is in conflict with evil. Since no clear distinction was made between the spirit of the living Christ and the indwelling Holy Ghost, the doctrine of the trinity was, in effect, a symbol of an essential dualism.[28]

The doctrine of the atonement also symbolizes this essential dualism:

> No mechanical or magical explanations of the significance of the crucifixion have ever permanently obscured the helpful spiritual symbolism of the cross in which the conflict between good and evil is portrayed and the possibility as well as the difficulty of the triumph of the good over evil is dramatized.[29]

Treating christological assertions as symbols of a metaphysical and ethical dualism was not new to Niebuhr in 1929. Four years earlier the discovery that the cross symbolized the essential dualism of human life had revitalized the symbol of the cross for him. This 1925 statement, which connects the rediscovery of the atonement with dualism, is not fundamentally different from later statements about the cross.

> It was only a few years ago that I did not know what to make of the cross; at least I made no more of it than to recognize it as a historic fact which proved the necessity of paying a high price for our ideals. Now I see it as a symbol of ultimate reality. . . . It is because the cross of Christ symbolizes something in the very heart of reality, something in universal experience that it has its central place in history. Life is tragic and the most perfect type of moral beauty inevitably has at least a touch of the tragic in it. Why? That is not so easy to explain. But love pays such a high price for its objectives and sets its objectives so high that they can never be attained. There is therefore always a foolish and a futile aspect to love's quest which give it the note of tragedy.[30]

Niebuhr's Christology developed beyond its fragmentary presentation in *Leaves from the Notebook of a Tamed Cynic* and *Does Civilization Need Religion?* It received its most complete elaboration in the 1939 Gifford Lectures. The dualistic background of his Christology was less obvious in this later writing, but the emphasis upon the Christ as a powerless ideal destroyed by the powers of the real world survived.

Niebuhr misunderstood Lehmann's criticism that he had not done justice to the mighty acts of God.[31] He thought the criticism was directed at his use of myth, when in fact the criticism was directed at a failure to understand the cross "as operative wisdom

48

and power." Niebuhr could not so understand the cross, because he first apprehended its significance as the very powerlessness of the ideal in the real world. This tension of the ideal and the real is constitutive of the shape of his political thought throughout his career.

Political Communities and Their Corruption

Niebuhr's analysis of group egoism developed as his Wilsonian liberalism dissolved under the pressures of post-Versailles interpretations of World War I. His theoretical handling of the corruption of political communities was shaped, as were most of his other insights to some extent, by his interpretation of the Great War. Between 1915 and 1928 he evolved from one "trying to be an optimist without falling into sentimentality" to "a realist trying to save myself from cynicism." [32] Throughout the period, his thought returned to the analysis of the ethical potentiality in group action. The answers he derived in this period did not remain satisfactory to him, but they did point to the structure of his later thought.

Niebuhr's second article[33] dealt with the conflict between the aspirations of the modern state and the aspirations of the individual. Focusing on the nations of Europe destroying Western civilization, he regarded both the mass grave and the common uniform as symbolic of the destruction of individualism by nationalism. The mass grave was particularly tragic because the ends for which men were being sacrificed were generally not important to them. The primary causes of the war were regarded as economic. Possible economic gains for the nation were not worthy of the sacrifice of individuals. The moral conscience of modern man transcended the nations, but the power of the nation forced individuals into common uniforms regardless of their individual aspirations. In a spirit of individualistic-universalistic protest against the claims of the nation he declares, "He [modern man] is a citizen of the world." [34]

Though Niebuhr recognized that nations were self-serving and narrowly pursuing economic self-interest, his underlying idealism was apparent. He hoped that, if nations were going to sacrifice men, they would find causes which justified the sacrifice. While not urging Wilson into the war, he revealed his openness to idealistic propaganda or policies. "Man is not unwilling to make sacrifices, but he has never longed more for issues that will hallow his sacrifices and make them worth while." [35]

The failure of Wilson's attempt to harness liberal idealism and nationalism drove Niebuhr to emphasize the egoism of the nation-state and to doubt the possibility of its policies transcending self-interest. In his growing disillusionment with liberalism, he occasionally evoked realism, although its shape remained far from clear. For example, in 1925 he rejected as liberal a tenet of political philosophy which he later would affirm as one of the cornerstones of political realism.

> The effort of liberalism to preserve peace between warring classes and nations by pitting self-interest against self-interest was bound to fail. It only served to aggravate the fears and hatreds which the groups and nations had for one another. The Great War came to reduce the whole philosophy of unrestrained self-interest and undisciplined power to an absurdity. [36]

By 1926 he wrote that Western civilization was completely secularized and its dominant motives were beyond the reach of ethical control. [37] In 1927 he felt that if the egoism of groups could not be morally qualified one would be driven to cynicism. [38]

Niebuhr regarded as almost impossible the task of persuading a nation to surrender its national interests for the sake of the larger society. He could not accept prudence as an adequate guide to statecraft, for World War I demonstrated how self-defeating were the counsels of political prudence. Given the situation of international anarchy, the formation of prewar alliances of the Triple Entente and the Triple Alliance were prudent actions. However, the dynamics of the alliances themselves were partially responsible for casting Europe into war. He argued for the interaction of rational and religious considerations to provide a basis for the qualification of blind national interest. He saw clearly the political nature of the problems of international politics, but his lingering idealism prevented him from imaginatively proposing political solutions. The conclusions of *Does Civilization Need Religion?* were not a permanent stopping place for Niebuhr; an article written in 1928 [39] indicates that, within a year, he had retreated from some of its positions.

Niebuhr took an antiworld government position which he was to develop and refine throughout his career.[40] Governments presupposed societies, and the most glaring fact of the international scene was the lack of an international society with social substance. He feared that international courts would inevitably be biased toward the status-quo nations that benefited from law and order.[41]

Niebuhr regarded international politics as plagued by the counsels of sentimentalists and cynics. Idealists who did not have a due respect for the difficulty of judging politics morally were of little help to the renewal of society; cynics who were lost in despair could not make recommendations for improvement. He pointed to the problem, but at this point in his career he lacked the resources for solving it. His failure to utilize the balance-of-power concept, which he had rejected as liberalism, and his continuing hope of transforming international politics denied him the intellectual resources he sought. He had learned the wisdom of the serpent, but that very wisdom prevented him from fully exploiting creative possibilities within traditional power politics or the innovations of international organization. He utilized the innocence of the dove, i.e., a hope for a transcendence of national interest, but this innocence prevented him from seeing the possibilities of creatively expanding the concept of national interest. The polarity between the ideal and the real was contained within his thought by 1927, but the tension between the two required further development before the mature political philosophy of Reinhold Niebuhr would appear.

Conclusion

Reinhold Niebuhr's deepening disenchantment with liberalism from his liberal Master of Arts thesis, through the merging of nationalism and liberalism in World War I, to its failure to express the realities of politics and the ideals of the religious man has been traced in this chapter. The disintegration of liberalism has been seen in his recognition of the need to account for the tragic element in history, in the dualism of his metaphysics, and in his analysis of the corruption of political communities.

The critique of liberalism deepened rapidly after the 1927 publication of *Does Civilization Need Religion?* In 1928 Niebuhr polemicized:

> This is the confession of a tired radical. I hope I will not remain tired. Time may give me new enthusiasms and save me from premature senility. But just now I am fed up. I am fed up with liberals, with their creeds, their idiosyncracies and their attitudes.[42]

But the critique was to go even further. In the 1930s he attacked liberalism from a Marxist perspective and in the early 1940s he turned an Augustinian-inspired theology against it.

Liberalism had failed partially because of its easy prostitution at the hands of nationalism. Niebuhr would continue to develop his political thought in relationship to American needs, but he never again was as uncritical a patriot as he had been during World War I. He kept a watchful eye on the German national scene; as early as 1924 he began to warn the American public of the poison of national socialism in Germany.[43] In the 1930s he was to hope in vain for an increasing awareness of class consciousness to restrain national egoism. Nationalism had become the dominant religion of modern man, and the search for ways to modify its force was to be one of his major preoccupations.

This chapter discussed how Niebuhr's major polemics against liberalism were directed at its too easy equation of history and progress. The attack took both theological and political forms and forced Niebuhr to express various types of dualism in discussing the social situation in religious terms. He stated his critique of the tradition in theological terms: "To identify God with automatic processes is to destroy the God of conscience; the God of the real is never the God of the ideal." [44]

The failure of his liberalism left Niebuhr without a body of political doctrine with which he could identify. His experience in the industrial conflict in Detroit, a growing awareness of the inadequacies of the Social Gospel, and contacts with the religiously inspired British socialists led him into socialism in the 1930s. The development of and disengagement from his socialism is the theme of the next chapter.

III. THE RISE AND FALL OF THE SOCIALIST ALTERNATIVE

The primary response of Reinhold Niebuhr to socialism occupied the 1930s and served as a transition stage in his move from liberalism to realism. Elements of socialism, considered by Niebuhr during that decade to be the most attractive political philosophy, are present in his earlier writing. His teacher at Yale, Douglas C. Macintosh, had recognized values in Marx's social philosophy and recommended them to his students.[1] His mentor and guide in political action in Detroit was the Episcopal Bishop Charles D. Williams who, while favoring the Single Tax of Henry George and hoping for socialist legislation, deplored class consciousness.[2] His work in Detroit had involved him in the industrial struggles of the 1920s, though not deeply in socialist theory. Niebuhr's association with the Social Gospel movement in the 1920s had left him with the mild form of socialism advocated by representatives of its progressive center.

Not until the depression and his teaching experience at Union Theological Seminary[3] did Niebuhr wrestle with socialism in a formal, disciplined manner. In New York City he encouraged socialist political theory in many forms, and he spent the decade of the 1930s weighing its strengths and weaknesses. By 1940 Niebuhr had withdrawn from the Socialist Party and abandoned his Marxist-informed criticism of liberalism. Elements of Marxist thought continued to be important in the 1940s, but decisively less so than in the previous decade. His critique of Marxist illusions plays a significant role in his thought of the 1960s and in his thought on American foreign policy. The organization of the chapter is topical rather than chronological. With minor exceptions (e.g., in the critique of Marxism) the topics are limited to his thought during the decade of the 1930s.

The Transition from Social Gospel to Socialism

Reflection upon the experience of the depression in New York City led Niebuhr to abandon hopes for significant reform through the two major political parties; he hoped that the socialists, through effective organization and concentration upon winning congressional seats, could rise to a position of power. In late 1929 he urged that the socialists abandon dependence on the programs of either the Communists or the American Federation of Labor. Dismissing laissez-faire economic theory as a boon to the privileged which hindered necessary progress, he advocated the removal of major sectors of the economy from private ownership, heavier inheritance taxes, increased income taxes, and extensive public welfare assistance as the necessary ingredients of political reform.

Niebuhr's essentially socialist political program was not thoroughly informed by Marxism in 1929. He cautioned that there were no guarantees that the new order would be more just than the old. He regarded Marxist hopes for the justice of the new order as romantic and the hopes of eliciting moral sensitivity from violence as illusory. His strongly held pacifist convictions prevented him from subscribing to Marxist doctrines of revolution, though many of his penultimate goals for society fit socialist programs.[4] As the depression deepened, so did his pessimism about the effect of liberal attempts to reform the system. In 1931 he wrote that the continued failure of the West to reorganize itself radically along socialist lines would probably lead to the system's violent end in a revolution.[5] Niebuhr's use of Marxist ideas in 1932 to criticize the social thought of Rauschenbusch indicates how far left he had moved.[6] He argued that their middle-class presuppositions had misled radical Christians to think that the just society could be obtained gradually in an evolutionary movement. The economic-social situation of the middle-class reformers allowed them to advance their class interests through relatively peaceful, democratic means. The political theory of the middle class did not adequately account for group egotism and the inevitable conflict between the dispossessed and the possessor. Niebuhr credited Rauschenbusch with seeing more clearly than most of his contemporary Christian social activists the depth of the social struggle. However, Niebuhr charged Rauschenbusch with expecting that society could be reformed through moral and educational means. The central weakness in Rauschenbusch's thought was the absence of a concept of the class struggle.[7] The Marxist idea of a class struggle expressed more adequately than any other model the strength of group egotism.

Niebuhr's analysis was Marxist, but his prescription in 1932 was still heavily influenced by the Social Gospel and particularly by its pacifism. He recognized the need for social coercion, but he hoped for nonviolent means of social change. For a brief period he tried to combine Marxist analysis with a Gandhian form of pacifist resistance. The nonviolent techniques of social change could be justified on a pragmatic basis because, in the long run, they were more effective. His choice of nonviolent techniques was so dependent upon pragmatic criteria that he denied any intrinsic difference between violence and nonviolence.[8] His reasons for wanting to evaluate techniques of social change on pragmatic grounds are understandable. His denial of an intrinsic difference between violence and nonviolence represents a polemic move against religiously based pacifism rather than careful analysis. Niebuhr's suggestion that the differences between violence and nonviolence were entirely pragmatic never satisfied many religiously grounded pacifists. His pragmatic defense of pacifism was one which would crumble as the depression deepened and as the opponents of social reform revealed little concern for the finer points of democratic politics. Acceptance of the Marxist analysis of the class struggle meant that pacifism held only a tenuous position in Niebuhr's political theory.

The Influence of British Socialism

The influence of the American Social Gospel movement upon Niebuhr's thought about politics is clear. A less important influence, but still one of considerable significance, was that of English Christian socialism. Middle-class Protestantism, since the middle of the nineteenth century, had tolerated the expression of Christian radicalism, but it had criticized the more truly proletarian discontent of Marxism. Charles Kingsley and F. D. Maurice represented to Niebuhr the English expression of mild socialism qualified by pacifism. This English socialism was more akin to the thought of the "utopian" socialists, Henri Saint-Simon and Charles Fourier, than to that of Karl Marx. In England both the chapel and the church had produced or nurtured a great number of social reformers. Though many radicals received their inspiration from the church and then moved away from it, in England much social radicalism was contained within the church. Statesmen like Arthur Henderson and George Lansbury combined their radicalism with deep religious convictions in a way that was fruitful for both social reform and religion. Radical Anglicanism seemed to Niebuhr, in the 1930s, to serve a particularly fine purpose in uniting a passion for justice with a symbolization of the mystery beyond social reform.[9] Looking back on his socialist period, the elderly Niebuhr preferred to stress the broadness of the socialist movement and to emphasize his debt to the Christian socialists at the neglect of his greater debt to Marx and the Marxists.[10]

Even while most deeply influenced by Marxist ideas, Niebuhr argued that social radicalism and Marxism owed their existence to Christian inspiration. Though critical of George Lansbury's withdrawal from politics because of pacifist scruples against sanctions, Niebuhr regarded him as "the symbol of the fact that in at least one western nation, Christianity remains organically related to the radicalism to which it gives birth."[11] In an early survey of the various Christian radical groups, he noted their differences and criticized some of their doctrine, but he was frankly appreciative of their accomplishments. The English left-wing Christians were far advanced over their American counterparts and primarily so because of their close relationship to the Labor

Party.[12] To a degree, the English radical Christians had accomplished in fact what Niebuhr urged for the American scene during his socialist period, an effective alliance between the Christian left wing and the secular left wing in a political party.

Niebuhr claimed that the English Christian socialists, particularly Sir Stafford Cripps and George Lansbury, had greater influence on his politics than any American socialist, less in the shaping of any political insight than in the personal examples of having combined Christianity and social radicalism. Niebuhr has quoted George Lansbury as saying that Christianity, not Marxism, was the source of his socialism, and that he only read Marx long after his socialism was set. Sir Stafford Cripps testified, according to Niebuhr, that he never would have been elected except for the organizing work done on his behalf by Methodist Bible study groups.[13]

Niebuhr did not follow either Lansbury or Cripps in their tendency to equate socialism and Christianity. Niebuhr maintained a distinction between his faith and his socialism which Lansbury would have regarded as a dichotomy. Though the conflict of party interest and their Christian faith plagued both Lansbury and Cripps, they did not reflect in their writings a sense of the inevitable gap between politics and ethics which characterized *Moral Man and Immoral Society*. Niebuhr maintained a sense of the mystery and eternal reverence of religion which Cripps obscured by his view of the church's vocation as the provision of the moral force for social reform. The deepening of the Marxist strain in Niebuhr's own thought also led him to differ with Lansbury on the question of pacifism.

The Attraction of Marxism

Several aspects of Marxist thought made it attractive to Niebuhr in the early 1930s. Donald B. Meyer has demonstrated the importance of the Marxist myth of the disinherited class, sense of catastrophe, and apocalypse in Niebuhr's thought. Meyer, however, underestimated the lure of political realism in Marxist thought for Niebuhr when he wrote, "the attractions in Marxism for Niebuhr did not root primarily in political realism. They were attractions of another order." [14] The central difference between *Does Civilization Need Religion?* and *Moral Man and Immoral Society* is the degree of Marxian analysis in the latter volume. *Does Civilization Need Religion?* raises doubts about the assumptions of liberalism, but *Moral Man and Immoral Society* reveals a complete break with it. Between 1927 and 1932, Niebuhr experienced a deeper sense of the difficulty confronting all programs of social reform, and Marxist thought helped him explain these difficulties. The privileged class resisted all efforts to improve the competitive position of the underprivileged class. Marxism took account of the severity of the class conflict and recognized that the social-political power of the privileged class would have to be destroyed before significant gains in equality could be achieved. Niebuhr was drawn to Marxian analysis because the Marxists seemed to have a realistic program for achieving their dreams of social justice. He deplored their moral cynicism, but he praised their realism. In evaluating the political strategy of the "Marxian Proletarian" Niebuhr commented: "If his cynicism in the choice of means is at times the basis of his undoing, his realism in implementing ethical ideals with political and economic methods is the reason for his social significance." [15] This realistic estimate of the means necessary to overcome the power of the privileged was what distinguished the Marxist from other less effective socialists for Niebuhr.

There have been other dreams of justice and equality. The distinctive feature of the Marxian dream is that the destruction of power is regarded as the prerequisite of its attainment. . . . We have seen how inevitably special privilege is associated with power, and how the ownership of the means of production is the significant power in modern society. The clear recognition of that fact is the greatest ethical contribution which Marxian thought has made to the problem of social life. [16]

The first article of Reinhold Niebuhr's new journal, *Radical*

Religion, made it clear that the editor was not primarily a democratic, revisionist socialist, but a Marxist. He was also a Christian, and he held that a Christian's relationship to Marxism ought to be a discriminating one. The journal defined the clarification of the relationship between Marxian and Christian thought as one of its central purposes. While Christians and Marxists held different world views and disagreed about ultimate presuppositions, there could still be agreement on practical objectives. The editor committed the journal and its Fellowship of Socialist Christians to agreement on the expectation of the collapse of capitalism, to a common rejection of sentimental moralism, to a recognition of the need for a social struggle, to the view that ideals were conditioned by material forces, and to the proposition that too close an alliance between religious institutions and the economic system muted the prophetic voice of the former. On the other hand, Marxist utopianism was rejected and the question of pacifism was recognized as an issue upon which socialist Christians would disagree.[17] During the 1930s, Niebuhr welcomed united front coalitions while resisting Communist control of the united fronts.

Late in the 1930s, while Niebuhr was developing his most thorough statement of the relationship of Christian theology to politics and becoming increasingly critical of the Marxist doctrine of man, he outlined his essential agreement with Marxist thought. Marxism furnished an analysis of the economic structure of society which was essentially correct. It correctly perceived the conflict between the proletariat and the bourgeoisie as inevitable. He agreed that private ownership of the means of production was the basic cause of periodic economic crises. Marxism was right in its judgment that the communal ownership of property was a prerequisite of social justice. He accepted Lenin's view that capitalism was responsible for the economic imperialism which characterized the advanced nations.[18]

Niebuhr was attracted to Marxism by aspects of its mythical content as well as by its realism and its social analysis. The record of his greatest fascination with Marxist mythology is found in *Reflections on the End of an Era,* which he has described as his "most Marxist work." [19] He urged that Christianity come to terms with Marxist mythology because it was more able to point to a meaning within the disintegration of Western civilization than either orthodox or liberal Christianity. He did not urge that Christianity surrender to Marxism, but he asked that the viable mythological insights of Marxism be recognized while using Christian insights to guard Marxist utopianism. He regarded history as inexplicable in its own terms, requiring a mythological interpretation to ascertain meaning amidst the chaos. The specific mythological insights which he adopted from Marxism included: the belief that capitalism was destroying itself through its own inner contradictions, the myth of the unique role of the disinherited class as the destroyers of the capitalist system, and a vision of a more just socialized society.

The Critique of Marxism

Niebuhr's Marxism was never unqualified. He remained free from the illusions of the fellow travelers and consistently criticized several central Marxist presuppositions. Reservations about Marxism held as a liberal evolved into qualifications of Marxism as a Christian socialist, and the polemical attacks of the cold war turned into the scholarly critique of Marxism as the ideological ferment of the East-West struggle abated. Taken as a whole, Niebuhr's critique of Marxism is a thoroughgoing indictment on three levels: (1) the failure of Marxism in its embodiment in political institutions; (2) the inadequacy of Marxism as a political philosophy; and (3) the dangers of Marxism as a religion.

Niebuhr's reports on his trip to the Soviet Union in 1930 were characterized by both positive and negative evaluations of the Communist experiment. He praised the enthusiasm of the society for its task of industrialization, but he feared that the virtue of efficiency was being exalted at the expense of other human values.

He understood why Orthodoxy as a supporter of the status quo before the revolution had to be attacked, but he did not regard the religious expressions of Communism as adequate to human needs. He appreciated the virtues of communal property, but he doubted whether the suppression of private initiative would contribute to the general health of the community. While welcoming the advance of industrialism, he feared unchecked Communism would bring it in a particularly ruthless manner. He applauded the rise of the industrial proletariat, but he decried attempts to force peasants into proletarian modes of living.

The evolution of Russian society increased his reservations about Marxism. The purges and trials conducted by Stalin convinced him of the sickness at the center of Soviet society. As World War II approached, he argued that there was not sufficient reason to prefer Communism over Nazism to sacrifice American lives in the defense of Russia. The Nazi-Soviet pact confirmed what Niebuhr had argued for years: Communism was being made to serve the aims of the Russian state rather than the Soviet Union being the bearer of the hopes of the worldwide proletarian movement. The responses of the American Communist Party to the changes in Soviet foreign policy revealed the center of its loyalty to intellectuals who had hoped it was beyond provincial nationalism. Niebuhr severely criticized the American Communist Party's attempts to reconcile its position with that of the Soviet Union. The real tragedy of modern civilization, for Niebuhr, was that the only alternative to its self-destructive system of capitalism was a tyrannical socialism. Niebuhr's disenchantment with Marxist theory was furthered by the deficiencies he observed in the societies which claimed to be founded on Marxist theory.

Niebuhr recognized that the evils of Stalin's dictatorship were partially due to contingent historical factors, but he emphasized the mistakes in Marxist political theory which made such a development likely. Marxist thought obscured the necessity for coercion in society by regarding coercion as a product of class oppression. Once the exploiting middle class was eliminated, the need for social coercion would disappear. The failure to see the inevitable need for coercion was connected with eighteenth-century optimism about man. It was also connected with Marx's reduction of the various sources of political power to one source. Political power depended upon the ownership of the means of production. Marxism concluded that once the means of production were responsible to the community, the political power would also be in the hands of the community.[20]

Marx did not envision an oligarchy arising to exploit the community for its own ends. According to Niebuhr, however, Marx's concept of the "dictatorship of the proletariat" had within it the seeds of the oligarchy of a ruling party. The denial of all political power to other than the representatives of one class destroyed all checks against the development of an oligarchy. The rise of managerial power in the twentieth century proved in both Communist and capitalist societies that the management of resources was a more important source of political power than the ownership of property. Marxist theory put the management of the country's resources into the hands of the group claiming to represent the proletariat and denied the necessity of checks upon their misuse of power. The very actions taken to secure the supremacy of the proletariat gave the oligarchy which spoke for the proletariat the elements of political prestige and the tools of social coercion.

> One pathetic consequence of this error is that the workers of a socialized concern, who are in theory the common owners of the property and are therefore prevented from holding any significant power, are rendered powerless against the managerial oligarchs who run the factory. The inevitable result is the accumulation of injustices more grievous than those which originally inspired the Marxist revolt against a free society.[21]

The political theory of Marxism granted one group an absolute monopoly of power and also exaggerated the inevitable self-righteousness of man by claims of scientific rationality for its social theory. The phenomenon of Communist dogmatism reinforced by totalitarian power made it particularly difficult for

Communist statesmen to understand the world in which their policies operated.[22] Niebuhr was very skeptical about the possibility of achieving a verifiable social science that was in important ways similar to the physical sciences; Marxism claimed to have done so. Marx himself was partially responsible for the claims of Marxist social science to infallibility. Niebuhr thought Marx's essential error was to identify the method of empiricism with the doctrine of materialism. From materialism was supposed to flow certain self-evident deductions. "All the propositions, dear to a revolutionary and apocalyptic idealism—universalism, collectivism, humanism, and socialism—are drawn, like so many rabbits, out of the hat of materialism." [23] Whether or not Marx's central error was to equate, as Niebuhr suggested, Lockean empiricism and materialism, Marx certainly confused descriptive and prescriptive language. The distinctions between the utopian socialists and scientific socialism are not so sharp as proponents of Marxist-Leninist science have imagined, and the pretense of scientific infallibility has given a note of fanaticism to the proponents of Marxism.

Niebuhr regarded the mythology of Marxism as its chief source of attraction to intellectuals. As his own study of Christian theology deepened, he became progressively a sharper critic of the religious elements of Marxism. His critique of Marxism on the religious level is the most original of the elements of his attack on Marxism. John C. Bennett has said, in commenting on Niebuhr's Marxism, "Today Communism has no opponent in this country who knows how to deal it a deadlier blow on the intellectual and spiritual level." [24]

Niebuhr thought Communism met his minimum definition of a religion and contained many ingredients of traditional religion.

Religion in minimum terms is devotion to a cause which goes beyond the warrant of pure rationality, and in maximum terms it is the confidence that the success of the cause and of the values associated with it is guaranteed by the character of the universe itself.[25]

Like Carl Becker, Niebuhr regarded the faith in the doctrine of progress as essentially a religious dogma. The Marxist faith in the dialectic of history leading to catastrophe and then utopia was also of the character of religious dogma rather than philosophy or empirical observation. The Marxist combination of penultimate pessimism with a note of ultimate optimism was particularly fruitful for political action. The innate determinism of Marxism was overridden by the sense of participating in, and acting consistently with, the flow of history. The particular role of the proletarian class in the Marxist world view incorporated elements of the Christian concept of the peculiar virtue of the dispossessed with messianic symbolism to make claims for the class beyond the competence of social science.

Communism was regarded by Niebuhr as having "at least one characteristic in common with all religion: it tends to oversimplify morals." [26] Rather than carefully balancing values, Communism was characterized by absolute devotion to the principles of equality and loyalty to the proletarian class. Puritanism made the virtues of the rising middle class supreme and "pure Christianity" made the ethic of love an absolute. In an analogous manner, Communism made the requirements of the proletarian class in achieving an egalitarian society supreme. Detailed analysis of the value presuppositions of Puritanism, the ethics of Jesus, and the Marxian ethic hardly reveal a simple ethic. In fact in the same article in a different context Niebuhr asserts, "Communism is a religion of mixed ethical values, but its energy proves that it is a religion." [27] Perhaps the most penetrating criticism H. Richard Niebuhr ever leveled at his brother's work was that his view of Christian ethics overly magnified the virtue of love. His brother's overemphasis upon the perfect love ethic of Jesus owed more to the tradition of Harnack than to a consideration of the fullness of the Christian ethic, according to H. Richard Niebuhr.[28]

The Marxist revolutionary creed encountered problems similar to those of other primitive creeds in preserving itself from the critical and relativizing tendencies of intelligence. Its response was typical of the responses of religious systems in the West. It created both a dogma and a church to define and defend the dogma. "Marx is its Bible and the writings of Lenin have achieved a dogmatic significance for it comparable to that which the thought of Thomas Aquinas had for the mediaeval church." [29] The Marxist confidence in the dialectic of history working out to certain anticipated ends seemed to Niebuhr sufficiently parallel to the religious trust in a higher power to regard Marxism as a religion.[30] Niebuhr's own inclination to regard discourse about God as language about a transcendent purpose which gave meaning to human history justified, for him, the definition of Marxism as a religion.

The illusions of Marxism, which were essentially religious, reinforced the tyrannical tendencies of Communism. The primary illusion was its utopianism. Great evils were approved on the grounds that every act was justified which would realize the classless society. The utopian illusions attracted intellectuals to Communism but obscured the injustices perpetrated in its name. "The important point is that the ruthless power operates behind a screen of pretended ideal ends, a situation which is both more dangerous and more evil than pure cynical defiance of moral ends." [31] The criticism of Marxism was in essence the same as the criticism of liberalism; both creeds were blinded by utopian illusions to the need for resolute political action for achievable moral ends. Marxist realism had exposed the illusions of liberalism, and Augustinian realism exposed Marxist illusions.

The Socialist Party

Niebuhr found resources within his understanding of the Christian faith to challenge the conventional American two-party system. He combined an inclination toward radical politics with the conviction that a Christian's political commitments were provisional and tentative because every political system was judged by the Kingdom of God. American political conservatism was never a live option for Niebuhr, and the failure of liberalism to be sufficiently realistic pushed him further to the left.

The major parties were forced by the facts of politics to remain ideologically within the limits forced upon them by their respective coalitions. The third parties, however, were able to take seriously the impending collapse of capitalism, the study of American society in terms of class analysis, and the socialization of the means of production. Niebuhr's acceptance of Marxist economic and social analysis drove him into the third-party movement, where such a view would be treated seriously. Niebuhr had taken the third-party alternative as early as 1928 in the League of Independent Political Action. In 1929 he dismissed the programs of both the Communists and the American Federation of Labor as irrelevant to the American political scene and urged a third-party movement.[32] He regarded the attempt to win congressional seats for socialist candidates as the best strategy. Elements in his program included the nationalization of coal, heavy inheritance taxes, heavy graduated income taxes, and broad public welfare measures. By 1932 he supported the Socialist Party ticket, and he continued to do so until 1940.

The collapse of German socialism and the rise of Nazism in 1933 encouraged Niebuhr's view that parliamentary, evolutionary socialism was inadequate to the crisis of the day. He regarded Germany as revealing in microcosm the problems and possibilities of Western civilization. Using lessons learned from Europe, more particularly Germany, to instruct the United States, he called for a rethinking of American radicalism. Next to the need for cohesion among the disinherited groups, he regarded as most important the disavowal of the revisionist hopes for parliamentary socialism. The revisionists, in Niebuhr's view, had held too absolute a loyalty to democratic procedure. The class which dominated a country economically could too easily exploit democracy for its own interests. He used his study of the German scene to instruct American radicals: "Recent events have proved quite conclusively that an uncritical attachment to, and an implicit trust in, the institutions of democracy will betray the workers in the hour of crisis." [33] However, the revisionists were wiser than the orthodox Marxists in admitting the need for greater subtlety in handling psychological and cultural forces. The Communist ideology was a major obstacle to any alliance of the disinherited on the American scene; effective cooperation required its revision. Niebuhr advocated, therefore, "a turn left and a turn right" in American radicalism.[34]

Niebuhr did not, however, ignore the unique features of the American scene. He thought that, if the vital rethinking of socialist positions could be carried out and the prodigious organization work undertaken, a radical movement could arise on American soil which exploited the American revolutionary tradition.[35] He was not completely clear about the connections between the American revolutionary tradition and the proletarian revolution, but he ought not to be criticized for simply transporting European models of action to the American scene.

Niebuhr was among the young militants who with Norman Thomas gained control of the Socialist Party in 1936. This victory for the left of the party gave it a new burst of energy, but by 1937 the hopes for the Socialist Party itself were fading, and Niebuhr urged a socialist-labor alliance. Labor was essential to any development of a mass left-wing party, but the refusal of the Congress of Industrial Organizations to give support to any but labor candidates restricted the socialists to an educational and protest role.[36] The creation of the American Labor Party broke the power base of the socialists in New York.

Niebuhr ended his association with the Socialist Party in the 1940 election when he voted for Roosevelt. Elements of socialist theory continued to play a significant role in his thought as late as 1947 or 1948,[37] but his loyalty to the Socialist Party ended with Roosevelt's third-term campaign. "All this means that Roosevelt, despite anti-third term traditions, is the only hope of maintaining the real gains which have been made in the past years of the depression." [38] Already the pragmatism which was ultimately to triumph was appearing as a source of criticism of socialism. "Doctrinaire radicalism which divides the progressive forces is just as bad as opportunism which loses sight of all ultimate goals." [39]

The failures of Russia, which were poignantly revealed in the 1937 Moscow trials, and the failure of German socialism in 1933 had discredited the alternative social system to a decaying capitalism. The failure of the Socialist Party in the United States to win mass support and the failure of its leaders to understand the international situation forced Niebuhr to regard it as irrelevant to the American political scene. By 1940 he regarded it as discredited: "Nothing is more obvious than that socialism must come in America through some other instrument than the socialist party." [40]

Donald B. Meyer's otherwise astute analysis of Niebuhr's relationship to third-party movements errs in maintaining that the creation of Americans for Democratic Action in the postwar years marks his return to the established two-party system.[41] While the founding of ADA did mark his abandonment of hopes for the Socialist Party, the discrediting of Marxist dogma had started before and continued after the founding of ADA in 1947. Niebuhr's founding role in and his continued support of the Liberal Party of New York State[42] is testimony to his refusal to settle easily into the two-party system. As late as 1967, Niebuhr confessed his embarrassment over the administration's Vietnam policy by hesitating to define himself as a Democrat in any other sense than that he had voted for Lyndon Johnson in 1964.[43]

Liberalism Under Marxist Criticism

Under the influence of Marxist mythology, Niebuhr argued that a vision of catastrophe was more adequate than the optimistic illusions of liberalism. Christian theology and Marxist mythology both contained optimistic hopes on the other side of destruction.

69

The Christian hope was otherworldly, while the Marxian hope was regarded as historical and, consequently, more prone to the dangers of utopianism. The catastrophic and apocalyptic tendencies of Marxism were no more the result of rational analysis than the evolutionary hopes of the liberals and revisionist Marxists. But Niebuhr regarded the view which wrested hope from pessimism more productive of moral action than either sheer optimism or pessimism.

Niebuhr slipped into the language of the inevitability of history while opposing liberalism. In his Marxist period he could write confidently that the "logic of history" and the "drift of history" were toward the collapse of Western civilization. When not engaged in polemics against liberalism and particularly while exposing the religious foundations of Marxism, he often rejected confident predictions on the direction of history. He regarded philosophies which attempted to predict the direction of history to be based upon mythology. According to Niebuhr, history did not provide the data upon which predictions of the future could be based. The ultimate direction of history is too uncertain to be a basis for social policy.

> It is a question whether any scientific world view, or view of history, could be made the basis of social action; . . . The facts of history are multifarious and infinite in variety. They do not lend themselves easily to precise conclusions, and certainly not to the kind of conclusions which base political action upon certain hopes and confident prophecies about future history. . . . The philosophies . . . harmonize the facts from a particular point of view which is determined not so much by the nature of the facts themselves as by the way in which a generation or an individual feels about the meaning of life and by what he regards as ultimate and important.[44]

There appears to be a contradiction in Niebuhr's rejection of confident predictions of the future and his criticism of liberalism for neglecting the destruction of Western civilization. Niebuhr, himself, knows when he moves from literal rendering of the facts to mythological speech, though it is not always clear in his works. He has no confidence that history can be predicted, and he would share the distaste of critics who deplore doctrines of the inevitability of history.[45]

Reflections on the End of an Era was written two years after *Moral Man and Immoral Society* in the midst of a deepened depression and increasing signs of war. It is more thoroughly Marxist and emphasizes the logic of history as thoroughly as does any of Niebuhr's works. The following are typical examples of historical dogmatism:

> The future belongs to the worker. . . . We may deprecate or welcome that fact but we can hardly deny its *inevitability.*

> Nevertheless the proletarian seems *as certain* to rule a new civilization as it is that the commercial and industrial owner held the significant power in the social order which is passing.

> His [the laborer's] victory is certain because the *logic of history* demands his type of society rather than the one which the owner is trying to preserve. . . .

> Thus modern society is forced by the conditions introduced by the machine to return to social ideals once held by early society. The more the intelligent portions of the community recognize this development as both *inevitable and desirable* the quicker will be the period of transition in which society now lives and the more certainly will the dangers of barbarism be avoided.[46]

Niebuhr resisted the temptation to date the fall of capitalism in his polemics against the system. But he agreed with Marx that its contradictions doomed it to destruction and its inequalities justified its extinction. Whereas *Moral Man and Immoral Society* had been doubtful about the achievement of radical changes through either evolutionary or revolutionary change, *Reflections on the End of an Era* confidently predicted the collapse of capitalism as a result of the trend of history and concluded that liberals were too blind to see the direction of the tide. The tide was running so strongly in favor of Marxism that if Christianity were to survive there must be a compromise between Marxian and Christian mythology. The secularized religion of Marxism was better able to affirm the moral meaning of the current class struggle than Christian orthodoxy. It was superior to liberal Christianity,

71

which would be finally discredited when its naïve trust in the evolutionary process was engulfed by social catastrophe.[47]

Niebuhr was polemicizing for social change in 1934, and many of his exaggerations were for political ends. He attempted to shatter the liberal mythology with a Marxist mythology, which he regarded as more adequate. There is a religious character to Niebuhr's prophecy that the day of judgment is darkness and not light in *Moral Man and Immoral Society*. The prophecy went beyond the facts, just as did liberalism's trust in inevitable progress, but he believed his prophecy more adequately encompassed the facts. However, for polemical purposes, Niebuhr occasionally allowed the myth of destruction to determine his reading of the facts and to neglect resources for improvement which others, less hindered by a myth of destruction (whether Marxist or Christian), could see. The most widely known example of this failure is his dismissal of the New Deal in its early phases. The New Deal was not bold enough to prevent the economic overlords from moving to the extreme right when they realized that power was slipping from their hands. He ruled out the possibility of a gradual transition from capitalism to socialism and predicted a drift toward fascism, which would sharpen the class antagonisms and initiate the class conflict.

> The imperilled oligarchy of our day, though it may pay lip service to the sweet reasonableness of these counsels [Keynesian economics], drifts nevertheless toward fascism. The drift is inevitable because it is more natural to hide wasted strength by a desperate venture of power than to arrest its decay by a prudent restraint upon its use. . . .
>
> The net effect of fascism must therefore be to guarantee that the end of capitalism will be bloody rather than peaceful. By destroying the last possibility of resolving the conflicts of modern society in democratic terms it makes a revolutionary end of these conflicts a practical certainty.[48]

The language of the "logic of history" and historical "inevitability" declined in inverse proportion to Niebuhr's critique of Marxism. The experience of the 1930s and 1940s taught him to be extremely wary of all schematizations of history, and gradually he moved in the interpretation of history from the category of "tragedy" to the motif of "irony."

The Critique of Pacifism

The second chapter of this study discussed how the peculiar combination of Wilsonian liberalism and the American nationalism of a second generation German-American led Niebuhr to disavow pacifism during World War I. The failure of Versailles and events following the war drove Niebuhr to affirm a pacifist position again in 1923. In the 1920s he became national chairman of the Fellowship of Reconciliation.

Niebuhr's pacifism collapsed under the Marxist-inspired critique of liberalism. He broke with the tradition of Christian social radicalism which had accepted a mild form of socialism while disavowing resort to violence. His acceptance of the Marxist class analysis and a catastrophic interpretation of the end of capitalism made it impossible for him to deny the use of all violence to the forces of social change. He concluded that, because the privileged class would resist the necessary changes with violence when the instruments of legal coercion failed, it was necessary to concede the right of violence to the underprivileged class. The privileged class could, by its economic power, social prestige, and control of the legal instruments of coercion, keep a pacifist proletariat in subjection. Violence and the threat of violence were essential ingredients of the class struggle. However, Niebuhr criticized what he regarded as the romantic illusions of the radicals in regard to the redemptive effects of violence. He urged that it be used sparingly and only where necessary. He promoted the development of instruments of nonviolent social change wherever the tactics of nonviolent resistance were relevant.[49]

Niebuhr's abandonment of pacifism led to his resigning from the Fellowship of Reconciliation in 1934. The Fellowship was split over the resignation of J. B. Matthews as executive secretary and over the extent to which it should be consistently pacifist. A poll revealed that only twenty percent of the Fellowship was unwilling to renounce all forms of violent coercion in the social struggle. Niebuhr's statement regarding his reasons for resigning from the Fellowship demonstrated his attempt to remain a pacifist regarding international war, while abandoning pacifism on the domestic front.

> While respecting this position of the pure and the qualified pacifists I am bound to admit that I cannot share their position. For this reason I am forced to associate myself with 20 per cent of the fellowship who are pacifists only in the sense that they will refuse to participate in an international armed conflict. Perhaps it would clear the issue if we admitted that we were not pacifists at all. We probably all recognize the terrible possibilities of violence. We regard an international armed conflict as so suicidal that we are certain that we will not participate in it.[50]

The article explaining his break with the Fellowship proclaimed that a primary difference with the Fellowship was that he regarded all issues of social ethics in nonabsolutistic terms. Pragmatism was evoked as the guide to whether policy at a particular time should be nonviolent.

Niebuhr's decision to regard the use of violence as a pragmatic issue soon led him to disavow the pacifism he had retained in the arena of international politics. In 1935, when confronted with the League of Nations' dilemma regarding the Italian conquest of Ethiopia, Niebuhr abandoned pacifism for the policy which he thought promised the greatest likelihood of restoring peace and some semblance of justice. Recognizing that economic sanctions and their enforcement could lead to war, he still argued that the League should enforce effective sanctions, including oil, against Italy. He criticized the politics of George Lansbury for whom he had great respect. Lansbury's refusal to support sanctions was, in Niebuhr's view, a confusion of the relativities of politics with the absolutes of the Christian faith. He praised Lansbury's insight that the League was serving Tory imperialism as well as Christian idealism but questioned his overly absolute pacifism, which refused sanctions because of the threat of war without providing alternative policies. The enforcement of international order required the resort to or threat of armed force because "no non-violent means of coercion can ever be guaranteed to be free of the peril of violence." [51] As World War II drew nearer he continued to call for resistance to the threats and claims of the German, Italian, and Japanese nations, but he never personally advocated American entry into the war prior to Pearl Harbor. As late as 1940 he continued to object to Roosevelt's rearmament policies. Though he had given up his pacifist position, he continued to try to limit carefully situations in which violence would be used and to argue against militarism.

Niebuhr's early criticism of the pacifism of liberal Christians focused on their tendency to confuse the religious and the pragmatic perspectives. Both religious and pragmatic approaches to pacifism were recognized as valid on their own terms, but confusion resulted when the two were mixed. Religious pacifism was legitimate as an ascetic response to the demands of an absolute love ethic. The absolute love ethic was a perfectionist ethic of nonresistance, and adopting it should cause one to renounce all responsibility for social justice which depended upon coercion, explicitly or implicitly. Religious pacifism was symbolically important, but politically irrelevant.

Pragmatic pacifism, which Niebuhr himself had advocated until 1932, was the attempt to mitigate the contest between opposing forces by means of social imagination, intelligence, and arbitration. Pragmatic pacifism utilized political arguments to demonstrate that violence should be avoided. Niebuhr recognized it as a useful corrective to the violent tendencies of group egoism. He could not, however, remain consistently pacifist on pragmatic grounds. His social analysis led to the conclusion that violence or the threat of violence was an indispensable element in the dynamics of social change. "A responsible relationship to the political order, therefore, makes an unqualified disavowal of violence impossible." [52] Niebuhr's argument against joining religious and pragmatic perspectives was a move to eliminate moral absolutes from the realm of political consideration. Politics was concerned with the weighing of relative values, and the weighing took place in the scales of history which considered all sorts of contingent factors. The testimony of the absolutist against violence was necessary, but not immediately relevant to pragmatic considerations. In fact his own pragmatism was set in and justified by particular religious perspectives. Having separated religious absolutes and pragmatic arguments for pacifism, Niebuhr could confine the religious perspective to a realm not immediately relevant to politics and advocate the use of violence when its discriminate use provided greater opportunities for justice than did the denial of violence. He recognized that he thereby justified particular policies which, while morally ambiguous in themselves, promoted the greatest good or the least evil. He accepted the implied principle that the end justifies the means in the sense that, in making ethical judgments about politics, it was necessary to subordinate one value to others. He rejected the principle insofar as it implied that one could make clear distinctions between ends and means.[53]

In 1940 Niebuhr attacked the merging of Christian pacifism and American isolationism and developed the fullest argument against pacifism in the church.[54] He considered pacifism appropriate as a nonpolitical expression of Christian perfectionism. Niebuhr appreciated the witness of the Mennonites who disavowed political problems and tasks.[55] He regarded such pacifism as an important symbol of the ideal. But he was more familiar with the pacifism which ignored the Christian doctrines of sin and justification by faith, and included a humanist optimism about man. Such pacifism was heretical, not because of pacifism per se, but because it failed to appreciate essential elements in the Christian doctrine of man. Using the term *heretical* very loosely, he judged pacifism founded on optimism heretical because it was true neither to the full standards of the gospel nor to the facts of human existence.

The theological grounds for Niebuhr's pacifism were stated

clearly in his 1940 exchange of views with Richard Roberts, a leading Canadian pacifist, in the pages of *Christianity and Society*. He asserted that the pacifists he most frequently encountered were unaware of the tragic character of human life. Pacifists tended to think that the struggle for power could be overcome by renouncing the use of violent means of social control. Their assumption followed from illusions about human nature which were opposed to the Reformation doctrine of justification by faith. Justification by faith accepted the contradictions in history between norms and achievements and pointed to divine mercy. Justification did not mean a perfection beyond history, but the possibility of love in history. He argued that the incarnation promised no escape from history as conflict. The redemption of Christ provided a revelation of mercy, not power to overcome the contradictions of history. War was not a mere incident in human history, but a revelation of the tragic character of all human history. Pacifists seemed to be unaware of the conflict within history until it was starkly revealed in war, and then they attempted to opt out "by a supreme act of renunciation." [56]

Niebuhr admitted that his relativism could easily give way to moral cynicism and agreed that it was necessary to keep alive the tension between the ideal and the realizable relative good. But he also pointed out that it was a Christian's responsibility to preserve whatever order and decency he could in society. For Niebuhr the distinction between the barbarism of the Nazis and the imperialism of the British Empire was sufficient for him to enjoin resistance to Nazi aggression. Roberts admitted the distinction, but regarded it an insufficient justification of war. Niebuhr recognized the evil of war but judged it less evil than an acquiescence to Nazi tyranny.

Niebuhr's critique did not remain unanswered. Pacifists replied in scores of articles and at least three pamphlets.[57] Each pamphleteer paid Niebuhr the compliment of regarding his attack upon their position as the most substantive in current Christian literature. Insofar as the critics admitted they were not attempting to provide an approach to international politics for a secular nation, their criticisms were not relevant to the task Niebuhr had undertaken. Criticisms based upon hopes of eliminating conflict through a more radical submission to the law of love fall prey to Niebuhr's attack and are of little interest to practitioners and theoreticians of international politics. The radical ethic of absolute pacifism is combined in one of Niebuhr's British critics with a high degree of utopianism. Macgregor writes:

> If only men were prepared to take God at His word, and to order their lives here and now by the laws of a transcendent Kingdom, then the power of God would answer the cry of faith, and the Kingdom would break in upon them anew and "take them unawares." [58]

One critic, John H. Yoder, draws the sharp distinction "between pacifism as a political policy for states and pacifism as an ethical principle for Christians." [59] He argues that Niebuhr fails to take seriously enough the difference between an ethic for an unregenerate society and one for redeemed Christians. Niebuhr's distinction between absolute pacifism and pragmatic pacifism is similar to the one Yoder demands.

Niebuhr and Yoder disagree sharply over the degree to which a Christian's political ethic is unique. Observation of the practice of Christians has prevented him from making Yoder's bold claims for Christian action. Yoder is correct that Niebuhr has not fully developed a doctrine of the Holy Spirit or stressed its working in the world. Nor does Niebuhr believe, as Yoder does, that the Christian community is free of the group egoism attributed to all groups in *Moral Man and Immoral Society*. Often critics have pointed to the lack of certain emphases in Niebuhr's thought which are part of orthodox Christian doctrine. In a time of radical questioning of the meaning and cogency of Christian faith, substantial criticism of a thinker requires more than merely pointing to the absence of emphasis of a doctrine. In terms of Niebuhr's apologetic method, it is necessary to show that the theologian has erred in his judgment of the human predicament, and Yoder has not undertaken that task. Yoder properly emphasizes the difference between what is and what ought to be, but he uses the distinction to substantiate a position which can derive an ethic for the Christian today directly from the authority of the teaching of Jesus. Niebuhr's prescription for what one ought to do always takes account of the relevant possibilities. In political ethics the delineation of the relevant possibilities is the responsibility of political analysis.

Yoder's emphasis upon the distinction between a Christian ethic and a social ethic for an unregenerated society would in dialogue soon force Niebuhr back to an accusation of self-righteousness against the Christian pacifist and to the additional charge that it is irresponsible to refuse to use the instruments of social coercion, clumsy as they are, for social justice and order. A certain imbalance in Niebuhr's thought results from excessively focusing on his hopes for radical social change and the approaching war in the 1930s. His response to a developing United States militarism and his position on the Vietnam struggle, which complete the story, are discussed in Chaper VI.

The Political Ethic

Though Niebuhr's political ethic in this period probably owes most to two theologians he heavily criticized, Luther and Rauschenbusch, there are five facets of the ethic which can be regarded as Marxian in inspiration. The acceptance of violence to achieve social change has already been mentioned. The tendency to regard the times as leading to a destruction of Western civilization owed more to Marxian analysis than to the direct inspiration of Amos. Niebuhr, however, regarded the Marxist "negation of the negation" as a secularized version of "the Day of the Lord is darkness and not light." A catastrophic view of history shaped his judgment of which alternative policies were relevant to the political situation. From Marx in particular he learned the large degree to which the claims for morality reflected the self-interest of a per-

son or a group. Marx's concept of social morality as ideology reflecting the economic position of the moralist revealed some of
the reasons behind the protests against the threatened violence of
strikes. Niebuhr's development of his political ethic in conjunction with the doctrine of sin was partially due to the connections
he saw between Marx's doctrine of alienation and his political
realism. An ethic without an awareness of man's brokenness was
inescapably idealistic. Niebuhr's ethic was in harmony with
Marx the socialist who emphasized the need for public ownership
and planning, but it was in opposition to Marx the utopian
revolutionary who envisioned a society without injustice and
competition. For a brief period, though regarding Marx's utopia
as illusory, he was willing to sanction such utopias for the sake of
furthering the struggle for social justice. The vision of the radical
soon faded, and he came to regret the closing paragraph of *Moral
Man and Immoral Society* in which he sanctioned the use of
illusion.

Niebuhr regarded his political ethic as an attempt to unite
political realism and morality. "An adequate political morality
must do justice to the insights of both moralists and political
realists." [60] The pursuit of equal justice within a society required
that the degree of coercion in the life of collective man be mini-
mized and that rational and moral factors be utilized in governing
its use. Agreeing with Augustine that the peace of the world is
achieved through strife, Niebuhr sought ways to unite the skill
of the political realist in the use of force and the wisdom of the
moralist in adjusting competing interests through reason and conscience. His attempt to unite realism and morality is seen very
clearly in *An Interpretation of Christian Ethics* in which he devotes chapters to criticizing the political ethics of both Christian
orthodoxy and Christian liberalism. In sweeping terms the charge
against the political theory and ethic of the church was that
orthodoxy had too easily dismissed the law of love for politics
while the modern liberal church had too easily affirmed its relevance. His statement of the problem of the Christian political

ethic and his criticism of the answers of both orthodoxy and liberalism depend upon his conception of the Christian ethic as the law of love. Like Harnack he treated love as the central motif and interpretative principle of Jesus' ethic.

Niebuhr had learned from Ernst Troeltsch that a final Christian ethic is not achievable. Each age must refashion its Christian ethic in view of the ideal ethic of Jesus and the conditions and presuppositions of the age. The church's attempts to produce a social ethic had not been notably successful, and the ability of the contemporary church to do so was in question. He undertook to state the ethic of Jesus in its most uncompromising form; it was an ethic of the ideal of love. The ideal of love could not be realized in human history, yet it was relevant to that history because it revealed the relativity of all other standards and lifted other norms to new heights. The norm of love was described as a transcendent norm which could not be fulfilled. The tension between the ideal and the real was overcome only in the Christian's faith.

Thus the Christian believes that the ideal of love is real in the will and nature of God, even though he knows of no place in history where the ideal has been realized in its pure form. And it is because it has this reality that he feels the pull of obligation. . . . Man seeks to realize in history what he conceives to be already the truest reality—that is, its final essence.[61]

The ethic of Jesus revealed the fulfillment of life to be that of self-sacrifice for another or a cause. All egoism was rejected as expressing sinfulness, and morality was understood as the limiting of egoism. Such an ethic was foreign to the needs of political life.

Whenever religious idealism brings forth its purest fruits and places the strongest check upon selfish desire it results in policies which, from the political perspective, are quite impossible.[62]

Whatever prudential elements appeared in the ethic of Jesus were regarded as inevitable by-products of an ethic which was founded on insight into man's nature; such elements did not detract from the radical character of the ethic.

The theology of Second Isaiah's vicarious, meek, suffering servant dominated Niebuhr's thought about the bearer of the Christian ethic. Jesus bore testimony to an ideal which was powerless in the world. The crucifixion was the ultimate symbol of love's fate in the world; the resurrection was a symbol of an ahistorical fulfillment of love. Niebuhr's portrayal of the ethic of Jesus revealed his background of perfectionism. Though not advocating asceticism, he still regarded it as the most logical outcome of the teachings of Jesus. His habit of wrestling with ideas in their extreme form colored his presentation of Jesus' ethic. He had abandoned the dualistic metaphysics which had characterized his liberal theology, but he continued to see the tension between the ideal and the real overcome only in faith. Even beyond the structure of his thought, his writing style continued to prefer dualistic modes of presentation or even the paradoxical expression.

The failure of the church to develop a satisfactory political ethic and the impossibility of Jesus' ethic in the political arena encouraged Niebuhr to utilize the resources of Western political philosophy in shaping his political ethic. His tendency to criticize the political philosophers of the past obscured how many insights he had drawn from them, and his steadfast refusal to sanction a systematic political theory made him appear as a critic of the tradition. His condemnation of the illusions of rationalism prevented his readers from appreciating the extent of his dependence on the liberal-rationalist tradition. He testified:

A prophetic religion which tries to reestablish itself in a new day without appropriating what was true in the Age of Reason will be inadequate for the moral problems which face our generation. . . . Critical intelligence is a prerequisite of justice.[63]

Niebuhr regarded Christianity as having in its faith a foundation and a roof for the structure of an adequate morality; the walls, uprights and diagonals, which held it together were the product of discriminate political and moral judgments.[64] A trust in the meaningfulness of human endeavor and a faith that the purposes of the moral life will ultimately be vindicated were prerequisites for an adequate morality in his view. He realized that an occasional moral philosopher could do without such religious presuppositions, but he regarded it as unlikely that many could act morally without them.

The relationship of love to justice remained an ever-present problem in Niebuhr's thought. In *An Interpretation of Christian Ethics* the principles of equal justice were regarded as an approximate expression of the law of love, which appropriately belonged to "a world of transcendent perfection." Perfect equality was not fulfilled either, but the principles of equal justice were relevant to the world of striving men. Love then remained a principle of criticism of all principles of social morality which in turn partially expressed the demands of love. Love also was a possibility for individual expression beyond the requirements of social coercion in the political order. *An Interpretation of Christian Ethics* emphasized the independence of the Christian ethic from culture. The emphasis upon the independence, which was partially an attack upon theological liberalism, rendered dubious the relevance of the ethic to that culture.

The tensions between the law of love and political realism understood in Marxist terms, or between a dedication to political relevance and an independent Christian ethic, resulted in an admittedly dualist ethic. The dualist ethic was elaborated more forcefully in *Moral Man and Immoral Society* than in *An interpretation of Christian Ethics*.

Morality was viewed largely in terms of the restraint of egoism. The egoism of individuals, sharply disapproved by the ethic of love, was amenable to religious discipline, whereas the egoism of groups was accepted as inevitable. "To some degree the conflict between the purest individual morality and an adequate political policy must therefore remain." [65] Niebuhr held to the standards of the "most uncompromising idealism" for the regulation of the personal life, but argued for the achievement of justice through the balance of power in the political arena. The two moralities are referred to as individual morality and social morality, or as the moralities of love and of justice. The gap between the two approaches is occasionally described as the gap between morals and politics. The acceptance of a "frank dualism" seemed more appropriate to Niebuhr than prematurely bridging the differences between the checks on individual and social egoism. The elaboration of this dualism was the central purpose of *Moral Man and Immoral Society*. The gap between individual and social morality which Niebuhr emphasized in the 1930s appeared so wide because he continued to speak of personal morality in perfectionist terms and social morality in terms of a Marxist-informed socialism. Also, he had not yet worked out the relationship between love and justice as fully as he would later do.

His polemics against importing irrelevant utopianism and perfectionism into political thought were more adequate than his attempt to divide individual and social morality. In one sense the individual does not exist outside the group and the moral question does not arise in isolation from the group. Acceptance of a dichotomy between individual morality and social morality encourages an obliviousness to the use of violence, intimidation, and false propaganda. Moral thought will be furthered by recognizing such acts as morally wrong even though reasons of state may require their use. The division into two moralities makes it harder to restrain the use of such tactics. A dichotomy between personal and social life, which sociologically speaking is impossible to justify, denies to social life the limitations which man's rationality attempts to place on his egoism. Niebuhr continued to work on the problem of an adequate social morality, and his treatment of the issue in regard to international politics is discussed in Chapter VI.

The Way to War

Niebuhr followed the political scene in Germany quite closely after his visit there in 1923. By 1930 he found the international economic situation and the political weakness of Germany combining to present a foreboding picture. He blamed the rise of political extremism in Germany upon the domestic economic crisis. The statesmen of the world were engaged in outlawing war and obscuring the economic issues which threatened the peace. Reparations and war debts created international tensions and prevented Germany's economic recovery. The money reaching the United States from the allies flowed back to Germany in loans, and the American control of the German industrial plant was increased. With the assurance of one sympathetic to Marxist dogma, Niebuhr regarded the high tariff walls and commercial rivalries of the nations as the sources of international conflict. "It is hardly necessary to argue at this late hour that the real root of international conflict lies in the sphere of economics." [66]

In 1933, the foibles of German civilization which Niebuhr had been analyzing since the early 1920s[67] conspired to produce Hitler's totalitarian state. From the failure of German socialism he drew lessons for American radicalism.

Niebuhr was particularly hostile to the church's failure to attack the anti-Semitism of the Nazis. While praising the church for trying to preserve its own independence, he criticized its quietism in regard to the "extravagances of Nazi terror." The Barthians had little to contribute to the whole struggle because, even though they were the element in the church most critical of the pretensions of the state, they would not fight for political alternatives. Outraged with the church's failure to oppose anti-Semitism, Niebuhr hastily charged, "Probably 75 per cent of the church population is avowedly nazi." [68] Detailed descriptions of anti-Semitic atrocities were coupled with a plea for a worldwide Christian protest against the German government. He did not expect much help from the German churches, but the terror had passed the point where sensitivity to the feelings of German Christians should muffle protest. In August of 1933 he protested not only against the admitted facts of government policy, but also against the execution of Jews in concentration camps.[69]

Niebuhr regarded the United States as another threat to peace. The United States had evolved a form of imperialism (a term he used to mean a high degree of influence across international borders) without the usual trappings of empire. The American imperialism depended upon American business and engineering. He argued that the human factors of politics were disregarded by engineers and businessmen. He regarded America as politically both the most powerful and the most ignorant of all nations.[70] He particularly feared any policies which would give the United States military power to equal its economic power. He thought the wedding of the two would blind the United States to the rightful claims of other nations. Regarding the labor movement in Europe as the most significant defense against imperialism, he pointed to the need for the development of a labor movement in the United States which would resist the development of American imperialism.

Niebuhr's concession that America was an imperial power did not lead him to argue for a world-power's active, responsible role in the interwar period, as it would in the postwar period. After recognizing the combination of American power and political ineptness, he counseled aloofness from the European struggles. He regarded the world, in 1934, as drifting toward the chaos of international war.[71] The situation had deteriorated too far to be significantly improved by American entry into the League of Nations. Too many nations were contemplating aggression to expect an international pact against aggression to have much significance. The imposition of economic sanctions would probably lead to the war they were intended to prevent. In 1934 Niebuhr regarded strict American neutrality as justified under all foreseeable circumstances.[72]

During the Ethiopian conflict, his policy recommendations focused on Britain. He urged the maintenance of the collective security apparatus; if sanctions involved a risk of war, the risk was justified. He continued his ambiguous policy of recommending collective security for Europe and neutrality for the United States. The immediate problem was to prevent the outbreak of a new major war so as to buy time in which to work for a new economic system. The basic problems were those of economic rivalry, and the enforcement of sanctions against Italy by the successful imperialist powers had the appearance of a peace maintained by satiated robbers. Still there was more than British interest at work in the League's opposition to Italy; the underdeveloped "conscience" of Europe was also being expressed. Yet the failure of British resolve to enforce oil sanctions against Italy discredited the League and revealed how little power, except that of Britain and France, was involved in the League. Niebuhr's writing on the Ethiopian question was quite typical of his later work on international politics with one exception; he demanded action, strove to preserve the peace through power politics, criticized the self-righteousness of the League, and attacked moralistic illusions, but he did not emphasize American responsibility in the crisis. His reluctance to urge American intervention in European politics prior to the war was due partially to his desire to restrain militarism in the United States and partially to a Marxist pessimism. He believed that the anarchy of capitalism was destined to destroy itself in war, and he hoped that the United States would remain aloof from the conflict. A sentence penned in commenting on the Ethiopian war is typical of his prewar pessimism: "It is therefore well to remember that the whole present structure of competitive capitalism is bound to lead to war." [73]

Gradually the two major policies which Niebuhr had endorsed were exposed to him as hollow. In 1938 he admitted that a capitalist nation could not remain neutral in a major conflict. Capitalist economic motivations would draw the United States into a European conflict again as they had done in the Great War. Neutrality and American capitalism were incompatible. He was also forced to admit that the democracies were unable to make a policy of collective security work. The experience of Manchuria,

Ethiopia, Spain, and China proved the inability of the League to prevent war through various collective security measures. In the spring of 1938 he thought that the proper use of economic power by the democracies might stop the aggressor nations while running the risk of war, but he doubted that the political will for such policies existed. For the United States he continued to recommend a policy of abstention from the impending conflict.[74] His policy of abstention was so thorough as to deplore the rearmament of the United States, even though a European war was immanent.[75]

Niebuhr saw more clearly than many that the irresoluteness of the democracies and the fanaticism of the fascists were leading the world to war in the late 1930s. His own policy recommendations, however, were also irresolute and characterized by a drift toward the inevitable chaos. He urged that the embargo on Spain be lifted, and he engaged in polemics against the pro-Franco Roman Catholic hierarchy of the United States. His hopes for Spain were in the direction of freeing nongovernmental forces in the United States to aid the loyalists. For a period he argued for a nongovernmental boycott of Japanese products, fearing that an official embargo would be regarded as a prelude to war. By the winter of 1938 he was urging an embargo against Japan. Gradually he drifted toward involving the United States against the various forms of fascism. He deplored the Munich settlement, but he realized that his criticism was less than relevant when made from the comparative security of the United States. His writing between Munich and the invasion of Poland stressed the need for Britain to eliminate its equivocation and to make clear to Hitler that it was prepared to resist further aggression. He praised Roosevelt's support of the "so-called democracies" but did not urge that the United States commit itself militarily to the European struggle.

Once war had come, though regarding Nazism as a judgment on the confusion and decay of Western civilization, Niebuhr regarded its defeat as the *sine qua non* of a return to health. Much besides the defeat of Germany had to be done to restore Europe, but the defeat of Germany was a negative prerequisite of the elimination of the injustice and anarchy of Europe.[76]

Niebuhr urged the United States to extend credits to the allies and to serve as the arsenal for the countries which were resisting Nazi aggression. He hoped, however, that the United States would itself stay out of the conflict. He believed it would, because he regarded it as unlikely that a democratic nation would go to war unless immediately imperiled. The division of opinion about the war in the United States convinced him that support of the allies was the most that could be expected. He engaged in campaigns against the strict isolationists, but he himself did not urge military intervention.

He persisted in the idea that a democratic nation could not be expected to engage in war until its interests were immediately affected with a rigidity uncharacteristic of his political thought. "We must accept the fact that nations, particularly democratic nations, do not enter a war until there is no other alternative, as both a political and a moral fact." [77] Neutrality for Niebuhr had the character of a law of politics which was forced upon democratic nations until their interests were directly challenged. The case for continued neutrality was strengthened in his opinion by the probable loss of civil liberties which would accompany intervention. Entry into the war would result in the war majority suppressing the sizeable minority which would resist the intervention. He renounced his previous criticism of Roosevelt's military preparedness measures and campaigned for increased aid to the allies short of war.[78] His chairmanship of the Union for Democratic Action in 1941 indicated his two major opponents at that time, "isolationism in the ranks of labor and reaction in the ranks of interventionists." [79]

When war came, Niebuhr looked back at the debates over whether the United States should enter the war and concluded that history had overtaken the debate. The choice was not so clearly in the hands of the American policy makers as had been supposed by both the isolationists and the interventionists.[80] The attack upon Pearl Harbor unified the Americans and removed the last obstacle which had prevented Niebuhr from recommending war. He accepted the war as a regretful necessity which should be prosecuted vigorously but without fanaticism. Niebuhr's work during the war involved him in relief work, semi-official work for the Department of War, and efforts for the German underground.[81] His writing and thought in this period are analyzed in the next chapter.

Conclusion

Though this book places the discussion of Niebuhr's socialism between his disillusionment with liberalism and his articulation of Christian realism, it does not suggest total breaks between those periods of his thought. The continuities are very significant indeed and provide the background against which the changes can be seen. The chapter has presented, as characteristic of Niebuhr's thought during the 1930s, a Marxist-inspired critique of liberalism which went beyond the critique he had developed of it as a liberal in the 1920s. In the next period of his thought the Marxist sources of the critique of liberalism, as well as liberalism itself, are criticized from the perspective of Christian theology.

The American entry into World War II revealed to Niebuhr the inadequacies of his previous understanding of international politics and the irrelevance of socialist or Marxist doctrine to the American scene. His support for President Roosevelt's domestic and foreign policies represented a major shift in orientation of Niebuhr's political thought. The shift was coincidental with the deepening of his theological study. As he moved more toward neo-orthodoxy, he argued briefly for a move left in politics while moving right in theology. Perhaps the move is logically possible, but Niebuhr could not correlate his Marxism with his theology or world events, and the Marxism became an object of his criticism.

Marxism provided a realistic perspective on politics and filled the vacuum in his political thought left by the decaying liberalism. It also faded, and there is not a single important idea in Niebuhr's developed political philosophy that depends upon Marxist philosophy. Some ideas from his Marxist philosophy remain, but they have found independent justification in his thought. Two areas of his thought were shaped during his Marxist phase and have been discussed in this chapter. His political ethic continued to evolve and is discussed in relationship to international politics in the concluding chapter. His rejection of pacifism, in its origins, had depended upon a Marxist analysis of the class struggle. The critique of pacifism was developed in theological and political terms separable from any Marxist dogma.

Though Niebuhr had forecast the dangers of Nazism at a remarkably early time and had warned Europe of the approaching war, he had not articulated a coherent policy for the United States prior to World War II. His prescriptions for foreign policy had been hesitant, and he had hoped the United States could remain out of the military struggle. The next chapter discusses his acceptance of the United States as an active world power. The founding of *Christianity and Crisis* as an interventionist journal is indicative of the Niebuhr who had accepted the hegemony of the United States. Any hopes that the United States could refrain from active political involvement with the rest of the world were dashed by the events of World War II.

Niebuhr's engagement with Marxism was very thorough. Though he never accepted it uncritically, he knew thoroughly the thought of Marx, the Marxists, and some of the revisionists; he tried to synthesize Marxist and Christian mythology; he accepted large parts of Marxist sociology; and he actively worked in united-front organizations. In his disenchantment with Marxism, he became a penetrating critic of it. He attacked it intellectually and politically. He became an advocate of a strong United States resistance to the Communist threat on the international scene, and he defined the cold war in terms of the defense of the values and ideals of the West.

IV. THE EXPOSITION OF CHRISTIAN REALISM

Reinhold Niebuhr's quest for political realism in Marxism was in vain, and he consequently turned to Christian theology as a resource for political philosophy. Theology had, of course, been an influence in all of Niebuhr's earlier writing, but in the late 1930s continued exposure to the faculty of Union Theological Seminary, serious study of Augustine, and the responsibility of preparing the Gifford Lectures resulted in his relating theology and political philosophy more thoroughly.

In a very general sense, the term *Christian realist* could be used to categorize most of Niebuhr's writing after World War I. Since the 1920s he had exhibited the attitude which he regarded as central to realism, i.e., "the disposition to take all factors in a social and political situation, which offer resistance to established norms, into account, particularly the factors of self-interest and power." [1] This study, however, discusses Christian realism as a phase of his thought, specifically that period of his thought which is most heavily influenced by theology and which precedes his renewed appreciation of liberalism. It is the phase in which Christian presuppositions were substituted for Marxist presuppositions in the attack upon liberalism.

The overall thesis of *The Nature and Destiny of Man* was that the two central motifs of Western culture, the sense of individuality and the conviction of the meaningfulness of history, were grounded in Christian faith. Liberalism had appropriated both motifs but had interpreted them inadequately. The first two sections of this chapter discuss Niebuhr's criticism of the optimism of liberalism which was due to errors in understanding man and history.

Niebuhr had criticized liberalism's view of man before the Gifford Lectures in 1939, but his doctine of man reached its most systematic statement in *The Nature and Destiny of Man*. Marxism, so influential in *Moral Man and Immoral Society* and dominant in *Reflections on the End of an Era*, was of minor importance to the constructive side of his thought. He no longer was combining Marxism and Christian mythology and, though he would concede that Marxism had helped Christians realize the resources of their own faith, he criticized Marxist illusions as sharply as liberal ones. Though *The Nature and Destiny of Man* represents his most weighty "theological" work, the argument is conducted in terms of political as well as theological analysis. In *The Children of Light and the Children of Darkness* he proposed a political philosophy for a free society. This study, while highly critical of liberalism, reduced the explicit theological content to a minor role.[2] It revealed Niebuhr's ability to write either in a secular style as he did as associate editor for *The Nation* or in a more theological style as he did for *Christianity and Crisis*.

Theology and political analysis are intimately related in *The Nature and Destiny of Man*. Like most of Niebuhr's systematic writing, this volume is oriented to the history of ideas. The adequacy of the ideas is judged by the degree of their correspondence to Niebuhr's understanding of the relevant social facts. Theological conceptions as well as political principles are judged by reference to their adequacy in comprehending man's social life. Theodore Gill's doctoral dissertation has emphasized the close relationship between theological and political analysis in Niebuhr and concluded that his politics cannot be understood without a grasp of his theology.

Reinhold Niebuhr's first importance to Christian thought today is as the creator of a Christian sociology. This attitude is not meant to question his eminence as a theologian: it is rather a recognition of what appears to be his theological method. There can be little doubt that the method proceeds more from the observation of social data to the recognition of theological conclusions than vice versa.[3]

Extensive criticism of his use of theological terms like *original sin* and the misunderstanding of his position which arose from such terms caused Niebuhr to regret using them. Original sin had connotations which obscured the realistic portrait of man which Niebuhr wanted to paint. *Man's Nature and His Communities* revealed the shift away from the language of orthodox theology which offended the modern intellectual community. He trusted that his "more sober symbols" would be apologetically and pedagogically more helpful than his earlier polemical use of orthodox symbols.[4] The abandonment of the symbol of original sin, however, implied no retreat from the position that man inevitably overreaches himself in a futile quest for security. The meaning behind the symbol was of importance to Niebuhr; convinced that the symbol was interfering with communication, he dropped it. *The Nature and Destiny of Man* represented, then, the mature Augustinian Niebuhr who had passed through liberalism and Marxism. It still lacked the full appreciation of the open, pragmatic, democratic, pluralistic society which was to characterize Niebuhr in the postwar years.

Christian realism is Niebuhr's response in theology and political philosophy to the cultural crisis in which World War II occurred. It is a critique of liberalism and a call to responsible action in international politics. This chapter discusses the two doctrines on which Niebuhr placed his greatest emphasis and which were specifically directed against illusions of liberalism—the doctrines of man and of history. It describes briefly his writing on World War II as the editor of *Christianity and Crisis*, which was the major journalistic outlet for Christian realism. Five theses of Christian realist thought on international politics which were developed in the context of the war and the immediate postwar situation are analyzed.

Niebuhr has been widely interpreted as a representative of neo-orthodoxy and as a political conservative. This chapter concludes by considering the appropriateness of regarding his thought as either neo-orthodox or conservative.

The Doctrine of Man

The Failure of Liberalism

"The essence of man is freedom," and liberalism, according to Niebuhr, did not realize it. The modern world view of liberal optimism interpreted man in terms of reason or nature. Rationalism, expressed as either idealism or naturalism, and romanticism both failed to comprehend man's ability to transcend logic and/or nature. Liberalism was true neither to the greatness nor to the depravity of man. Or, as he put it in his more polemical moods: "The liberal soul is pedestrian and uninspired. . . . The liberal soul produces neither warriors nor saints, heroes nor rebels, and it is ill at ease when confronted with their fury and their passion." [5] The full charge was that liberal optimism attributed evil to contingent facts which could be overcome, failing to see that evil was inextricably bound to man's freedom. Social engineering and social science could not fulfill the hopes of their advocates because man, in his freedom, could not be organized or analyzed by the means appropriate to the physical sciences.

Niebuhr regarded the modern view of man as being overly confident of the goodness of man. Though noting minor strains of pessimism in the various modern anthropologies he surveyed, he regarded optimism as the prevalent note. The pessimism of Hobbes, Rousseau, and Nietzsche, according to Niebuhr, was only provisional. That of Freud, on the other hand, was thoroughgoing and in fact was regarded as indicative of the despair which would confront modern man if his illusions were dispelled.[6] Whether the various anthropologies interpreted man in categories of reason or of nature, they agreed that man existed basically within a realm of harmony and order. Political anarchy, economic depression, social chaos, and mass hysteria were insufficient to destroy modern man's self-confidence and trust that, with the proper education and reformed institutions, he could correct his temporary setbacks. The easy confidence of the American population remained unshaken by the Great War, and part of Niebuhr's polemic against overestimations of man's goodness was a translation of postwar European thought into the American idiom. He drew upon Brunner and Heidegger in his exposition of the doctrine of man, but when he generalized about the modern view of man he meant the optimistic elements noted in various anthropologies, plus a widespread popular movement of confidence in the United States which asserted that man is the master of his own destiny. The mood of optimism was accompanied by a rejection of any doctrines that indicated man's misery and egoism were inevitable. Liberal theology, philosophy of education, and sociology jointly rejected the concept of original sin. Niebuhr reinterpreted the concept of sin and attacked optimism at the same time. Only in an ethos which appreciated the concept of sinful man was the Christian scheme of redemption and salvation relevant. The ethos which encouraged hopes of redemption through education and/or organization could not appreciate the Christian conception of sin, nor could it adequately account for the chaos of modern civilization.

Doctrine of Sin

The ambiguity of the human situation is the starting point of Niebuhr's analysis of sin. Man is a creature of nature, bound to a particular time and place and to particular environmental features which shape his destiny. But man is also a creature of spirit which means, for Niebuhr, that he sees and understands his situation. He can see, articulate, and try to avoid the contingencies of nature. Man's awareness of the limits within which he lives means he transcends them in some sense. Man tries to understand his particular place in the world in terms of the whole. He tries to regulate his conduct by universal standards. But inevitably, Niebuhr believes, the particular perspective corrupts the universal, and the particular interest colors the view of the general interest. Though freedom is analyzed more fully below, it is relevant to note here the relationship between freedom and sin. Man is free to transcend his immediacy, although he cannot finally escape his finiteness.

Man is, in Niebuhr's phrase, "both strong and weak, both free and bound, both blind and far-seeing." [7]

This ambiguous position of man produces the anxious man. The man who sees beyond his limits is anxious about his finiteness and desires to overcome it. Like Kierkegaard, Niebuhr regards such a state as temptation, not sin. Theoretically man can make the proper response to his situation and accept its insecurities by trusting that they will ultimately be overcome. Niebuhr draws upon Heidegger's analysis in *Sein und Zeit* to explain how anxiety is simultaneously the cause of man's achievements and the precondition of his sin. Man knows his life is limited, but he does not know where the limits are. No achievement represents perfection, and there is no place for man to rest in his struggle to escape his finitude. Anxiety is inevitable and, given man's nature, necessary, but only when the situation is misinterpreted does it produce a rebellion by man against the law of love.

Man's inevitable misinterpretation of his situation is due to the presence of a prior evil, the origins of which remain mysterious. The influence of Augustinian theology has suppressed the dualism of Niebuhr's earliest writings, and he uses the devil or the serpent as a symbol that the situation is misinterpreted to man. This misinterpretation is due to the human situation, which partakes of both "unlimited and limited knowledge" and cannot be reduced simply to an intellectual mistake due to one's conscious overestimation of his powers and knowledge. Niebuhr uses the Genesis myths to point out that sin is a mixture of error and conscious perversity.

Man's condition of anxiety produces sin if man lacks trust that the insecurities of history, the abyss of meaninglessness, and death will be overcome by God. Given the possibility of trust in a redeemer God, man's anxiety need not, in theory, lead to either pride or sensuality. Therefore, the root of sin is properly defined for Niebuhr as unbelief or lack of trust. Given unbelief, man's anxiety drives him to (1) claim unconditioned significance for himself or

(2) try to escape the possibilities of freedom by immersing himself in some natural vitality.

Niebuhr has written extensively on sin as sensuality, or the attempt to eclipse the self by finding an idol in a process or another person. His primary concern, however, has been with the expression of sin as pride. He distinguishes between four forms of pride: pride of power, pride of knowledge, pride of virtue, and spiritual pride. Though all four forms of pride are relevant to his political analysis, it is the various forms of the pride of power which are most directly relevant and which have received the greatest amount of attention from critics.

The will-to-power is not due, as Karen Horney suggested in *The Neurotic Personality of Our Time,* to the insecurities of a competitive civilization. Rather than having an ephemeral cause which can be eliminated, it is a perennial expression of man's attempts to overcome the basic insecurity of human existence. Will-to-power expresses what Niebuhr understands to be "sin in its quintessential form." [8]

Niebuhr has made a provisional distinction between the pride of the man who possesses power and that of the man who seeks power. Man in his freedom never reaches the position of complete security; the most secure monarch may be driven beyond the bounds of prudence in seeking still greater security. A distinction between the security-seeking of the establishment and that of the rising class must be made, but beneath the distinctive expressions lies the common attempt to extend their egos and to establish their security.

This will-to-power is regarded by Niebuhr as constituting part of the essence of politics. It is to be expected, it can be sublimated and checked, and the most outrageous forms of it can sometimes be controlled. It cannot be eliminated, for it is constitutive of the nature of man. Therefore Niebuhr is inclined to be critical of political ideas which ignore the will-to-power. The outer limits of policy are set by what is regarded as possible, even though policy is not directly derived from the nature of man. Niebuhr's views about man function in his political analysis as similar convictions functioned for Madison. Politics on the practical level may only rarely rise to the level of argument about the nature of man, but the view of man held by the policy makers may ultimately be decisive. Most politicians may operate with a set of platitudes about man. Though not carefully defined, such conceptions are important, as the authors of *The Federalist* realized.

The early writings of Niebuhr emphasizing the universality of sin suggested the leveling of all moral distinctions. For example: "Forgiving love is a possibility only for those who know that they are not good, . . . and know that the differences between the good man and the bad man are insignificant in his [God's] sight." [9] John Bennett and others criticized the tendency to obscure degrees of moral responsibility and objective evil results.[10] In the Gifford Lectures, Niebuhr tried to maintain the position of the common fallenness of all men while distinguishing between the consequences of their acts with the formula, "equality of sin but inequality of guilt." In part this emphasis met the earlier criticism, but Niebuhr's perfectionist background still prevented him from making the fine distinctions of moral responsibility which Bennett had suggested were desirable. From the perspective of the rigorous ethic of Jesus, all men were sinners; from the perspective of practical politics, the self-righteousness of men who were aware of their relative righteousness and forgetful of their basic alienation unleashed fanaticism. Niebuhr's emphasis upon sin as pride prompted him to stress the virtue of a humility grounded in a recognition of the sinfulness of all men. The context of Niebuhr's writing on the equality of sin indicates that it was the universality of sin which he was most concerned to establish." [11] On the basis of his doctrine, he could have said that "all men are equally sinners," thus avoiding the implications that "all sins are equal." In *The Nature and Destiny of Man*, guilt was defined as the "objective and historical consequences of sin." A definition of guilt which severs it from feelings and complexes violates the common usage of the term and would require a good deal of argument to sustain it. Niebuhr, however, in his concern to maintain discriminatory canons while retaining his egalitarian conception of sin, did not argue the case for his "objective" definition of guilt.

Doctrine of Freedom

For Niebuhr, freedom distinguishes man from the realm of nature. "His essence is free self-determination." [12] Niebuhr's discussion of freedom and sin attempts to avoid the errors of both overly consistent Augustinianism or Pelagianism by simultaneously maintaining man's radical spiritual freedom and the inevitability of his sin. This is possible only if man's freedom is closely related to his sin.

Liberalism failed to understand the depravity of man because it rejected the wisdom contained in the traditional Christian discussion of sin. It failed to appreciate the greatness of man because it underestimated the radicalness of man's freedom. It hoped to eliminate conflict between men because it did not understand that man's sin was inextricably connected with his freedom.

Freedom for Niebuhr means that man chooses between real alternatives. That is, man's choices are what they seem to be and what morality requires them to be, choices of actions that influence an undecided future. In addition to choices by individuals of particular acts, man chooses his total end. Man chooses the gods he will serve.

Niebuhr regards Heidegger's analysis of human nature as the most profound, modern, nontheological analysis. Of particular importance to Niebuhr was Heidegger's view of man as the creature which reaches beyond itself, beyond its environment, beyond its time, and beyond its reason. Man can stand apart from himself and judge himself as an object. Man is confronted with endless potentialities, and no arbitrary limits to his choice do justice either to his ability to conceive of new possibilities or to his unlimited striving. In addition to the freedom of choice, which is a crucial question for moral philosophy, Niebuhr is affirming the choice of an ultimate principle of meaning.[13] This quest for an ultimate principle of meaning which transcends the world reflects man's awareness of his self-transcendence and approaches the search for God. Yet the God sought by free man must be more than reason, for man transcends even his reason.

Niebuhr's debt to Kierkegaard, particularly to *Begriff der Angst*, is obvious in *The Nature and Destiny of Man*. The anxiety which Kierkegaard called "the dizziness of freedom" contains the possibility of choosing false gods or the true God. Like Kierkegaard, Niebuhr argues that no explanation but the affirmation that sin posits itself is sufficient to account for man's inevitable free choice of false centers of his existence. The sense of responsibility for one's sin is authentic because the sin is freely chosen.

The freedom of choice within the limits of the possibilities of creation and history and the affirmation of the freedom of transcendence in man's essential structure do not lead Niebuhr toward voluntaristic social theory. He traces the errors of seventeenth and eighteenth-century political theories to their tendency to underestimate the degree of freedom contained within the human psyche and to overestimate the degree to which social forces were subject to man's will. For example, Hobbes contradicted his denial of man's freedom of the will by positing the creation of the state *ex nihilo* by an act of man's will. The French Enlightenment viewed the realm of nature as an essential harmony which would be restored when the interference of governments was eliminated. Competing egos were regarded as essentially harmless unless the government interfered. The shallowness of such thought, which was fully developed by Adam Smith, was made evident by its failure to explain how man, in his freedom, could overrule the laws of nature through government.

The dialectic between theology and politics in Niebuhr is revealed strikingly in his discussion of human freedom. The controversy over man's freedom is traced through the history of both theology and political theory. The paradoxical character of affirming both the inevitability of sin in man's freedom and his responsibility is admitted, but the paradox is retained in view of the inability of alternative views to explain man's behavior in the political realm.

Politics and Scientism

For Niebuhr, politics is an art and not a science. He is critical of attempts to treat social studies as sciences comparable to the natural sciences. The study of man in society is more difficult than the study of nature because: (1) every social event takes place within a great number of dimensions, and events can be correlated plausibly within many different schemes; (2) the recurrences in history are not simple; therefore, social events cannot be reliably predicted; (3) inasmuch as men are free, the causes of social events depend upon their secret motivations. To the extent that men are determined, their actions are theoretically predictable, but particularly in the realm of politics secret motivations often upset predictions. Social studies involve a more complex causal chain than do the natural sciences and must take into account the unpredictability of the human agent. Results in social studies cannot lead to the compelling conclusions possible in the natural sciences. Niebuhr's quarrel with social science revolves around the false claims of some social scientists to use the prestige of science to reinforce their own partial perspective on society.

The fact that the observer of human society is an interested man with the fears, hopes, and ambitions of the men under study distinguishes his report of the movement of social groups from his report, for example, of the movement of stars. Weighing social events involves the observer in the drama of human life, and the interest of the self prevents the use of pure abstract intelligence. Even though the involvement of the self can be reduced by training, social reporting has more in common with taking a Rorschach test than with analyzing a chemical compound. Judgments on the Russian revolution, the Spanish civil war, or the election of 1964 inevitably reflect the interested self. While the field of historical observation provides opportunity for the development of

102

disinterested observation, events like the fall of Rome or the Reformation still prove remarkably difficult to analyze apart from social and religious convictions relevant to the contemporary situation.

Niebuhr's critique of the pretensions of scientism also noted that science depends upon certain presuppositions which James B. Conant has called "conceptual schemes." The vaunted empiricism of social science often obscured the role of these presupposed conceptual schemes and produced conclusions dependent upon the previous assumptions in the name of science.[14] Niebuhr's point that things themselves are not observed in society is applicable to nature as well. Sociology revealed its "obsolete viewpoint" (*überwundenen Standpunkt*) by assuming the perfectibility of man and the idea of progress.[15]

Though Niebuhr deplored the influence of ideology upon social studies, he regarded it as inevitable. His doctrine of sin provided him with Christian grounds for retaining the lesson he had first learned from Marx. Man's view of the social situation is largely influenced by personal and group interests. The influence of ideology or the world view which implicitly supports one station in life at the expense of empirical accuracy affects the social scientist as well as any other citizen. This influence of self-interest can be transcended, and religious humility joins hands with skepticism in freeing one from ideology.

Niebuhr's political philosophy is based upon the analysis of political ideas from the history of political discussion, checking these ideas against empirical data whenever possible. The very generality of some of his concepts leads him to oppose reducing politics to science. For example, echoing Hume, he assumes that political men must take human egotism for granted. His analysis of the inevitability of human sin due to the conjunction of freedom and sin corresponds to the expectation of statesman and constituent alike. It is the folly of the social scientist to try to reduce this general tendency to specific causes. John Dewey, among others, attributes this egoistic corruption of political judgments to the battle between science and dogmatism. The church and state have resisted the purifying effects of science and been kept under the sway of authority. Dewey's elaborate theory to explain a common phenomenon reflects his own crusade for the social sciences, but the universal character of egoism has long been recognized, and it requires no detailed explanations.[16] The search for specific causes of aggressiveness, characteristic of social science, is based upon the postulate that man can transcend this aggressiveness once its specific causes are understood. Niebuhr regards theories which ascribe aggressiveness to educational patterns, the division of property, the existence of the state, or the restrictions of civilization upon man's sexual impulses as inadequate in their comprehension of man's freedom and tendency to sin.

The optimism of social science has been quite apparent in the study of international relations. Several of the important academic chairs in international relations were established after World War I in the midst of optimism and a conviction that war could be eliminated if only its causes were properly understood. Niebuhr's criticism of social science was directed against the optimism which accompanied it in the early decades of this century and not against the rigorous application of thought to political problems. Niebuhr's *Moral Man and Immoral Society* laid the ground for Hans J. Morgenthau's *Scientific Man vs. Power Politics*, which asserted that the study of politics was best undertaken with an Augustinian or Hobbesian doctrine of man and that the virtues of natural science were not necessarily transferable to the human struggle for power. The story of the Morgenthau-Niebuhr alliance and their endeavor to apply the insights of the history of political theory to international politics belongs to Chap. VI.

Theology of History

Niebuhr attacked the optimism of liberalism's philosophy of history on two levels. The first and more secular level, that the historical optimism obscured the tragic character of life and history and disregarded the historical evidence of tragedy, was discussed in the first chapter. The second attack revealed the significant influence of Augustine on Niebuhr.[17] Niebuhr's writing, particularly in the 1940s, developed the theme that liberalism's view of redemptive history was antithetical to Christian doctrine.

Many diverse forms of modern philosophy shared the conception, according to Niebuhr, that the meaning and fulfillment of history was to be found within time. The historical process was one of development, and the fact of development gave meaning to the whole. The ambiguities of history would be overcome within history as the result of the "logic of history" or the evolution of the free man and the gradual disappearance of the sources of man's frustration. Niebuhr found that this confidence in redemptive history inspired such diverse thinkers as Comte, Condorcet, Dewey, Hegel, Herder, Kant, Leibnitz, Marx, Mill, Spencer, and Wells.[18] Niebuhr noted that there were minor dissonances of romantic pessimism, but "the new song of hope" was the dominant anthem of modern culture.

Charles Cochrane's thesis, that the decay of classical spirituality was due to the inadequacy of the doctrine of recurrence, was accepted. Classical man failed because he attempted to meet new challenges with old solutions. The pagan apologists with whom Augustine did battle attempted to return to the past and to meet a unique spiritual crisis (the decline of Rome) with remedies which had given comfort in other situations. Augustine developed the biblical view of time within Western culture. His insistence upon a linear interpretation of history, stressing the uniqueness of events and finding tentative meanings within the process but reserving the final meaning of history for the judgment of God, provided the church with intellectual resources that classical culture lacked. Niebuhr applauded Augustine's contemptuous rejection of the cyclical theory of time and history. "He ridiculed classical arguments 'dragging us from the straight road and compelling us to walk on the wheel . . . which if reason could not refute, faith could afford to laugh at' (*De Civitate Dei*, xii, 17)." [19]

In his bold style of isolating and comparing distinctive traits of various epochs, Niebuhr generalized about the classical, Christian, and modern views of history. Classical and modern philosophies of history regarded history as intelligible. Modern culture found this intelligibility in terms of the process itself, while classical culture found it in reference to the Platonic forms or changeless archetypes. The classical world agreed with the modern world that time and history were intelligible, but not that they were self-explanatory. Christian faith, on the other hand, regarded neither time nor history as simply intelligible. Christian faith had recourse to the mysteries of creation and providence to give meaning to time and history. History was not the same as the recurrences of natural time, but it was movement toward a significant future. The ultimate sources of meaning were beyond the process itself. The modern view of history has rightly observed that both nature and institutions develop. The lack of this insight plagued premodern social theory. But from this insight the modern world deduced the illusion that the development would fulfill life and eliminate its errors.[20]

A philosophy of history which finds history intelligible within its own terms and hopes for redemption through development is not receptive to the Christian message nor able to report accurately the ambiguities and tragedies of history. The Christian faith is a message of hope to a despairing world which is taking history seriously. Niebuhr's experience as an apologist was that, before the message of hope and redemption could receive a serious reception, the audience had to be convinced that history itself was not simply intelligible and redemptive. Christian faith presupposes a degree of pessimism, and as an apologist Niebuhr often found it necessary to encourage pessimism so that the message of an ultimate hope could be heard. The dual motivation of encouraging the development of a climate favorable to the gospel and of honestly describing historical reality entered into Niebuhr's polemics against the optimism of liberalism.

The apologetic and political interests which dominated Niebuhr's thought merged in his rejection of the prevailing confidence in the intelligibility and the progressive fulfillment of history. The confidence of modern man obscured his vision, ill prepared him for his confrontation with the barbarism of modern politics, and rendered him oblivious to the deepest insights of the Christian faith, which presupposed man's acknowledgment of his own inadequacy and tragedy. Niebuhr did not regard himself as a pessimist, but he thought that only the Christian faith could overcome the provisional pessimism resulting from empirical observation of man's social life.

Niebuhr has stressed that the ultimate principles of the interpretation of history are not, in the narrower use of the term, rationally derivable. The historian is necessarily selective, and his choice of interpretative principles is trans- or ultra-rational and similar in character to a religious choice. History is not reducible to logic or to the rules of organic development. Niebuhr has, therefore, concluded that there can be no Christian "philosophy" of history, strictly speaking. He has tentatively suggested that the notion of a philosophy of history is obscure, "because a philosophy of history will reduce the antinomies, obscurities and the variety of forms in history to a too simple form of intelligibility." [21] He has, however, argued for a Christian theology of history, i.e., a view of history which boldly acknowledges that its points of reference, principles of interpretation, and so forth are rooted in Christian symbolism and which emphasizes that human history is only comprehended fully by that which transcends history. For Niebuhr the arguments of historical relativism are convincing, and ascribing meaning to history is only possible from a standpoint of faith. Ascribing unity to history depends upon presuppositions about time which are not derived from historical analysis itself.

Robert E. Fitch has summarized Niebuhr's philosophy of history in this period as consisting of three propositions and a focus. The focus is the revelation of wisdom about God and man in the events of the life and death of Christ. These events are the clue to the meaning of the rest of history. From an understanding and an existential appropriation of these events flow Niebuhr's theology of history. The three propositions which characterize Fitch's outline of history are: (1) "history has unity by faith but not by sight"; (2) "history cannot be redemptive"; and (3) "history provides a disclosure of meaning but not a fulfillment of meaning." [22]

Christianity and Crisis and the War

Though until Pearl Harbor Niebuhr never advocated that the United States enter the war, he did encourage policies which would involve the United States more deeply in the European conflict. He vehemently attacked isolationists and all who would obscure the threat of Nazism to Western civilization. The history of his political journalism and involvement prior to the war was discussed in the previous chapter. However, treatment of Niebuhr's editorship of Christianity and Crisis was delayed until this chapter because it more completely belongs to his Christian realist period.

The first issue of Christianity and Crisis made it quite clear that the journal was dedicated to opposing Christian and secular forms of perfectionism and pacifism. The journal was committed to active participation in world politics and opposed to isolationism in its many forms. It emphasized the need for discriminate judgments in politics. The failure to discriminate between the degree of evil in British and Nazi imperialism, for example, was neither empirically nor morally justifiable. The journal announced that, though it would analyze various political and theological issues, the most pressing problem at that time was the defeat of the Nazis. The threat of tyranny was regarded as more evil than participating in war to stop tyranny, and Christianity and Crisis attempted to present an interpretation of the faith which would be relevant to the task at hand.[23]

The second article of the first issue carried the headline, "The World After the War." While admitting the difficulty of articulating war aims, the editor encouraged the democratic leaders to do so and argued that five great problems would have to be dealt with: (1) the reconstruction of Europe and the definition of Germany's role therein; (2) the reorganization of the national and international economic systems; (3) the disarmament of the nations; (4) the solution of the security problems of the small nations; and (5) the establishment of a world political order and the abridgment of national sovereignty.[24] This listing represents the journal's most far-reaching suggestions of postwar settlements. Although the editor returned again and again to the discussion of war aims and to just postwar settlements, his reach never exceeded the country's grasp as far as it did in that first issue.

The discussion of Niebuhr's approach to the war in Chapter II emphasized that he was not technically an interventionist, i.e., he did not urge the United States to join the war. However, the failure of the United States fully to aid Britain evoked his wrath. The following quotations reflect the moral fervor with which he urged increased United States involvement as he argued that the decisive reason for Christians to act to repeal the Neutrality Act of 1939 was the act's immorality.

We demand the immediate repeal of the Neutrality Act because it is one of the most immoral laws that was ever spread upon a federal statute book. Its immorality was accentuated by the misguided idealism which was evoked in its support. The essence of immorality is the evasion or denial of moral responsibility. . . . Morality consists in the recognition of the interdependence of personal life. . . .

As with men, so with nations. An irresponsible nation is an immoral nation, while a nation that is becoming dimly aware of its responsibilities and acts accordingly is moving toward morality. The Neutrality Act of 1939 was the culmination of a recent immoral trend in American life which needs to be recognized for what it is and dealt with accordingly.[25]

Throughout the war Niebuhr continued to comment, at least biweekly, on the war's progress. He generally supported President Roosevelt's conduct of both the war and diplomacy. His major differences with the political leadership of the United States were on three issues: (1) he disagreed with the program of saturation bombing; (2) he disagreed with the policy of demanding unconditional surrender of Japan and Germany; and (3) he urged more positive steps by the government toward the postwar world it hoped to mold. Niebuhr's occasional writings during the war followed the twists and turns of military and political strategy. If these occasional writings do not together represent a contribution to the theory of international politics, neither do they reveal any major mistakes in judgment as to the course of events of the war.

As the war reached an end, Niebuhr emphasized the positive tasks of rebuilding. He foresaw that the assumption of responsibility by Russia, Britain, and America for the shattered world would evoke charges of imperialism. He saw no way to avoid the charges, and in fact he accepted the conclusion that the United States in assuming responsibility would not be consistently wise in the exercise of power. He hoped that the concern of the idealists for the rule of law would qualify the realists' tendency to trust completely some new balance of power. This meant that the major powers would have to assume responsibility for building a world organization, for protecting the rights of the small nations, and for encouraging the development of the rule of law.[26]

Niebuhr urged the country to remember that the spirit of vengeance had lost the peace of World War I at Versailles. Germany had suffered more than enough in the war and should not be punished after the war. The judgment of the victors, acting as judges in their own case, could not be just. Though recognizing that leading figures in the Nazi hierarchy and war criminals should be punished, Niebuhr vigorously urged that the victorious allies distinguish between the Nazis and the Germans and that punishment not be applied to Germany as a nation.

After the war he continued to labor tirelessly in refugee organizations and in groups sending aid to Europe. He was a member, in the fall of 1946, of a U.S. State Department mission investigating the educational program of the United States military government. He continued in the postwar years to plead publicly and privately for the humane and wise treatment of the defeated peoples. His collected papers in the Library of Congress contain numerous letters written to aid refugees, dozens of items of correspondence related to relieving postwar suffering, letters concerning the provision of books to German scholars, and evidence of hours of work invested in raising funds and in sponsoring CARE packages.[27]

Following the war, *Christianity and Crisis* reaffirmed that its original purpose had been to interpret Christian faith in a manner relevant to the threat of tyranny. Its editor committed it in the postwar period to political realism and the new opportunities for creative politics, pledging its emphasis would be on repentance rather than despair. In terms of the general outlines of foreign policy it counseled: (1) strategic firmness and a creative economic policy; (2) support for the United Nations; (3) international control of atomic energy; and (4) support for the principles of trusteeship in problems of colonialism.[28]

Theses of Christian Realist Political Philosophy

The Defense of Democracy

Niebuhr wrote his major treatise on democratic political theory during the period in which allied victory in Europe was being assured. He gave the Raymond W. West Lectures at Stanford in January, 1944, immediately after the Yalta Conference and finished rewriting them during the August liberation of Paris. The volume, *The Children of Light and the Children of Darkness*, was conceived as a corrective to the illusions of optimism which Niebuhr regarded as supportive of democracy. Democracy as a theory for the organization of community was stronger than the

111

illusions in which it was submerged, and he thought it would be stronger for being grounded on a more secure understanding of man than it had previously exhibited. The essay articulates one of his perennial concerns, that men who would be morally responsible in politics must also be politically wise, and it also provided an ideological defense for a system that had been recently on the military defensive.

He regarded the second world war as bringing home to Americans, the way the first world war had done to Europeans, the refutation of all optimistic estimates of man's moral capacities. The book gave expression to the concern that, to the extent democratic ideals were connected to optimism, they too might be discarded along with optimism. The optimism he regarded as having been invalidated was the optimism of the bourgeois classes who, seeing their own group advancing culturally, socially, and economically, had mistaken their rise for the direction of mankind. There were still traces of Marxist rhetoric in the volume, but they had little importance in the argument. The traces of Marxism were apparent in his prediction that "in any event, bourgeois civilization is in process of disintegration." [29] He then argued it was necessary to save what was permanently valid in democracy even if bourgeois society was doomed. In 1944 he did not have much evidence that bourgeois civilization was doomed, even though he gave vent to such predictions; what he was certain of was that the experience of World War II refuted dreams of an early achievement of human community on a world scale.

The thesis of the book, that neither idealism nor cynicism served the cause of democracy, was captured in a sentence that became one of the most quoted of the Niebuhr aphorisms: "Man's capacity for justice makes democracy possible; but man's inclination to injustice makes democracy necessary." [30] This theme is played throughout the volume with the claim being that inasmuch as man is a "child of light" or a moral creature he can achieve a degree of community and harmony. Politics can, to a degree, be the art of seeking the good of the community. On the other hand, to the degree that a man is a "child of darkness," or one who is basically self-serving, his egoism needs to be checked to protect the community from his will-to-power. Politics is also the struggle between men for the control of the society's resources and institutions. Democracy, according to Niebuhr, provides the possibilities of fulfilling man's benevolent side, but it also provides ways of checking his will-to-power. The greatest danger to man is his own unchecked power, and democracy is peculiarly well endowed by its systems of checks and balances, elections, and separation of the divisions of government to guard against the misuse of power.

The intellectual defense of democracy needed to be undertaken in full light of the recognition of man's vital capacities and his tendencies to use those capacities to fulfill himself at the risk of destroying his fellows. Neither optimism nor cynicism about man would suffice if democracy were to be understood as a perennially valid form of human organization. Neither liberalism nor Marxism sufficiently understood man's nature, and this lack vitiated their respective political theories. Niebuhr attempted to articulate a deeper analysis of man to serve as the basis for reflection upon political communities. The dynamics of human nature led him to conclude that, granted all its problems, democracy still gave the fullest expression to man's vitalities. Other considerations led him to regard foreign policy as the Achilles' heel of democracy, and these are discussed in the following section.

The Weakness of Democratic Foreign Policy

Niebuhr has not put much confidence in the ability of democratic states to conduct foreign policy since the exposure of the weaknesses of the Treaty of Versailles. During World War II he saw Western civilization threatened jointly by the barbarism of Nazism and the ineptness of the democracies. He viewed the foibles of the Western democracies' foreign policies prior to U.S. entry into the war as revealing structural problems in the whole foreign policy enterprise of the democratic states.

He thought the isolationism of the United States and the pre-Munich complacency of Britain were both due to the inability of democratic leaders to force their populations to sacrifice before their own national interest was directly threatened. Hitler was able to force the German people to sacrifice for the creation of an armed force; creating a comparable armed force prior to the direct threat of war was not a viable alternative for the democratic states.[31]

From Niebuhr's perspective, democracy was supported by liberal culture, which trusted that all differences could be accommodated. The culture had few resources for estimating the tragic dimensions of history. A determined foe could count on an inept and irresolute response by his democratic opponents. Niebuhr thought that Hitler had estimated the weaknesses of liberal culture accurately and that from his estimate of the weaknesses he had grown confident that he could destroy it.[32]

A further weakness of democratic foreign policy was the inability of democratic leaders to offend significant minorities in the country by acting against their wishes for the sake of the broader national interest. Niebuhr regarded the Franco victory as the first of many defeats suffered by the democracies. He thought that Roosevelt had understood the dangers present in a Franco victory and that fear of the Catholic hierarchy, with its connections with the big-city democratic machines, had prevented him from acting. Resolute leadership could not be counted on in a democracy; moreover even resolute leadership could not overcome the natural lethargy of the population if opposed by a force as significant as the Catholic hierarchy.[33]

The masses of a population could not be expected to understand the quickly shifting orientation of a country's foreign policy in a world of power politics. A country with a tradition of isolationism had peculiar problems in adjusting to the needs of the hour. To the extent that the leaders of a democracy depended upon the foreign policy consensus of the nation, they were limited by opinions formed in a previous situation rather than the immediate crisis. Also, democracy was always tempted to mold its foreign policy in the shape of its demagoguery.

The prewar failures of democratic statesmen impressed Niebuhr, and through him the Christian realist school, with the weaknesses of democracies in foreign policy. The eventual victory of the democracies did little to dispel this conviction. The postwar situation provided some evidence that republican forms of government were ill equipped for the subtleties of international politics, and Niebuhr continued to argue that oligarchic forms of government were better equipped than republican forms for the formation and execution of foreign policy.

Universal Ideals Obscure National Egoism

The politics leading to World War II confirmed in Niebuhr's thought the thesis that, while the pursuit of national self-interest was only slightly qualified by the broader values recognized by the nation, universal ideals often served as a disguise for the pursuit of national self-interest. Nations, like men, could only rarely admit the extent to which their policies were directed to furthering their own interest.

> Every national organism seeks to defend itself, and possibly to extend its power and prestige, in competition with other nations. Every nation claims that in doing this it is fighting not only for its own existence but for certain values which transcend its existence.[34]

The residual loyalty of nations to broader values refuted the cynics who thought international politics were totally lacking a moral dimension. However, the use of moral values as ideological cover for the inevitable pursuit of national power and prestige refuted the idealists who thought international politics were simply guided by moral choices.

The claim that nations were fighting for broader interests was not wholly false, or it would not have achieved the credibility it did. However, the claims of Germany, Russia, Britain, France, and the United States to represent universal values had all been

115

contradicted by their neglect of these values when more pressing interests of national power were concerned. The anti-Bolshevist and antifascist policies of Germany and Russia were discredited by their alliance. The loyalty of Britain and France to democracy was belied by their acquiescence over the fall of Spain. The United States could not act until its security interests were directly attacked at Pearl Harbor.

Niebuhr's analysis of the element of deceit in the pretensions of nation-states to be pursuing universal values was similar to his view of individual men justifying their narrow, self-seeking actions by appeal to broader values. The nations did what individual men did, but in the case of the nation it was more blatant and more nearly inevitable.

World Government Cannot Be Realized

Niebuhr regarded the defeat of Nazi Germany as the *sine qua non* for a new order in Europe. He hoped that the elimination of Hitler could be followed by trends toward national interdependence, the abridgement of national sovereignty, the elimination of trade barriers, and the achievement of higher degrees of justice nationally.[35] As the war ground to a halt, he wrote, "We cannot have world security without much more abridgement of national sovereignty than either the great or small nations are willing to grant." [36] He agreed with the proponents of world government that security from recurring wars demanded world government in some form, but he could not therefore conclude that world government was possible. More probably the world would continue to live in relative insecurity from war. His theological convictions merged with his estimate of the international scene to conclude that man's international relations would be plagued by conflict. The very organizations which secured order on the national scene encouraged disorder on the international scene.

He argued that, imperfect as the Dumbarton Oaks and Yalta proposals for an international organization were, they should be supported rather than risk all by promoting an unrealizable world government. The political basis for creating a world government did not exist in 1945; "the traditions and habits, the collective instincts and impulses of the nations run counter to the ideal concept." [37]

Though Niebuhr served as a United States delegate to a UNESCO conference and praised the work of the organization in promoting cultural understanding, in his role as an adviser to George Kennan's postwar Policy Planning Staff [38] he played the role of critic whenever world government proposals were discussed. His position was to promote all possible international cooperation and organization, but not to allow utopian visions of world government to interfere with the complicated task of securing the precarious order and justice that was available within the existing system.

Niebuhr's critique of world government plans, in addition to attacking the plans in detail, has emphasized two major points.

The fallacy of world government can be stated in two simple propositions. The first is that governments are not created by fiat (though sometimes they can be imposed by tyranny). The second is that governments have only limited efficacy in integrating a community.[39]

His political philosophy emphasized the organic factors which produced national community rather than the legal structures which bound the community together. Governments were the result of many factors working together for national cohesion. The factors of economics, language, race, religion, cultural and historical consciousness were all relevant to the formation of a government. Community, for Niebuhr, is prior to law; government is a function of community and only secondarily a creator of it.[40]

While encouraging the development of a worldwide community, Niebuhr recognized that at present the forces of particularism are stronger than the attraction of any universalism on the world scene. A few alliances, growing economic interdependence, cultural exchanges, and the United Nations are heavily out-

117

weighed by the factors of diverse cultures, ideological differences, and nationalism.

The United States Should Assume Global Responsibilities

Niebuhr's attitude toward the world role that the United States ought to play changed as the United States' involvement in world politics grew. Prior to World War II, he had advocated the development of a system of mutual security with the United States remaining neutral. Before Pearl Harbor, he had urged that the United States help stiffen the allied cause without advocating U.S. entry into the war. Following American entry, he argued for active U.S. involvement in the postwar settlement, and he argued that the power of the United States required that it assume a role of world leadership after the war.

His writing on the war, which filled the columns of *Christianity and Society* and *Christianity and Crisis* and appeared frequently in *The Nation,* focused primarily on the political issues of the war. *Christianity and Crisis* and *Christianity and Society,* the less-Marxist successor to *Radical Religion,* were both founded by Niebuhr. In both he often wrote on religious or theological issues and tended to use theological concepts freely in his political analysis. Niebuhr's writing for *Christianity and Society* was much less inhibited than that in *Christianity and Crisis,* which reached a broader audience. *Christianity and Society* was read largely by people quite close to Niebuhr's position, and he rapidly produced editorials for it in his most polemical style. *The Nation,* on the other hand, generally did not carry Niebuhr's writing on theological issues. His political analysis in it was much freer of theological terminology than his writing in either *Christianity and Society* or *Christianity and Crisis.* He wrote and worked actively on the perennial Christian concern of relief and refugee work. He wrote essays and reviews interpreting the character of Germany and probing the spiritual aspects of the struggle. He commented on diplomatic conferences and the twists and turns of American policy. He objected repeatedly to the policies of obliteration bombing and unconditional surrender. However, the major emphasis of his writing was on urging the United States to adopt far-sighted political policies in order to secure the peace at the end of the war.

Niebuhr realized that the power of the United States would tempt it to act pridefully and arrogantly. He feared that the United States could become imperialistic, but even more he feared that the United States would not act to reduce the international anarchy that would be the heritage of World War II. Throughout the war he urged the U.S. and Britain to bear responsibility for rebuilding Europe and restoring order in Asia. He knew that a failure of the Anglo-Saxon alliance to achieve a cooperative relationship with either Russia or China meant continued instability in world politics. He recognized the difficulty of maintaining a partnership with a victorious Russia, but throughout the war he thought wise statesmanship could preserve the wartime alliance after the struggle. He argued that, despite the unsatisfactoriness of a peace settlement dictated by the great victorious powers, failure for the major powers to agree would be tragic. While welcoming the late-war proposals for an international organization, he stressed that only great-power cooperation could provide a lasting settlement and avoid another world war.

Niebuhr thought prophetic religion contained resources which the United States needed in its new global role. Prophetic religion ought not to let the U.S. remain secure in feelings of national righteousness. The U.S. needed a sense of the severe judgment which was part of great responsibilities. He thought that God had chosen Britain and the United States to play a particularly fateful role in the postwar world arena.[41] He was quite willing to demythologize the assertion to mean that at particular times various nations and classes have special missions. The task of the churches was to contend against the American tendency toward irresponsibility and complacency in national life.[42] There was also an opposite impulse in American life toward imperialism which needed to be countered.[43] In his attempt to expose the cultural weaknesses of the U.S. which encouraged isolationism on the one hand and imperialism on the other, he advocated a humble acceptance of responsibility and urged that it be undertaken in full awareness of what was at issue religiously as well as politically.

> We must not have an easy conscience about the impurities of politics or they will reach intolerable proportions. But we must also find religious means of easing the conscience, or our uneasy conscience will tempt us into irresponsibility.[44]

After the Cairo and Teheran conferences revealed very little planning for postwar Europe, Niebuhr argued for a new European unity which would prevent international chaos and war. He feared that a division of Europe into spheres of influence would guarantee future conflict. He criticized the allied leaders for being so preoccupied with the war that they were unable to plan for the peace.[45] At the time of President Roosevelt's death, however, he credited him with achieving a "higher form of political maturity than this nation has previously achieved." He praised the President for his conduct of both the war and negotiations and noted that, if the proposed measures of international accord were inadequate, the fault lay primarily in the situation rather than in Roosevelt.[46]

Though the cold war frustrated hopes for a postwar coalition guaranteeing mutual security, Niebuhr's arguments in favor of an internationally responsible United States were still relevant. The meaning of a responsible United States in the post-World War II world is analyzed in chapter VI.

Relationship to Neo-Orthodoxy and Conservatism

Neo-Orthodoxy

The view which treats Reinhold Niebuhr, along with Karl Barth and Emil Brunner, as a leader of the neo-orthodox movement is not entirely mistaken. There are certain broad affinities in the thought of the three. They all contributed to the attacks upon liberal culture, politics, and theology. They all found inspiration in Reformation thought. They each emphasized, though in somewhat different ways, the gap between the sacred and the secular. The doctrines of sin and justification by faith in Christ played determinate roles in all their theologies. Also, they all regarded man's existence and history as provisionally tragic.

However, Reinhold Niebuhr's thought on politics cannot be deduced from the theology he held in common with other representatives of neo-orthodoxy; his political thought and those of Brunner and Barth had very little in common. Brunner's political thought has a conservative note which is foreign to Niebuhr's thought. Barth's political thought is impossible to define within the normal frame of reference of political philosophy, but his specific political judgments reveal a long history of disagreement with Niebuhr. Niebuhr's political judgments are consistent with his theology, but his neo-orthodoxy did not determine his political judgments. Neo-orthodoxy itself seemed to be compatible with either radicalism or conservatism. The purpose of this inquiry is to state briefly the nature of Niebuhr's dependence upon Brunner and Barth and to point to the significant differences in their thought.

Niebuhr indicated consistently that, insofar as he was in debt to the neo-orthodox or crisis theology of the continent, he owed more to Brunner than to Barth. The debt to Brunner is most obvious in *The Nature and Destiny of Man*. Niebuhr studied and was very impressed by Brunner's *Der Mensch im Widerspruch*.[47] The question of the volume, "What is man?" is the question of *The Nature and Destiny of Man*. Brunner's discussion of the themes of man as sinner, man in the image of God, the connection of man's freedom with his sin, and the greatness and the misery of man are handled in ways with which Niebuhr felt no need to disagree in his Gifford Lectures. Brunner's reliance upon the Reformers while correcting their doctrine with the insights of biblical criticism and science is also, in broad outline, similar to Niebuhr's position. The tendency to examine secular answers to the problems posed by an existential analysis and to reject them in favor of theological answers, again, is similar to the method of *The Nature and Destiny of Man*. The similarities between the two works are striking but are due to both authors working on the Augustinian-Reformation tradition in an awareness of the prewar crisis in man's understanding of himself, not to conscious, unacknowledged borrowing. One of the distinguishing characteristics of the two studies is the increased seriousness with which Niebuhr treats the political world. The discussions of politics in *Der Mensch im Widerspruch* are perfunctory. Brunner's tendency in *The Divine Imperative* to reflect a view of the state emphasizing only its negative, police functions is criticized in Niebuhr's *Human Destiny*. According to Niebuhr, Brunner's theory of natural law served the forces of social reaction by favoring the use of coercion by the forces of the status quo while denying them to the forces of revolution.

Niebuhr's debt to Brunner is clearly expressed in his own belated admission:

> I read Brunner's book some time before giving my lectures, and profited greatly from his analysis of the doctrine of sin in his *Man in Revolt*. Subsequently I became involved in tracing the doctrine through as much of history as I could encompass. In the process I lost sight of Brunner and did not refer to his work, though, as he confesses, I had written appreciatively to him about the book. It was a grievous error not to acknowledge my debt to him, though my omission was occasioned by finding no specific agreement or disagreement with him which would require a footnote. I may say that Brunner's whole theological position is close to mine and that it is one to which I am more indebted than any other.[48]

Reinhold Niebuhr has been interpreted as a Barthian. It is a common error on the level of journalistic writing. However, scholars have also regarded Niebuhr as a Barthian, although an American Barthian. As careful a scholar as Charles C. West has attempted "to show him as the Barthian he truly is."[49] West did not hesitate to show significant differences between Barth and Niebuhr. However, his minimization of the role of Niebuhr's substitutes for natural law and natural theology and his emphasis upon the role of revelation in Niebuhr's thought tended to support his case that Niebuhr was under Barthian influence. John C. Bennett, in an appreciative review of West's book, criticized his attempt to make Niebuhr appear to be closer to Barth than Niebuhr would admit.

I believe that he [Charles C. West] is quite wrong in his assumption that these [substitutes for natural law and natural theology] are peripheral to Niebuhr's thought and that Niebuhr is really more Barthian than he admits because the effective criterion for his theological thought is revelation.[50]

It is the fact that he has been interpreted as a Barthian rather than any decisive influence on Niebuhr's political thought that requires a brief discussion of Niebuhr's rejection of the Barthian position.

The bulk of Niebuhr's references to Barth are critical. In many articles written since 1928, he has attacked aspects of Barth's thought.[51] Though deploring features of Barth's theology, Niebuhr directed his strongest polemics against Barth's politics.

Barth's religious socialism collapsed much earlier than did Niebuhr's. Barth never found an alternative political program; though his theology became more transcendent, his occasional political judgments and his political silence carried weight. Niebuhr's 1928 article criticized Barth for his lack of "creative social activity." [52] In part this was the criticism of a continental theologian by an American activist, but it was also an expression of concern for the lack of moral vigor in the new theology. He asserted in 1931, "If the Barthians are socialist, I think it is not unfair to them to say that they don't work very hard at it." [53] Niebuhr feared that Barth's religious perfectionism and his shock at the failure of Christian socialism had combined to produce a defeatist attitude toward social justice.

In 1934 Niebuhr deplored the tendency, seen particularly in Gogarten, for Barth's theology to be exploited for reactionary ends.[54] He thought Barth's theology was compatible with either social liberalism or radicalism, but it did not seem to be involved in healing the wounds of Germany. He repented of some of his polemics against liberalism after observing how orthodoxy could be used by the forces of social reaction.[55]

He welcomed Barth's opposition to the Nazis, wishing that it had come sooner and noting that ten years earlier it might have had great significance in central Europe. Barth opposed Nazism as a theologian on two grounds: (1) it was a political religion, and (2) National Socialism was not a *Rechtsstaat*.[56] Niebuhr regarded Barth's Christian opposition to Nazism as an abandonment of his earlier refusal to relate politics and faith. Barth regarded it as a shift of emphasis.

Niebuhr's criticism of Barth continued after the war. He interpreted Barth as suggesting that Christians had no guidance for the pressing political decisions required by history. The "crisis" theology, however well suited for a crisis, was inadequate for the daily decisions which determined the nature and outcome of the crisis.[57] Niebuhr criticized Barth for failing to use the resources of secular political wisdom in aiding him to make important political-moral distinctions. He expressed this attack in two points: (1) Barth's focus was consistently too eschatological for him to worry about the "nicely calculated less and more" of which political decisions are composed; and (2) Barth was overly pragmatic, refusing to utilize moral principles and trying to look at each event anew.[58]

Niebuhr attributed Barth's silence on the Hungarian rebellion to a "marxist creed . . . in his subconscious," "ill-disguised anti-Americanism," and a series of political misjudgments.[59] Even if Niebuhr had recognized the particular features of Barth's neutrality as legitimate, this silence on Hungary would have been intolerable. Even Communists criticized the action and broke with the party. Niebuhr asserted, "Surely one could have expected as much of the world's most eminent Protestant theologian as of the assistant editor of the *London Daily Worker*, who publicly disavowed all his former illusions." [60]

Niebuhr's debate with Barth reveals more clearly than many of his controversies with liberal social reformers: (1) his fear that theology can be a means of escaping from social responsibility; (2) his openness to empirical studies; (3) the need for principles of social morality; and (4) the willingness to judge theological systems by their ability to produce political justice and wisdom.

Conservatism

Niebuhr's political thought moved from the left to a radical left position and then back to the right. The question raised by this section is, how far did the swing back to the right go? Is it helpful to regard Reinhold Niebuhr's political thought at any stage as conservative? Though there are sufficient grounds for finally rejecting the term *conservative* as applicable to Niebuhr's thought, the investigation into the reasons why his colleagues, friends, and a major interpreter have regarded him as conservative reveals interesting features of his thought.

Eduard Heimann doubted that the suggested political move left and theological move right programmed in *Reflections on the End of an Era* would hold together. He was correct, and the developing theological consciousness of the Christian realist contributed to the suppression of Marxism within Niebuhr's thought.

Heimann emphasizes the pragmatism of Niebuhr's thought as the source of his conservatism. Heimann believes that the essays of John Bennett, Arthur Schlesinger, Jr., and Kenneth Thompson in the volume, *Reinhold Niebuhr: His Religious, Social, and Political Thought*, conclude that Niebuhr's political philosophy is "a pragmatism which finds its proper application in an authentic conservatism." [61] The three interpreters do deal extensively with his pragmatism, but none of them classify Niebuhr as a conservative. Schlesinger emphasizes the resurgent liberalism qualified by pragmatism as the final stage of his thought. Bennett explicitly denies that Reinhold Niebuhr should be regarded as a conservative.

There is some danger in ending on this note because it may seem that Niebuhr has merely substituted a conservative creed for the radicalism of his earlier career. This is certainly not true. . . .

In recent writings Niebuhr makes clear that he cannot be classified with the "new conservatives" who also appeal to Burke.[62]

Heimann erred in naming Bennett, Schlesinger, and Thompson as authorities who recognize Niebuhr's conservatism; his argument linking pragmatism and conservatism, however, requires further investigation. Conservatism in Heimann's opinion is the logical outcome of pragmatism. Pragmatism as a political philosophy urges the preservation of what is through accepting necessary changes. "For if we change what no longer works as far as is necessary to make it work again, then this is preservation by means of change, change for the sake of preservation." [63] Pragmatism is a viable political philosophy, in Heimann's view, when its presupposition of a sound and viable political structure is realized, but it lacks resources for radically altering the structure. Pragmatism "loses its applicability when that which exists cannot be preserved." [64] In Heimann's view the economic scene, both domestically and internationally, is characterized by structural problems for which pragmatism provides no solutions. Heimann, a socialist, disagrees with Niebuhr's break with socialism and he regards his pragmatism as influential in the break. Niebuhr's pragmatism binds him to the modification of the status quo in a day when an adequate analysis reveals that radical social change is required. However, Heimann's short essay leaves the hard questions unanswered. He does not prove that the present economic system is headed for disaster. Nor can he quote Niebuhr to prove that the latter is opposed to changing the economic system domestically or internationally. Niebuhr's rejection of socialism does not in itself make him a conservative; there are many alternatives to socialism on the political spectrum. Niebuhr's participation in and leadership of Americans for Democratic Action and support for programs commonly identified in American politics as liberal make a classification of Niebuhr as one who supports the status quo with modification difficult to sustain. Niebuhr's sense of the movement of history does not allow him willingly to defend that which is destined to change. Heimann's real disagreement is with Niebuhr's current refusal to read the movement of history through socialist glasses. The next chapter will discuss the combination of liberalism and pragmatism which Niebuhr developed in the postwar years and argue that pragmatism has been more closely allied with liberal politics than conservative politics in the United States.

Will Herberg also regards Reinhold Niebuhr as a conservative. Herberg refers to "Niebuhr's brand of conservatism" which admittedly is not the conservatism of those who describe themselves as conservatives in American politics. Exact definition of this peculiar conservatism is not provided except for reference to the fact that "it is enough apparently to establish a kinship with Burke." [65] Herberg thinks Niebuhr's awareness of the relative character of political institutions and his "emphasis on the historic continuities of social life" made Niebuhr's political thought conservative.[66] Although Herberg is correct that these elements are present in Niebuhr's thought, neither element is proven by Herberg to be foreign to the broad stream of American political liberalism. Herberg himself could be regarded as among the "new conservatives," but more substantial arguments need to be produced to place his mentor in that group.

Gordon Harland regards Niebuhr's conservatism as an important ingredient of his political philosophy. Harland reflects the emphases of both Heimann and Herberg. Niebuhr's conservatism is implied in his criticism of liberalism and related to both his "prophetic radicalism" and his pragmatism. Harland admits, while wanting to retain the term *conservative*, that Niebuhr is not associated with American conservatism nor with the defense of the status quo. His relationship to "historic conservatism" is essentially, for Harland, Niebuhr's respect for its emphasis on factors of power and organic processes of social cohesion rather than abstract schemes.[67] Harland's work indicates how difficult it is to label Niebuhr a conservative. Harland retains the term, conceding that it is not the common use of the term and failing to provide an alternative definition.

Niebuhr himself has encouraged his classification as a conservative in three ways: (1) he has recognized wisdom in political conservatism; (2) he has evoked the names of Edmund Burke and Winston Churchill as political guides; and (3) he has attacked liberalism. The attack upon liberalism, already discussed, has been revealed as largely an attack upon humanistic optimism. The use of Edmund Burke has been casual and unsystematic in Niebuhr's writing; he used Burke as a weapon against abstract idealists and the errors of the French revolution. The references to Burke in Niebuhr all come from selected passages in *Reflections on the Revolution in France* and emphasize what Niebuhr elsewhere describes as political realism. The references to Churchill do not commit him to the total political outlook of Churchill but indicate deep respect for his uniting moral purpose and artful politics in the defense of Britain against Nazism.[68] He praised Roosevelt for similar brilliance in leading the United States in the struggle. In Niebuhr's usage and in common political usage, Churchill was regarded as a conservative and Roosevelt as a liberal, yet in foreign policy they had many of the same virtues. The qualities of realistic politics which Niebuhr occasionally praised in political conservatism were not intrinsically related to conservatism.

Niebuhr did not use the term *conservative* in a precise sense. He considered a careful definition of the term unnecessary. In his chapter on "The Foreign Policy of American Conservatism and Liberalism," he wrote, "Perhaps it is as useless to define the ideal conservatism as to restore exact meaning to the word liberal." [69] In that context he did not define conservatism precisely but pointed to its characteristics, including: (1) support for the status quo; (2) loyalty to aristocratic interests; (3) commonsense wisdom; (4) awareness of the factors of power and interest: (5) pragmatism; and (6) politics understood as the art of the possible. Except for the first and second characteristics, neither of which Niebuhr valued highly, these characteristics were as applicable to liberals as to conservatives, particularly liberals of the character of Franklin D. Roosevelt. Niebuhr's failure to define his terms and to use them carefully is partially responsible for the treatment of him as a conservative. When he praised conservatism in the following statement, for example, he should have used the term *realism*: "In part, this conservatism is the product of Christian rather than 'idealistic' approaches to the perennial facts of human nature." [70] His desire here was to emphasize the need for historical, empirical approach and for the consideration of factors of human egoism. The term *realism* is much more appropriate than the term *conservatism*, which denotes a predisposition to defend existing political institutions and connotes a defense of privilege neither of which is intrinsic to Niebuhr's political philosophy.

The rejection of the term *conservative* as applicable to Niebuhr's political philosophy leaves unanswered the degree to which his political philosophy is in debt to pragmatism. The definition of this pragmatism and its relationship to his Christian faith on the one hand and his political liberalism on the other is the subject of the next chapter.

Conclusion

This chapter has argued that the failure of both Western liberal culture and its Marxist alternative encouraged Niebuhr to elaborate a doctrine of man, a doctrine of history, and a political philosophy grounded in Christian theology. The theological critique of liberalism displaced the Marxist critique of liberalism. He regarded his theology as standing in the Augustinian tradition, and he appropriated Augustine's political realism.

His occasional and more formal writing during the war and in the years immediately before and after the war turned again and again to the themes of the peculiar dangers surrounding American foreign policy and the need for America to assume a major responsibility for the protection of Western culture and international order. American society labored under illusions which made responsible foreign policy difficult to achieve. Niebuhr attacked what he regarded as the most dangerous illusions and gave ever-increasing attention to international politics.

Various factors were operative during Niebuhr's Christian realist period which hinted that it would not be his last attempt to mold a political philosophy adequate to support American foreign policy. He became aware that his critique of liberalism was not completely consistent with his admiration for Franklin D. Roosevelt's achievements in both domestic and foreign policy. Having defended democracy in its embattled hour, he realized anew its resources in both its liberal foundations and its pragmatic adjustments to changing situations. The critique of his theology by astute theologians and the ability of secular liberal friends to utilize his political thought while ignoring his theology made him search for another language in which to express his insights about man.

Christian realism was not repudiated by Niebuhr, but aspects of it were dropped and significant alterations in his thought took place in the postwar years. Most noticeable was an increased respect for pragmatism and liberalism during the period in which he did his most important writing on international politics.

V. A PRAGMATIC-LIBERAL SYNTHESIS IN CHRISTIAN POLITICAL PHILOSOPHY

The previous four chapters of the study exhibit the evolution of Niebuhr's thought. The development of his philosophy was traced from his early liberalism, through the refutation of that liberalism by historical events, through the Marxist critique of liberalism, and into the theological attack upon liberalism. This fifth chapter describes Niebuhr's return to political liberalism. He does not return to the idealistic Wilsonian liberalism of his youth but to the more pragmatic liberalism of Franklin D. Roosevelt.

This period of his career is the most important for his thought on international politics. It is in this postwar period that Niebuhr devotes primary attention to international politics and gains a reputation as a theorist in international relations. Much of the thought of this period is discussed in Chapter VI, which deals explicitly with his philosophy of international politics. This chapter discusses briefly the characteristic trends of his thinking and examines the political philosophy which supports his thought on international politics.

Arthur Schlesinger, Jr.'s essay on Niebuhr's political philosophy indicated that a new synthesis had been achieved in Niebuhr's thought in the postwar period.

> The penetrating critic of the Social Gospel and of pragmatism, he ended up, in a sense, the powerful reinterpreter and champion of both. It was the triumph of his own remarkable analysis that it took what was valuable in each, rescued each by defining for each the limits of validity, and, in the end, gave the essential purposes of both new power and new vitality.[1]

There were aspects of Niebuhr's thought which were not yet clear in 1956 when Schlesinger announced the synthesis. He saw the synthesis, but he could not anticipate how far the new de-

131

velopment in Niebuhr's thought would revise previous opinions. The failure was not Schlesinger's, but it was an inevitable result of a characteristic of Niebuhr's writing. His brother has noted the difficulty of understanding Reinhold Niebuhr due to the hiddenness of his presuppositions. "Reinie's thought appears to me to be like a great iceberg of which three-fourths or more is beneath the surface and in which what's expressly said depends on something that is not made explicit." [2]

The publication of *Man's Nature and His Communities* in 1965 brought together the various strands of revision which had been taking place in Niebuhr's political philosophy since the war. The book reveals more clearly than any other work the presuppositions of his political philosophy which were guiding his occasional and theoretical writings on international politics. It recants previous polemics against liberalism and reflects the reliance on liberalism and pragmatism which characterized his work. The long essay on political idealism and realism is his solution to the problem he regarded as the most important in political philosophy. It relates liberal principles of social morality to the factors in politics which inhibit the realization of those ideals in an attempt to resolve the problem that he had wrestled with since his earliest writing.

The significance of the work for an interpretation of Niebuhr's thought is best expressed in the "Introduction" to the volume.

> This volume of essays on various aspects of man's individual and social existence is intended to serve two purposes: namely, to summarize, and to revise previously held opinions. . . .
> The systematic essays are intended to "revise" previously held opinions only in the sense that they seek to give a systematic account of the revisions which have taken place in the author's mind in a whole lifetime of study and of writing books too frequently. [3]

This chapter discusses his revised doctrine of man, the understanding of history as ironical, his perspective on American history, the sources of his increased pragmatism, the sources of his renewed appreciation of political liberalism, and a proposed solution to the idealist-realist debate.

The Egoistic Self

The differences between the analysis of man's nature in *Man's Nature and His Communities* and *The Nature and Destiny of Man* are due primarily to the disappearance of the theological vocabulary. The themes of *The Nature and Destiny of Man* (man as created in the image of God, man as sinner, original sin, *justitia originalis*, the biblical doctrine of grace, the kingdom of God, the *parousia*, the last judgment, and the resurrection) are not the themes of *Man's Nature and His Communities*. Human nature is still the subject of analysis and the focus is still on man the political animal, but the style has changed. Though *The Nature and Destiny of Man* is important as a work in the philosophy of history or political philosophy, it is clearly within the theological circle. Its argument is frankly apologetic and inclines the reader who agrees with the argument to move into the theological circle. In contrast, *Man's Nature and His Communities* translates a theologically inspired view of man into nontheological terms. The argument does not lead a sympathetic reader into the theological circle. Some theological insights are confirmed through empirical studies, but the reader is not given the impression that the conclusions require theology.

Man's Nature and His Communities represents, in part, Niebuhr's attempt to revise his description of the human situation in the light of the criticism of his Gifford Lectures. He conceded that the attempt to revive the vocabulary of original sin had been an error. It had not been possible to free original sin from the connotations which were anathema to the presuppositions of liberal culture. Looking back on the effort he wrote: "But these labors of modern interpretation of traditional religious symbols proved vain." [4] Criticism of his theological language by political philosophers who were in substantial agreement with his understanding of man had influenced him to describe the human situation in a more secular style.[5] His growing respect for Erik Erikson's thought is represented by the adoption of some of the

133

language of ego-psychology for the description of the human situation. The differences between *The Nature and Destiny of Man* and *Man's Nature and His Communities* is partially one of intellectual evolution and partially simply a change in style. Throughout his career Niebuhr could write articles in either a secular or a theological mode. The pieces in *Christianity and Society* or *Christianity and Crisis* are characterized by a much more frequent usage of theological terms than articles he wrote concurrently for *The Nation* and *The New Leader*.

As early as 1956 Niebuhr's reply to William J. Wolf's critique of his doctrine of man had indicated dissatisfaction with aspects of his own thought. He admitted that his formulas of "equality of sin and inequality of guilt" and "redeemed in principle but not in fact" were unsatisfactory.[6] He never did satisfactorily meet the issues (within theological symbolism) which these formulas were designed to answer. In *Man's Nature and His Communities*, he again wrestled with the issues, but without the neo-orthodox theological symbolism.

Niebuhr's move away from the theological symbolism of *The Nature and Destiny of Man* led to a misunderstanding with Paul Tillich. Tillich reported to a colloquium in honor of Reinhold Niebuhr on October 20, 1961, that Niebuhr had recently admitted he now agreed with Tillich's description of the human situation. There still remained differences between them, but after years of debate, Tillich implied that Niebuhr now agreed with him.

A week ago we had a wonderful talk in Cambridge for one to two hours, and he said to me quite spontaneously, "I have accepted your point of view in this respect. We cannot use any longer the language of the tradition if we want to communicate anything to the people of our time." As an example, he gave me his use of the words *sin*, and especially *original sin*, in his book. . . . The words *original sin* shouldn't be used at all. He accepted—if I understood him rightly—something like *universal estrangement* instead of the term *original* or *hereditary sin*.[7]

In reply to Tillich's address, Niebuhr confirmed the former's report about their agreement that traditional theological symbolism was often irrelevant, but disagreed with Tillich's translation of the tradition into ontological terms.

He accurately reports the conversations we had at Harvard before the Colloquium, in which I confessed that I had made a mistake in hurling the traditional symbols of Christian realism—the fall and original sin—in the teeth of modern culture when I sought to criticize the undue optimism of the culture. Both these symbols, though historically significant, are subject to misunderstanding in a secular culture. . . . I still think that Paul Tillich's translation of these symbols into the ontological terms *essential* and *existential* man is too Plotinian in that it implies, if not asserts, that the whole temporal process is a corruption of the eternal. Thereby one precious Biblical concept, embodied in the idea of the goodness of creation, may be obscured. I would now rather translate these historic symbols into descriptive, rather than ontological, terms.[8]

The hint provided here, that a further attempt at a description of the human predicament would be made, was fulfilled in *Man's Nature and His Communities*.

Niebuhr's translation of the historic symbols into descriptive terms (a) retains the emphasis upon freedom of his earlier writing, (b) expresses sin as overly consistent self-seeking, (c) interprets love as self-giving, and (d) discusses grace as the gift of security. Man's self is subject to impulses toward both self-seeking and self-giving. These impulses are expressed in all of man's relationships. True human fulfillment is found when one generously gives oneself to a cause or to another self, but such self-giving presupposes that the self is not desperately seeking its own security. The self is never consistently freed from seeking its own security, but if it can presuppose security it can relate creatively to others. The impulse toward self-giving is the basis of morality, but morality itself cannot give the self the capacity to relate to others. That capacity comes only as a gift. The capacity is given originally by the family which nurtures and protects the person. But even as the family promotes self-giving by nurturing the relatively secure person, it promotes self-seeking by promoting the family's good at the expense of, or at least at the neglect of, the good of other families. All personal lives and all achievements of human community reflect this double impulse toward self-giving and self-seeking.

Niebuhr thinks this description of the human condition is consistent with the aphorism of Jesus, "He who finds his life will lose it, and he who loses his life for my sake will find it." [9] Orthodox doctrine, both Catholic and Protestant, has obscured the insight by distinguishing too sharply between common and saving grace. It has thereby encouraged a view of righteousness within the community which the "long history of religious self-righteousness" refutes.[10] It has also erred in thinking that self-regard could be suppressed. The perpetual paradox that the human self is both self-giving and self-striving has been hidden. The self fulfills itself by being inclined away from preoccupation with the self by various forms of social pressures and responsibilities.[11]

Niebuhr's analysis continued his battle against claims for the perfection of either the individual or society. It was subject to those charges which had been leveled at him throughout his career, that it did not emphasize strongly enough the sanctification of the individual, the uniqueness of the church, and the possibilities of human achievement in society. The charges could not imply, however, that Niebuhr had not examined these possibilities. He had examined them in the light of his understanding of man and in his reading of history, and he had found the claims unsupportable.

The analysis of man retained the tough-mindedness of his Marxist and Christian realist periods. The sober estimate of man, however, was now set in the context of liberalism. The emphasis upon the continuity between the religious and the secular, or saving grace and common grace, and the openness to psychology indicated the revised direction of his thought. The rigorous apologetic mood of the Gifford Lectures was absent from Niebuhr's latest book. Rather than asserting the greater intellectual adequacy of Christian theology in understanding man, he was insisting upon the complementing of theological insights by other methodologies. The tough-mindedness was, to Niebuhr's mind, the fruit of empirical and historical observation rather than the result of either Christian or Marxist presuppositions.

Reflections on History

The word *history* contains a certain ambiguity. It refers both to events which have occurred and to the record of those events. Niebuhr uses *history* as a series of events in the life of man when he argues that, though history itself is not meaningful, it bears all the meanings which can be found. His own writing of history emphasizes the interpretation of events over the recording of the events for their own value.

Niebuhr's focus was on the story and the meaning of the story rather than on the detail of the occurrences. He had many friends who were professional historians, and he was willing to defer to friends like Professors Arthur Schlesinger, Jr. and Wilhelm Pauck on questions of the verification of the events. He did not seek to escape from the discipline of the historians, but neither did he shoulder its burdens. He wrote and waited patiently for specialized historians to correct him if he had erred. He tried to stand humbly before the historians while offering to them his understanding of the meaning of the events they tried to verify and relate. In his preface to *The Irony of American History,* he expressed this humility: "I must add that I have no expert competence in the field of American history; and I apologize in advance to the specialists in this field for what are undoubtedly many errors of fact and judgment." [12] Reactions to his writings on the history of America were, of course, mixed. Evidence of the positive response of the historians is noted in Professor Henry F. May's 1968 article on *The Irony of American History.* He began his article: "In 1952 many historians of the United States were deeply impressed by Reinhold Niebuhr's *The Irony of American History.*" [13]

137

Niebuhr's usual practice in arguing for the acceptance of an idea was to trace its history. In discussing *justice* he would trace the idea of justice from its Greek and Hebrew roots, through the early years of Western civilization, to its emergence in medieval Europe, into the complexities and various alternatives of the concept in Reformation, Renaissance, and Enlightenment thought, and for a conclusion he would analyze its contemporary meaning. Or if he were attacking a policy of the government, for example Vietnam, he would trace with biting irony the mistakes of the various administrations which had led to the present quagmire. So if it is true that his reflections upon history lacked the precision of a careful history, his social criticism and philosophy utilized more historical detail than philosophers usually consider.

The deftness with which he generalized about historical epochs drove both his students and his family to historical research. The Niebuhrs' family life was often the center of far-ranging debates over the interpretation of history and what was history as opposed to sheer interpretation. Mrs. Ursula Niebuhr's Oxford education combined with the discipline of teaching ever-questioning Barnard undergraduates often gave her the advantage in debates over historical points. Particularly on British history she often corrected her husband. *The Irony of American History* is dedicated to their son, Christopher, whose approach to historical materials stands in contrast to his father's. Christopher's mind retains massive amounts of the detail and his rapid-fire delivery of the detail overwhelms his listeners. In later years, Christopher often corrected his father to the father's alternating pride and chagrin.

A visitor to Reinhold Niebuhr's retirement home on Yale Hill in Stockbridge, Massachusetts, shortly before his death was inevitably awed by the power and depth of the elderly Niebuhr's mind. He also felt in Christopher the vitality that reminded many of Reinhold in his youth. In their talk he saw the mastery of the slightest detail by Christopher and sensed the father's impatience to get on to the overarching interpretation of the data. Ursula tended to be more modest in her generalizations than Reinhold as she emphasized more the counterpoints which forced the qualification of the broader generalization. She laced her conversations with a critical wit which forced one to participate in the encounter every bit as completely as one did when engaged with her husband. The conversations at the Niebuhr home inevitably involved the problem of the historical, from the history of Stockbridge at which they all were experts, through problems of biblical history in which Ursula had an edge, to the issues of American history in which Christopher mastered the details and Reinhold was allowed to interpret. The pace of the dialogue was breathtaking, and visitors left the beautiful stone-wood house in Stockbridge awed and better informed than upon their entry.

The Irony of History

Niebuhr's adoption of irony as the major motif of his interpretation of history is significant. Its adoption reveals the decreased importance of three previous motifs, and it also indicates a trend toward a less dogmatic and more empirical approach to history. The second chapter indicated how the liberal motif of progress had been unable to deal with the tragic character of history. The third chapter discussed the failure of the Marxist dialectic of history to dominate Niebuhr's thought. The fourth chapter indicated that the motif of tragedy was of continued importance to Niebuhr. Even the volume of essays entitled *Beyond Tragedy* regarded a provisionally tragic interpretation of the human situation as essential to the Christian apologetic.[14] His first full treatment of irony as a motif for interpreting history appeared in *The Irony of American History* in 1952.

Robert E. Fitch's essay on Niebuhr's philosophy of history neglected to examine carefully the evolution of Niebuhr's thought about history and tended to blur the distinctions between pathos, irony, and tragedy. While he admitted that Niebuhr's development of the theme of irony is as recent as 1952,

Fitch argued that it had been important to his thought since 1934.[15] Fitch's essay tended to stress the continuity of Niebuhr's philosophy of history and to blur some distinctions between his philosophy of history in his Marxist, Christian realist, and pragmatic-liberal periods. There is, of course, a continuity; it is the same man thinking about the problem of history. An argument which stressed the continuity of the philosophy of history while acknowledging the significant differences between Marxism and Christian realism could only with difficulty stress the centrality of the philosophy of history in Niebuhr's thought. Fitch's case hangs upon his supposed discovery of the use of irony in *Reflections on the End of an Era*. Unfortunately for Fitch's purpose, Niebuhr had used the term *pathos*, not *irony*, to interpret the aspect of history which he described.

> One of the pathetic aspects of human history is that the instruments of judgment which it uses to destroy particular vices must belong to the same category of the vice to be able to destroy it. Thus some evil, which is to be destroyed, is always transferred to the instrument of its destruction and thereby perpetuated.[16]

The term *pathos*, as defined by Niebuhr,[17] fits the feature described more adequately than does irony.[18]

Fitch's other evidence for the development of the theme of irony in Niebuhr's thought deals with tragedy and humor, not with irony as a category for the interpretation of history.[19] Fitch's failure to marshal proof for Niebuhr's early use of irony as a motif for the interpretation of history allows the interpretation that (1) Niebuhr's distinctions between pathos, tragedy, and irony were important to his thought, and (2) the shift from tragedy to irony was correlative with other shifts in his thought. The gradual replacement of tragedy by irony in his philosophy of history indicates a new openness to human accomplishment and a less dogmatic approach to history in the post-World War II era.

Irony was differentiated from pathos, for Niebuhr, by the actor's increased degree of responsibility. It was differentiated

140

from tragedy by the fact that the involved weakness was an unconscious fault rather than a conscious resolution.[20] Irony was more than comedy, though it contained a comic element. Irony revealed a hidden relationship in the incongruity which was the essence of comedy. The most succinct definition of irony is found in Niebuhr's volume, *The Irony of American History*. "Irony consists of apparently fortuitous incongruities in life which are discovered, upon closer examination, to be not merely fortuitous." [21] Ironical situations are characterized by a tendency to dissolve when the actors become aware of the irony. For the awareness means the discovery of "the hidden vanity or pretension by which comedy is turned into irony." [22]

It was the possibility of the United States turning away from the hidden vanities and pretensions of American life that prompted Niebuhr to write on the ironies of American history. He no longer was as bitter in his castigations of America's liberal culture, for he saw that it had realized a higher degree of justice than its critics thought possible. Yet he still thought the United States was hindered by "pretensions of virtue, wisdom, and power." His book, *The Irony of American History*, was more the work of a moralist than a historian or philosopher of history. It was the work of a moralist who wanted to free his country from illusions which hindered its wise conduct of foreign policy. Niebuhr's use of the category of irony was an attempt to convict the American nation of certain pretensions and thereby to free it for a more creative role in world politics.

Even in Niebuhr's special use of irony, it is not particularly a theological concept. Niebuhr relates it to his theology, however, and claims that it is the normative way for Christians to view history.

Yet the Christian faith tends to make the ironic view of human evil in history the normative one. Its conception of redemption from evil carries it beyond the limits of irony, but its interpretation of the nature of evil in human history is consistently ironic. This consistency is achieved on the basis of the belief that the whole drama of human history is under the scrutiny of a divine judge who laughs at human pretensions without being hostile to human aspirations. . . .

The Biblical interpretation of the human situation is ironic, rather than tragic or pathetic, because of its unique formulation of the problem of human freedom.[23]

The Christian view of history is not tragic because it is not necessary that man do evil. He can choose the good, but in his pride he does not. The development of the concept of irony inclined Niebuhr away from the more pessimistic notes of his Marxist or Christian realist writings. Developing the ironical interpretation of history, he wrote:

Nevertheless, a purely tragic view of life is not finally viable. It is, at any rate, not the Christian view. According to that view destructiveness is not an inevitable consequence of human creativity. It is not invariably necessary to do evil in order that we may do good.[24]

The Ironies of American History

Niebuhr's commitment to American ideals and to the country drove him to the role of social critic. Some of his criticism was polemic and some was prophetic preaching. A favorite form of critique for him was irony, the form of which was discussed above.

He was drawn to the figure of Don Quixote perhaps through Unamuno whose writings on death and the decline of Western civilization had influenced him earlier.[25] Don Quixote had refuted the ideals of chivalry by espousing them. The reader whose mind was stimulated by the author Cervantes could see the refutation of the ideals even though Don Quixote himself was oblivious to the absurdity of his portrayal of values of knight erranty.[26] As Cervantes had laughed at chivalry through Don Quixote, Niebuhr set out to laugh at the foibles of a bourgeois American culture. The laughter he desired to provoke would be accompanied by understanding of the hidden incongruities of American life. He hoped that an understanding of the ironies of American history would help to dissolve those ironies and to reduce the pride and pretensions of the country.

Condemnation of the weakness of the United States accomplished little; the use of irony, he hoped, would avoid the hostility of injured pride and result in an "abatement of the pretensions which caused the irony." [27]

Niebuhr first attempted the task of revealing to the country the ironies of which it was only dimly aware in the book, *The Irony of American History*, in 1952. This task was continued in a book of essays published in 1958 under the title *Pious and Secular America;*[28] in 1963 he jointly authored with Alan Heimert of Harvard *A Nation So Conceived* [29] which had a similar purpose. *The Democratic Experience*[30] which Paul E. Sigmund coauthored in 1969 had a similar thrust in Part I, though it reflected on the broader democratic experience of Europe also and was less explicit about the use of "irony." In all these books he argued that history was not tragic. Men did not have choices only between evil alternatives, for they could with sufficient understanding of their own predicament act creatively. The books revealed a similarity of purpose and sometimes of examples as he ranged over the data of American history to attack American illusions.

Niebuhr piled ironies upon ironies, using the term so frequently that it seemed to lose the rather careful meaning he had given it. The fact that the dreams of agrarian, isolationistic innocence of the young America had been reduced to irrelevance by the growth of the United States was regarded as ironical.[31] The fact that American idealists attempted to escape the realities of international politics by articulating schemes for world order was labeled irony.[32] The awareness that the nation had been better able to assure its security in the days of its youth than in the day of nuclear power was seen as irony.[33]

The height of irony to Niebuhr was that the foe, Marxism, in the hands of the Soviet Union, had transmuted weaknesses in liberal culture into a dangerous creed that threatened to destroy democracy.[34] The ideas of man's control of his destiny, equality, the innocence of man which had fueled liberal illusions, were combined into a religio-political mythology in Marxism, which, protesting against the ills of bourgeois culture, threatened mankind. Bourgeois culture and Communist culture shared illusions, and their conquest of the power of nature through the science which was to save man threatened the world. Against the misunderstandings of the cold war and the discredited mythologies involved in the struggle, Niebuhr responded in the spirit of scripture: "He that sitteth in the heavens shall laugh (Psalm 2:4)." [35]

In the four books mentioned above, Niebuhr attacks the complacency, sentimentality, utopianism, and parochialism which he thinks the American rise to power has encouraged in Americans who held on to oversimple views of their heritage. He uses irony in a rather general way as a label for an incongruity between American myths and reality. Marcus Cunliffe, professor of American history at the University of Manchester, in the preface to the English edition of A Nation So Conceived points to the central purpose of all four volumes by writing: "The second value of the book is in providing a sample of a special category of current American historiography—that which is devoted to the destruction of clichés." [36]

An irony of Niebuhr's writing on the ironies of American history was that he gave as little attention as he did to racial strife in the four books. In the introduction to the latest published volume this omission was noted: "In the United States, we are conscious, as we were not a few years ago, how difficult it is for democratic politics to deal with the problem of race, especially when it is reinforced by economic handicaps." [37] The book itself dealt with the problem of race in the United States only slightly and superficially. The other three books on American history had only one chapter of eight pages and a few scattered references to the race problem in the United States. Editorials and magazine articles did focus on aspects of the race problem as did the seminar he gave in his retirement on social ethics, but the race problem as such did not penetrate into the center of his concerns about American history. If there is irony in the manifestation of militant blacks charging liberal whites with failure to take their liberal creeds, The Constitution of the United States, and The Declaration of Independence seriously, it is even more ironical to find Niebuhr, to whom many militant black theologians look as an ally, guilty by omission of neglecting blacks in American history. Niebuhr has not tried to exclude himself from those Americans who are subject to illusions about the American past. However, his major article, "The Negro Minority and Its Fate in a Self-righteous Nation," [38] written during the summer of 1968 in his old age and ill health in the style of his reflection on the ironies of American history, filled the gap which his books on history had left.

Pragmatism

In retrospect, Niebuhr's debt to pragmatism can be seen in all periods of his thought. However, he openly welcomed the philosophy of pragmatism only in the fourth period of his thought. His attacks upon liberalism had obscured the pragmatic quality of his thought, and it had been particularly hidden by Marxist and Christian dogma. The philosophy of William James had been important to Niebuhr as a young student,[39] and Niebuhr's methodological presuppositions continued to reveal the influence of James. In the 1930s Niebuhr cooperated with and argued against John Dewey. In the 1940s he came to appreciate the pragmatic liberalism of President Roosevelt. In the 1950s he explicitly advocated Christian pragmatism.

Niebuhr's pragmatism is characterized by a rejection of all ideologically consistent political schemes. History is full of novelty, and the stuff of political life cannot be put into neat generalizations. Attempts to state principles of politics on divine, natural, or rational grounds have all been undermined by the relativizing forces of history. Every institution of government should, in Niebuhr's opinion, be regarded pragmatically, i.e., the social critic or philosopher should always be aware that an institution which served well in the past may be outdated and require modification. Institutions of government are to be examined, not in the light of Marxist, liberal, or Christian canons, but with regard to their usefulness for man's common life in a particular situation. This pragmatism forces the teacher of social ethics to refrain from expounding the moral law for political life and inclines him to study how tentative, regulative principles of morality function in history. Though occasionally he will protest against the use of any principles in judging politics, his more consistent position is that principled judgments and action on the basis of such judgments are essential. For example, he attacked Barth's "extreme pragmatism, which disavows all moral principles" [40] at the time of the Hungarian revolution of 1956.

William James

Unfortunately Niebuhr did not provide a precise record of his debt to William James. His intellectual autobiographies all indicate his move toward pragmatism, but they do not discuss William James. The question of influence is inevitably a difficult question to answer satisfactorily, though one quotation provides a clue to the importance of James. "I stand in the William James tradition. He was both an empiricist and a religious man, and his faith was both the consequence and the presupposition of his pragmatism." [41] Four aspects of Niebuhr's thought reveal sufficient similarities with William James's definition of pragmatism to regard him as a pragmatist even if the exact degree of dependence on James is indeterminable. His thought is strikingly similar to that of James in social ethics, epistemology, and apologetics. His avoidance of optimism and pessimism in the expectations of improvement in man's political life is also foreshadowed in James's meliorism.

In social ethics Niebuhr follows pragmatism. He regards some form of pragmatism or utilitarianism as the only way of making moral judgments about social and political questions. Both means and ends are judged pragmatically, and any conflict between the two is also weighed pragmatically, i.e., a judgment is reached in terms of the concrete interests involved. He recorded his commitment to pragmatism in social-ethical theory in bold terms:

> When viewing a historic situation all moralists become pragmatists and utilitarians. Some general good, some *summum bonum*, "the greatest good of the greatest number" or "the most inclusive harmony of all vital capacities" is set up as the criterion of the morality of specific actions and each action is judged with reference to its relation to the ultimate goal.
>
> The choice of instruments and immediate objectives which fall between motive and ultimate objective raises issues which are pragmatic to such a degree that they may be said to be more political than they are ethical.[42]

Niebuhr's ethic is not simply William James's ethic. It preserves a dualistic note inherited from Augustine and Luther that is not important to James. It is also informed by a vision of Christian perfectionism by which James's ethic was untroubled. In the practical conclusions reached, it tended to be more consistently "tough-minded" than was the ethic of William James.

The prestige of Paul Tillich has supported the view that Niebuhr had no epistemology. Tillich began an essay entitled "Reinhold Niebuhr's Doctrine of Knowledge" with the assertion: "The difficulty of writing about Niebuhr's epistemology lies in the fact that there is no such epistemology. Niebuhr does not ask, 'How can I know?'; he starts knowing." [43] Tillich then asserts that the omitted factor reappears in disguised form. He argues that Niebuhr's lack of epistemology is the source of his criticism of ontology. The remainder of the article criticizes Niebuhr for refusing to accept Tillich's ontology. Niebuhr's thought does appear weak when judged by the canons of Tillich's ontology. Skepticism regarding Tillich's ontology, however, is not the same as the lack of all epistemology. Niebuhr never wrote a formal essay on epistemology, but he considered the problem at length in three books[44] and in several essays on related subjects. Tillich's refusal to acknowledge Niebuhr's consideration

147

of the epistemological question was due partially to his desire to reveal Niebuhr's lack of ontology, but it was also due to the strangeness to Tillich's thought of Niebuhr's epistemology. Niebuhr stood in the empirical tradition of William James, which was anathema to German idealism.

Niebuhr combines a high degree of skepticism about claims of metaphysical or religious knowledge with a frank acceptance of the achievements of the sciences. Man as inquirer seeks knowledge which will be useful to him. Knowledge consists of an awareness of the coherences in life. These coherences are more easily attainable in realms unqualified by human freedom and human self-interest. The skepticism about metaphysical or religious knowledge combines with his doctrine of the free but self-interested self to make him a critic of attempts to establish a "scientific morality." On the other hand, he welcomes the refinements in social research which are moving toward greater accuracy in predicting the political behavior of man.[45]

Niebuhr shares the modern world's confidence that the sciences will continue to produce new knowledge in their respective spheres. He finds the subject and object dilemma in epistemology rationally unanswerable, but he assumes that there is an ultimate congruity.[46] He assumes a large degree of coherence in a basically ordered but unfinished world.[47]

> The whole of reality is characterized by a basic coherence. Things and events are in a vast web of relationships and are known through their relations. Perceptual knowledge is possible only within a framework of conceptual images, which in some sense conform to the structures in which reality is organized. The world is organized or it could not exist; if it is to be known, it must be known through its sequences, coherences, casualities (*sic*) and essences.[48]

If asked, "How do you know?" Niebuhr would answer by describing the process of verifying the idea. The process of verification would involve the coherence of the idea with other ideas, logic, or the observable world.

It is natural to test the conformity to the particular coherence in which it seems to belong. We are skeptical about ghosts, for instance, because they do not conform to the characteristics of historical reality as we know it.[49]

Niebuhr's position, so far presented, is in harmony with the following statement by William James: "Truth for us is simply a collective name for verification-processes. . . . Truth is *made*, just as health, wealth and strength are made, in the course of experience." [50]

Niebuhr has confirmed that the following quote from James represents his approach to the epistemological question:[51]

It matters not to an empiricist from what quarter an hypothesis may come to him: he may have acquired it by fair means or by foul; passion may have whispered or accident suggested it; but if the total drift of thinking continues to confirm it, that is what he means by its being true.[52]

Like James, Niebuhr assumes that most of man's intellectual achievements represent modification of previously held ideas.[53] Niebuhr characteristically works through a problem in political thought by assembling the various answers to the problem, checking each possibility, and accepting the one which is verified in the sense of cohering to other needed ideas and experience.

One level of Niebuhr's Christian apology is very close to that of James. They both have abandoned traditional natural theology because of dissatisfaction with the arguments for the existence of God and an antagonism toward rational systems which they thought prematurely closed a developing world.

Both apologists recognized an area of life which was beyond the reach of empirical studies. Neither had a bias toward rejecting theological statements as meaningless. Both personally possessed lively religious convictions. James's formula sums up one level of their agreement on apology:

If theological ideas prove to have a value for concrete life, they will be true, for pragmatism, in the sense of being good for so much. For how much more they are true, will depend entirely on their relations to the other truths that also have to be acknowledged.[54]

Niebuhr made use of this form of pragmatic apology for theological ideas when he pointed toward the quality of the Christian's life as verification of the Christian insight. "The only way of validating such a faith is to bear witness to it in life." [55] The use of the argument of pragmatic utility for religious beliefs is shown in quotations from three of his works:

This is a final enigma of human existence for which there is no answer except by faith and hope; for all answers transcend the categories of human reason. Yet without these answers human life is threatened with scepticism and nihilism on the one hand; and with fanaticism and pride on the other. [56]

Since supreme omnipotence and perfect holiness are incompatible attributes, there is a note of rational absurdity in all religion, which more rational types of theologies attempt to eliminate. But they cannot succeed without sacrificing a measure of religious vitality. [57]

Life has a center and source of meaning beyond the natural and social sequences which may be rationally discerned. This divine source and center must be discerned by faith because it is enveloped in mystery, though being the basis of meaning. So discerned, it yields a frame of meaning in which human freedom is real and valid and not merely tragic or illusory. [58]

The argument from the utility of a theological conception is one important level of Niebuhr's apologetic and one which he seems to have taken from William James, though it was available elsewhere.

A fourth similarity in the thought of Niebuhr and James is the hopeful pragmatism to which the former came in the post-war years. One need not conclude that Niebuhr had once been a pessimist to recognize a more hopeful note in his analysis of the self and society in his latest writing. He did not adopt Spengler and Unamuno as his disillusionment with liberalism grew, but he was influenced by them. He found the provisional pessimism of Marxism helpful in qualifying the idealism of the social revolutionary. His theology had insisted that the Christian message was heard best in a world aware of the tragic quality of history. His final thought, that of a Christian informed by liberalism and pragmatism, was close to the position described by James as meliorism.[59] He could see that some of the conditions of a healthy political order were already present, but so were forces resisting health. The political philosophy of liberalism could be affirmed and the values of liberty, equality, and fraternity pursued, but the struggle was not over nor was the outcome secure. The fourth period of Niebuhr's thought was not a return to his earliest liberal optimism nor was it a continuation of his more pessimistic Christian realism. As in James, pragmatism and liberalism interacted to produce a sober, goal-oriented philosophy which could lay claim to a middle position between optimism and pessimism. Niebuhr's meliorism, however, was closer than that of James to the latter's category of "tough-minded" political thought. Niebuhr retained a larger degree of eschatological perspective than did James, and he also was more inclined than James to emphasize the inevitable corruption of political community. This higher degree of "tough-mindedness" was one of the chief differences between Niebuhr and John Dewey, the most famous exponent of pragmatism after James.

John Dewey

Niebuhr attacked Dewey's thought repeatedly,[60] and the followers of Dewey have not been reticent in counterattacking.[61] The interest in the basic disagreements between Niebuhr and Dewey should not obscure their common debt to William James nor the similarities of their thought. They both considered the context in reaching a decision on political policy. They joined in opposing the great systems of philosophical rationalism. Both represented their thought as developing rather than defending a system. Neither thinker gave a completely naturalistic account of man, for both knew that man was continuous and discontinuous with nature.[62]

There is sufficient reason to regard the Niebuhr-Dewey controversy of the 1930s as an intramural affair. Both men were liberals who owed much to William James and pragmatism. Both were associated, during the depression, with a variety of causes and a collection of ideas loosely described as socialist in inspiration.[63] The intramural character of the debate increased its importance in the minds of many residents of Morningside Heights, as institutional interests and departmental concerns could not easily be separated from some of the arguments.

Niebuhr's quarrel with Dewey was not primarily a theological one. In fact, Niebuhr reviewed John Dewey's *A Common Faith* in rather positive terms. Dewey's form of naturalism was not attacked from a more orthodox Christian perspective. The one note of mild criticism in the review, which might be interpreted as complimentary, was that Dewey did not suspect how close his creed was to the teaching of prophetic religion.[64]

Niebuhr's attack upon Dewey focused on what creative social intelligence could be expected to accomplish.[65] Both Niebuhr and Dewey admitted that the social order had always been dominated by force. Dewey hoped that the new social sciences could change the way society was administered. Niebuhr hoped for a radical realignment of the balance of power in society, but he did not expect reason to control force.

> Professor Dewey has a touching faith in the possibility of achieving the same results in the field of social relations which intelligence achieved in the mastery of nature. The fact that man constitutionally corrupts his purest visions of disinterested justice in his actual actions seems never to occur to him.[66]

Arthur Schlesinger, Jr., has used the following categories to delineate the differences between the two thinkers:

> In the case of Dewey, it should be said that his disdain for the New Deal and his commitment to socialization proceeded naturally enough from his disregard for power in society and from his faith in human rationality and scientific planning; but for Niebuhr, who was realistic about man and who wanted to equilibrate power in society, the commitment to socialization was both the price of indifference to the achievements of piecemeal reform and a symptom of despair. Where Dewey spurned the New Deal because of his optimism about man and his belief in science, Niebuhr seemed to spurn it because of his pessimism about man and his belief in catastrophe.[67]

Schlesinger came close to understanding their common rejection of the New Deal, but the differences are much more subtle; the polarities of optimism and pessimism will not stand serious scrutiny any better than Niebuhr's own treatment of Dewey as a "child of light." Nor can it be argued convincingly that Dewey disregarded power in society while Niebuhr was indifferent to piecemeal reform. Throughout the decade of the 1930s, Niebuhr wrote editorial after editorial for reform, fought for unpopular reform causes, and gave himself to left-wing political activity. Certainly he hoped, under Marxist influence, for a radical transformation of American society, but this hope did not lead him, as it did more consistent Marxists, to oppose reforms for the sake of increasing class polarization. Niebuhr himself did not criticize Dewey for disregarding power but rather for relying too heavily on the possibility of conflicting claims being adjusted through discussion, democracy, and education.[68] Morton White's observation, in the context of criticizing Niebuhr's thought, is closer to the full breadth of the two social philosophers than is Schlesinger: "All we have here is the recognition that men are somewhere between the serpent and the dove, and while Niebuhr puts us closer to the serpent, Dewey puts us closer to the dove." [69]

Dewey and Niebuhr concurred during the depression on the need for a third political party to lead the country into socialism. Both expected radical changes in the economic and social structure of the country and thought the changes would come through revolution, if not achieved by democratic reform. Their deep differences were seen in their criticism of Marxist radicals. Niebuhr criticized them for romantic illusions concerning the possibility of eliminating force from human affairs. Dewey criticized them for lacking a rigorous social science. In their appreciation of democracy the same fundamental difference could be seen. Niebuhr regarded democracy as the best governmental system for the adjustment of power; Dewey praised democracy for enabling the social ideals of men to be tested by experience, making possible the selection of the most rational policy.

Niebuhr's central criticism of Dewey was drawn from Marxist sources; later it was to be based upon the Christian doctrine of man. Dewey's faith in "creative social intelligence" did not take adequate account of how social science was subject to misuse by self-interested men. Social science was easily converted to ideological uses by men less interested in truth than in pursuing their own ends. Niebuhr was left unimpressed by the analogy of the success of science in nature because he regarded man as distinctively a historical being. Dewey emphasized the continuity of man, nature, and society.

> The intelligent acknowledgment of the continuity of nature, man and society will alone secure a growth of morals which will be serious without being fanatical, aspiring without sentimentality, adapted to reality without conventionality, sensible without taking the form of calculation of profits, idealistic without being romantic.[70]

Niebuhr emphasized the discontinuity between man and nature. It was precisely in man's freedom over the patterns of nature that man's distinctive qualities resided. The study of man in history was not subject to the same means of inquiry that had proven so fruitful in the study of nature. Niebuhr's charge that the social sciences were not developed to the same extent as the natural sciences was irrefutable. He regarded the theory, that this qualitative difference between the two areas of study was due to a "cultural lag" which would be overcome, as the "pathos of liberalism." The social crisis was not due to the lack of research and education but to the clash of self-interested groups. These groups adopted whatever social science was available to the justification of their own purposes. He admitted the need for reason in planning social action, but he regarded Dewey's estimate of the hopes for rational arbitration of social conflict as overly optimistic.[71] He could agree with Dewey that reason was a practical instrument for solving problems, but he thought that reason was a fragile instrument used by particular men and groups to justify their own interests.

Niebuhr never wrote extensively on Dewey's approach to international politics. However, the gap between their understanding of international affairs was as great as any difference between them. Niebuhr was particularly opposed to schemes for world government or the outlawing of war. Dewey revealed a robust confidence in the outlawing of war.[72] He believed that the "people" of America had a particularly significant role to play in dismantling the war institution. His analysis focused on the reasonableness and utility of outlawing wars and providing alternative means of settling international disputes. His theory lacked any feel for the Hobbesian state of anarchy which prompted nations to seek desperately their own security. Dewey's political analysis did not indicate the dynamic evils of Hitlerism and Stalinism although both were already rather conspicuous in the world.

Niebuhr charged that the failure of educators to realize the seriousness of the mid-1930 social crisis was partially due to the comfort and security of their essentially middle-class position. Similarly, in his opinion, the tendency of the educator to see the solution of the social crisis in the training given to the expert reflected a certain class bias. Liberal hopes that the evolving intelligence of the general community would lead to reform were refuted by the nonexistence of such a community. Society was composed of competing classes, and the perspective of each class was limited by its own economic interest.[73]

Dewey's political model, like Plato's, subordinated class conflict to the needs of education. Class antagonisms could be overcome by rational adjustment, and the rational adjustment of these antagonisms required educational reform. Educational reform and political reform are related and interdependent in both Plato and Dewey. Niebuhr protested against the tendency to obscure the perennial problems of politics under the vocabulary of education. His criticism of Dewey's discussion of politics in educational terms and his use of theological vocabulary for the discussion of politics gave an unfortunately obscurantist cast to his critique. Niebuhr regarded Dewey's tendency to develop "a political theory in the form of a philosophy of education," [74] and his hopes for resolving political problems through science as attempts to escape from the realm of politics. Niebuhr remained skeptical of all attempts to eliminate political conflicts through some program of increasing social science, but the original source of this skepticism was his Marxist tendency to regard the social sciences as easy prey to ideological perversions. This polemic against reducing politics to science became one of the defining characteristics of the realist school.

Christian Pragmatism

In debt to William James and in dialogue with John Dewey, Niebuhr developed a new form of pragmatism by combining it with Christian theology. In an important article he argued that pragmatism was the new direction in the field of Christian political and social ethics.[75] The acceptance of pragmatism meant the dissolution of the traditional dogmas of both the left and the right. Christian pragmatism meant, to Niebuhr, a recognition of the complexity of the issues of economics and politics, a commitment to justice, and an acceptance of a sense of responsibility for political life.

The synthesis of pragmatism and theology relativized all political ideals by criticizing them from the perspective of theological absolutes. The theological absolutes, however, were sufficiently transcendent to prevent their interference with the promotion of the highest degree of justice possible in a given situation. All absolutes could be corrupted, and the Christian absolutes had been corrupted repeatedly; but properly used they provided ultimate intellectual defenses against tyranny, anarchy, and nihilism. The absolutes which the theological tradition offered were: the authority of God beyond the authority of all men, the moral law revealed as the law of love in Christ, the dignity of person, and the reverence for the "orders" of community life.

Pragmatism prides itself upon its openness to helpful contributions from other philosophies. Particularly in the area of political philosophy, pragmatism is open to influences from other bodies of thought. For James, Dewey, and Niebuhr, liberalism informed their pragmatism. Niebuhr's exultation over pragmatism's dissolution of the dogmas of the left and the right is partially intrinsic to pragmatism, partially a new confidence in liberalism, and partially a Christian nonchalance about particular social and political dogmas. The Christian influences in Niebuhr's pragmatism were often subtle and stemmed from his theologically grounded doctrine of man.

Liberalism

Niebuhr's liberalism in politics is rooted deeply in his theology. The connections between his theology and his liberal politics is nowhere seen more clearly than in a brief article entitled, "Freedom," written for a theological dictionary. In that article he argued that mankind has belatedly come to realize the need for shaping its institutions of order so as to secure the greatest freedom for man. Man's freedom is rooted in his essential nature; it is his freedom more than any other quality which distinguishes man from nature.

> The community must give the person a social freedom which corresponds to the essential freedom of his nature, and which enables him to express hopes and ambitions and to engage in interests and vitalities which are not immediately relevant to the collective purposes of the community, but which in the long run enrich the culture and leaven the lump of the community's collective will and purpose.[76]

The connection of liberty-producing political institutions and the freedom of man's essential nature is a bold step which many theologians and political philosophers have refused to take. The linkage is an indication of the theological roots of Niebuhr's political liberalism.

The Practice of Liberalism

Niebuhr's admiration for Franklin D. Roosevelt grew after his first vote for him in 1940. His respect increased as he saw Roosevelt beguile a conservative and isolationist nation into adopting programs of social welfare and international responsibility. His commitment to what Niebuhr understood to be liberal ideals was clear as was his commitment to resolute and successful political action.

Niebuhr wrote that Roosevelt had learned from Wilson's errors and that his commitment of the United States to a continuing role of world responsibility marked a new level of maturity in American foreign policy.[77] He recognized that Roosevelt operated within the framework necessitated by the pride and power of the great nations. The concessions were not regarded as simple expediency but a wise recognition of the limits the sovereignty of nations placed upon international politics.

Niebuhr's praise for Roosevelt's foreign policy balanced tribute to his political vision and to his command of pragmatic politics. The lend-lease act which drew the United States deeper into the European conflict was particularly praised by Niebuhr as an example of political sagacity. "Roosevelt was no systematic political thinker; but he saw the main issue clearly and acted upon his convictions with as much consistency as the confused state of American public opinion would allow." [78]

Niebuhr judged political ideas in terms of their results. The verification of political theory in terms of its products revealed his deep pragmatism, even though he often introduced such judgments with the words of one of his favorite texts, "By their fruits ye shall know them." The achievements of the Roosevelt era forced Niebuhr to admit that liberalism, shorn of its illusions and pragmatically oriented, had greater resources than he had anticipated. Roosevelt became the symbol of pragmatic liberalism for Niebuhr.

Niebuhr has said that he heartily approved of being interpreted as a liberal and, as evidence of his liberal politics, pointed to his founding role in the Americans for Democratic Action.[79] Niebuhr helped merge the Union for Democratic Action into the broader Americans for Democratic Action and presided with Elmer Davis over the new organization's first conference in Washington, D.C., in 1947. He continued to serve actively as a leader until his illness in 1952 forced him to curtail his activities. Niebuhr was influential in the early hard line that ADA took against Communist policy and in insisting that the United States play a responsible role in resisting Communism. In penning the first draft of an ADA statement on foreign policy, he wrote:

> The foreign policy of the United States is determined by the responsibilities which we have acquired as the most powerful nation in the free world and by the necessity of exercising our responsibilities in the continual contest between the world-wide tyranny of communism.[80]

Niebuhr viewed ADA as a tool for implementing Roosevelt's pragmatic liberalism on the domestic front and opposing the spread of Marxism on the international front while avoiding the errors of idealism. Niebuhr's identification with liberalism in the form of the Americans for Democratic Action is clear in a letter written in 1954 to David C. Williams:

> It's thrilling to belong to an organization which began its existence with a challenge to communism from the liberal standpoint, and is now leading the liberal forces in this nation in resisting the corruption of McCarthyism.[81]

Ten years after ADA's founding, Niebuhr still thought of its two central presuppositions as representative of the achievements of Franklin D. Roosevelt: first, liberalism had to be realistic in international politics, and second, the balances within a democratic society needed continual refining to insure that higher degrees of justice be attained.[82] Gradually Niebuhr's polemics against liberalism became more discriminate and his harsh criticism was directed toward idealism and optimism. This shift reflected both his increased awareness of his own liberalism and an inclination to define liberalism differently.

The Theory of Liberalism

Niebuhr's critique of liberalism has served as a healthy antidote to utopianism. In his later years, he has often emphasized that his attack upon liberalism was exaggerated and overstated. Earlier discussion of Niebuhr's definition of liberalism emphasized that his real interest was to attack various expressions of facile optimism.[83] The reason Niebuhr could, in his later years, describe himself as a liberal is that he had never rejected the major part of liberalism, and the aspect of liberalism which he attacked was not integral to it.

Daniel Williams, while concurring with Niebuhr's attack upon utopianism, believes that Niebuhr's method of isolating single traits has led him to state his criticism of liberalism in an exaggerated manner, obscuring some of the truth represented by liberalism.[84] Niebuhr's reply to Williams ascribes his inexact definition of liberalism as due to defining "liberalism too consistently in terms of its American versions." [85]

Niebuhr does not escape criticism by claiming that the liberals he was attacking were American. For liberalism as a political philosophy in the New World was freed of some of the very optimism which characterized liberalism on the continent of its birth. Certainly there have been a sufficient number of dreamers in America, and many of these gave expression to their hopes in the Social Gospel. But the mainstream of American political thought has revealed a pragmatic or realist shape. The liberalism of the Adamses and Madison was tempered by a realism not too different from Niebuhr's.[86] Enlightenment optimism was present but not prevalent in the founders of the American republic.

John Adams' rejection of Condorcet illustrates the contrast between the optimism of some French democrats and the sobriety of the American democrats.

Thus Condorcet was untroubled. Instead of bemoaning the fact that the Americans were Blackstonian historians, he proudly welcomed them into the fraternity of the illuminated. American constitutionalism, he said, "had not grown, but was planned"; it "took no force from the weight of centuries but was put together mechanically in a few years." When John Adams read this comment, he spouted two words on the margin of the page: "Fool! Fool!" [87]

The liberalism of the New World was not so self-consciously bourgeois as that of the old because the middle class had not had to break feudal patterns, nor was it on the defensive against conservatism and radicalism. The Enlightenment "heaven on earth" received minor support in the United States, but as the grievances of the New World were less anguished than those of the old, the political leaders could set about improving and insuring some satisfactions on earth.

The comfort and sobriety of the country's founding fathers were not unrelated. The impending millennium of Enlightenment political thought had its American supporters, but they were not in the majority, nor did they have the power to act on their vision. Louis Hartz's study of the influence of liberalism in America emphasizes the differences between European and American liberalism, and chief among their differences is the failure of optimism to dominate American liberalism.

Thus the American liberals, instead of being forced to pull the Christian heaven down to earth, were glad to let it remain where it was. They did not need to make a religion out of the revolution because religion was already revolutionary. [88]

The study to this point has discussed Niebuhr and liberalism within the terms of his definition of it, which assumed optimism as the necessary and central ingredient of liberalism. Niebuhr has admitted that this understanding of liberalism is defective. An alternative understanding of political liberalism reveals the continuity of Niebuhr's political philosophy with liberalism.

Beginning with Niebuhr's own description of liberalism as being in its broadest sense synonymous with the democratic protest against feudal society, several of the central ideas of liberalism as a political philosophy can be delineated. "The ideas at the heart of the liberal faith . . . are ideas of freedom and also ideas about the conditions, political and social, of making freedom secure." [89] These ideas arose out of older ideas and institutions; but in the seventeenth, eighteenth, and nineteenth centuries they were elaborated in the manner which is regarded as liberal. The word *liberal,* in the sense of a body of political ideas, is of relatively recent origin, gaining currency in the last century. The ideas of freedom which are characteristic of liberalism are connected with the rise of the modern state, the expansion of commerce and industry, the rise of the city, and the dissolution of the medieval religious consensus.

The idea of natural law had a long history, but the change from the emphasis on natural law to that of natural rights of man was a characteristically seventeenth-century shift. Locke moved the idea of natural rights to the center of man's political thought. The idea of natural rights was based on certain illusions: radical individualism, the myth of state of nature, and the myth of a social contract. But the insistence that man as man had certain rights survived the criticism of those illusions. These rights of men were to be guarded against the encroachment of the state, which in liberal thought was both necessary and dangerous. The rights claimed by Locke for all men against the state were available to only a few, and Locke, as Mill after him, did not possess clear ideas of how the rights he claimed for the aristocrats could be extended to all men. The socialist attempts to extend Locke's natural rights to all men do not necessarily imply a rejection of the idea of freedom which Locke held. The elaboration and application of the seventeenth century's ideas of freedom has resulted in both Whigs and socialists adopting

162

liberal concepts of freedom. The Whigs retain more of Locke's aristocratic bias, while the liberal socialists improve on Locke by attempting to realize the rights he demanded for all men by social planning. The rights claimed by liberalism were the right of spiritual privacy, the right of resistance to established authority, the right to limit the authority of a government over its citizens, the right to criticize the government in speech and press, the right to a just opportunity to secure material possessions, and the right to personal liberty insofar as it did not infringe upon the welfare of others in society. While not all liberals would agree with such a statement of liberal demands, it does represent the essentials of the liberal creed. The list does not enter into the claims and counterclaims of the political economists, for the term *liberal* can with some justification be associated with directly opposing claims in economics. In political philosophy, however, the term does have a general structure which can be defined, theorists who can be regarded as liberal,[90] and governments in which the incarnation of liberalism can be seen. Understanding liberalism as a collection of ideas about the freedom of men and the limitation of government to secure those freedoms does not necessarily imply any dependence upon a vision of moral progress in history. Many liberals did believe in historical progress, but some did not. Many believers in historical progress were not liberals in the political-philosophical use of the term. The idea of historical progress has its own history and needs to be analyzed in its own terms.

Niebuhr eventually dissociated liberalism from utopianism and admitted that his reactions to utopianism had been extreme.

My second account of a gradual revision of my originally held opinions must deal, of course, with my rather violent, and sometimes extravagant, reaction to what I defined as the "utopianism," i.e., the illusory idealist and individualist character, of a Protestant and bourgeois culture before the world depression and two world wars.[91]

Man's Nature and His Communities does not criticize liberalism per se; rather, it attacks the excessive utopianism of modern culture and the counterreaction of nihilistic cynicism. It attempts to map out a program of moderate realism which promotes the liberal goals while taking account of the factors of power, inertia, and self-interest. The alliance of Christian pessimism and liberalism is seen in Niebuhr's preference for John Milton over John Locke and in James Madison over Thomas Jefferson. The voluntarism and individualism of Locke's conception of the social contract is criticized without taking the opportunity to attack liberalism itself.

Idealism and Realism

The central problem for Niebuhr in political philosophy has been the nature of the relationship between man's ideal communities and man's real political life. Mistaken answers to the problem, particularly optimistic and moralistic answers, have hindered the formation and execution of United States foreign policy. Niebuhr has labored, throughout his career, to clarify this relationship. In its most extreme expression the problem of the ideal and the real was revealed in Niebuhr's Christology; the ideal was powerless to coerce and was crucified by the political powers of the historical situation. In more moderate expressions, the problem was seen in the attempt to persuade wartime leaders to aspire to a more just and well-organized peace than wartime expediency encouraged. Niebuhr's writing, at its extremes, revealed both the self-giving spirit of Christ and an understanding of the self-seeking strategem of Machiavelli. His major emphasis, however, has been to persuade the American public of the need for wise and responsible foreign policy. He has assumed American policy would be self-seeking, and he has tried to teach that neither consistent national egoism nor idealistic expressions of national righteousness and self-sacrifice would best serve American foreign policy. The major essay in *Man's Nature and His Communities* returns to this perennial issue in his thought and outlines a balanced approach to the idealist-realist controversy.

The essay on idealism and realism traces the idealistic and realistic motifs from Plato to Hans Morgenthau.[92] The movement in Niebuhr's thought from Christian realism to a less consciously theological position and to an increased pragmatic-liberal orientation is seen in his increased criticism of Augustine's realism. As late as 1953, though Niebuhr was critical of Augustine, he affirmed his realism. In 1965 Niebuhr was sharply critical of Augustine's realism and identified himself as a "moderate realist" rather than a "realist." The contrast of the tribute to Augustine in 1953 and the criticism of him in 1965 reveals the change in Niebuhr's realism.

Thus Augustine . . . proves himself *a more reliable guide than any known thinker*. A generation which finds its communities imperiled and in decay from the smallest and most primordial community, the family, to the largest, and most recent, the potential world community, *might well take counsel of Augustine in solving its perplexities*.[93]

The political thought which served as inspiration in 1953 began to appear irrelevant to modern democracies in 1965 as the resources of liberalism penetrated more deeply into Niebuhr's mind.

An analysis of Augustine's and Luther's dualism and consequent "realism" affecting political communities must yield the negative conclusion that the realism was too consistent to give a true picture of either human nature or the human community, even before the advent of free governments, and *was certainly irrelevant to modern democratic governments*.[94]

The essay improved on his earlier writing on democratic theory by expounding the realism of James Madison. His analysis of power and interest presented the deepest pre-Marxist observations on the influence of class interest and the need to manage rather than eliminate factional interest.[95] His increased respect for Madison reflected his own assurance that political liberalism could be combined with realism and also his view that the

institutions of representative government had outlived the bourgeois ideology and optimism which had often supported them.

The argument of the essay exposes the dangers of overly
consistent realism or idealism. Man is both self-seeking and inclined toward a moral life. His moral ideals can be achieved only
through policies which account for the self-seeking aspirations
of various men and groups. He does not expect the realization
of man's political ideals, not even of his own liberal democratic
ideals of toleration, liberty, and representative government.
However, man cannot succumb to cynicism, and the wisest
policy is one which strives to maximize the degree of possible
justice. Justice, as a principle for Niebuhr, consists of both
equality and liberty. The goal of tolerable justice for a society
involves the achievement of the maximum possible degree of
liberty and equality within a framework of order. The ideals
of political liberalism are utilized by Niebuhr, but he does not
confuse what he regards as normative with his description of
political reality. Political reality is necessarily separated from
the ideal, but it is in need of constant improvement and criticism
by reference to the ideal.

Conclusion

Reinhold Niebuhr's thought, after World War II, was increasingly influenced by pragmatism and liberalism. By 1965
the contrast between Niebuhr's thought and his Christian realism of the World War II years was significant. The contrast is
most obvious in the comparison of *Man's Nature and His Communities* to *The Nature and Destiny of Man*. The movement
in his thought which has been the subject of this chapter was
to a pragmatic-liberal synthesis upon a base of Christian theology. The pragmatism and liberalism, which were American
in origin, have been expressed in the contemporary world in
the achievements of Franklin D. Roosevelt's administration. The
theology has been a demythologized form of the Augustinian-

Pascal-Reformation theology which had characterized his Christian realist period. The insights into man and his communities were not radically different from the Christian realist period, but the language in which they were expressed was different.

The attitude toward political liberalism is quite different from the polemics against it in the Christian realist period. This changed attitude is due both to the recognition that the tendency to equate liberalism and optimism was mistaken and to the recognition of the achievements of liberal institutions and policies.

The increased affirmation of pragmatism was done in the context of the assumption of insights from political liberalism and Christian theology. This combination meant that his thought had deep affinities with the thought of James Madison, though it drew insights from the whole history of political theory.

The pragmatic-liberal synthesis was a characteristically American way of approaching political reality, and Niebuhr's criticisms of American optimism and moralism are part of a continuing dialogue in the history of American political thought. His writings on the incongruities of American history have attempted to expose American illusions and in so doing to free the United States to exercise a role of responsible leadership in world politics.

VI. THE UNITED STATES' ROLE IN INTERNATIONAL POLITICS SINCE WORLD WAR II

There has been a mutual influence between Reinhold Niebuhr's thought on foreign policy and his understanding of other philosophical issues. So far, the study has traced the evolution of Niebuhr's political philosophy in the context of his thought on broader philosophical issues. From time to time, the chronological development of the study has required that issues of foreign policy be analyzed at some length, but the major treatment of Niebuhr's thought on American foreign policy has been reserved for this chapter.

This chapter presupposes the political philosophy of Chapter V. It discusses Niebuhr's influence in the realist school and analyzes three of Niebuhr's central foreign-policy concepts: national interest, power, and imperialism. It is in his contribution to the realist school, his thought on the three topics mentioned, and his handling of the relationship between morality and international politics that Niebuhr's distinctiveness as a thinker about American foreign policy is most clearly seen. Following the discussion of the role of democracy in the world, a conclusion suggests in summary form what his contribution to American thought on foreign policy has been and indicates certain deficiencies in his thought.

The discussion and argument of the chapter rely upon numerous occasional pieces which were often written in the heat of a particular crisis. However, the emphasis is not upon what Niebuhr wrote about particular problems. The focus of the chapter is on the broad outlines of Niebuhr's thought on American foreign policy in the post-World War II period. The chapter attempts to describe Niebuhr's philosophical thought about

American foreign policy, not post-World War II foreign policy problems as seen by Niebuhr.

Father of the Political Realists

Niebuhr's role as one of the major founders of American political realism has been widely acclaimed.[1] George F. Kennan has entitled Niebuhr "the father of us all."[2] Niebuhr's *Moral Man and Immoral Society* preceded by half a decade the turn toward realism of *The Nation* and *The New Leader*. Though political realism found other leaders in E. H. Carr, Nicholas J. Spikman, and Hans J. Morgenthau, Niebuhr's was the first significant volume of the new school. Writing in 1941, John C. Bennett recognized Niebuhr as the initiator of a new movement in political and theological thought:

> In this country Niebuhr has been the spearhead of a new tendency toward what is often called "realism" among American religious thinkers. More effectively than any one else in America he mediates to us insights that are common assumptions in European theology and he does so with moderation.[3]

There is a second sense in which Niebuhr can be regarded as the father of political realism. His thought has laid the foundations of political realist philosophy in the doctrine of man. The dependence of Hans J. Morgenthau on Niebuhr has been confessed; the content and footnotes of *Scientific Man vs. Power Politics* document that dependence. Though the realists display many differences, they agree that the doctrine of man is important for political theory. All of them reflect some debt to Niebuhr in their doctrines of man.

Kenneth W. Thompson regards the early years of the Policy Planning Staff of the State Department, founded in 1947 by General Marshall, as the period in which the realists most clearly influenced policy. The Policy Planning Staff brought together George F. Kennan, Paul H. Nitze, Louis J. Halle, C. B. Marshall, Dorothy Fosdick, and as advisers, Hans J. Morgenthau and

Reinhold Niebuhr. From the writings of these persons, Thompson believes five common elements can be deduced, all of which are prominently present in Niebuhr's thought and can be used as standards by which to define political realism. The common elements are: (1) the tendency to avoid moral absolutes in international politics; (2) a rejection of the escape from power politics attempted by writers on international relations in the 1920s and 1930s; (3) a distrust of concepts of human perfectibility and moral progress in human affairs; (4) a passion for the study and interpretation of history; and (5) the conviction that a rather explicit conception of man is helpful to political thought.[4]

The divisions within the realist school are beyond explicit categorization. An attempt has been made by Theodore R. Weber to describe a two-party split within the realist school.[5] Weber argued that the realists divide on the question of the application of norms to political life. One group, which he called the prudential realists, included Ernest Lefever, William Lee Miller, and Kenneth Thompson. A second group, including John C. Bennett, Paul Ramsey, Edward L. Long, George Kennan, and Robert Batchelder, he entitled casuistic realists. The chief difference between the two groups, according to Weber, is whether in a particular situation action ought to be derived from moral principles or from a calculation of the probable political consequences of the action.[6] Weber's classification has many deficiencies. None of the realists would accept Weber's dichotomy as descriptive of his differences with the other group. One of Weber's prudential realists, Kenneth Thompson, has contradicted his classification by emphasizing the role of moral principle in his book, *The Moral Issue of Statecraft*. Furthermore, the fundamental contrast in the methodology of Christian social action is more apparent between the thought of John C. Bennett and Paul Ramsey, classified together, than between Kenneth Thompson and Bennett, supposedly in opposing groups. To the degree that the realists have adopted Niebuhr's thought about ethics and politics, it would be impossible for them to divide into two camps, one emphasizing principles and the other, results. Niebuhr's polemics may obscure his dialectical balance, but the bulk of his writing has emphasized the utilization of principles of social morality to inform one's choice of policy alternatives.

Raymond Aron has criticized the realists for "mixing theory and praxeology"; [7] he believes this mixing has contributed to their failure to make rigorous distinctions between the historical particulars and the permanent characteristics of international politics. The realists have tried to distinguish the contingent from the perennial in international politics. Such an attempt is the chief purpose of Niebuhr's major work on theory, *The Structure of Nations and Empires*. Aron is correct, however, in his assertion that they mix theoretical and practical considerations. In fact, they judge theoretical insights by practical results and tend to explain practice in terms of broad theoretical considerations. The school has demonstrated an affinity for moving in and out of political power and the academic community. Its major journalist, Walter Lippmann, published works on social philosophy, and its major theologian wrote hundreds of journalistic pieces. The school as a whole, and Reinhold Niebuhr in particular, have favored the form of the political essay which combines theoretical reflection and policy recommendations. A distinguishing feature of the Policy Planning Staff was its commitment to the development of "an applicable body of theory." [8]

The next three sections of this chapter consider central concepts in the realist body of theory as understood by Niebuhr. The section on morality compares Niebuhr's discussion of morality and international politics with Morgenthau's thought.

The United States' National Interest

The United States and its allies effectively dominated the world at the end of World War II; no nation could directly challenge the will of the Allies. The common interests of the Allies, however, had consisted primarily in the defeat of the Axis, and from the alliance came the protagonists of the next chapter of the struggle between sovereign nations. Niebuhr had hope for continued postwar cooperation and the building of new structures of order,[9] but tensions among the Allies during the war convinced him that the major powers would try after the war to advance their own interests and that the most desirable state achievable would be a relatively stable balance of power.[10]

The collapse of the wartime alliance led to the cold war, one of the three chief characteristics of international politics in mid-twentieth century. The rivalry between the two major nations was aggravated by the revolutionary fanaticism of Communism. The utilization of Communist ideology made the Soviet Union a more complex and a more dangerous opponent than Nazi Germany. The cold war, in Niebuhr's analysis, was a struggle to preserve the values and institutions of Western civilization from the revolutionary fervor of a dangerous creed. There is no evidence that Niebuhr ever advocated the rollback of Communism or the elimination of socialism where it existed, but he did hope for and expect a withering of the Communist appetite for active revolution. He was a consistent cold warrior (i.e., he advocated serious competition in all spheres to meet the Communist challenge), but he did not permit the cold war to become a preoccupation that blinded him to other foreign policy considerations.

The second major characteristic of international politics in the postwar period was the revolution in military technology. The nuclear weapon and intercontinental ballistic missile altered significantly the way international problems were met.[11] The problem of security was particularly heightened for the United States, and the two major protagonists ironically became the guarantors of each other's survival. J. Robert Oppenheimer's simile captures the way Niebuhr regarded the irony of nuclear deterrence:

> We may anticipate a state of affairs in which the two Great Powers will each be in a position to put an end to the civilization and life of the other, though not without risking its own. We may be likened to two scorpions in a bottle, each capable of killing the other, but only at the risk of his own life.[12]

The issue confronting Niebuhr was not only how the United States should act regarding a series of issues around nuclear weapons, but whether the whole character of international politics had changed.

The third characteristic of the international political situation after the war was the merging of the movements for nationalism and modernization in the non-European world. European nationalism was transplanted to the colonial world and combined with the revolution of rising expectations to unleash revolutionary political forces. In Niebuhr's mind, United States national interest required encouraging this process without sacrificing international order and the loyalties of European allies.

The challenge of the three revolutions combined with the traditional features of international politics to confront a new world power with awesome responsibilities. United States foreign policy was primarily a response to these revolutionary developments, though it was responsible for the development of nuclear weapons and had abetted the nationalist movements. Niebuhr, as a realist, expected United States foreign policy to pursue the interests of the American people. As a moderate realist or a pragmatic liberal, he defined those interests very broadly. The primary goal of United States foreign policy was the preservation of order, not the secure order of domestic politics but rather a more or less stable balance of power which would prevent major breakdowns in the system. The United States ought not, in the pursuit of order, to assume the responsibility of policing the world to quell all revolutions or all threats of war.[13] He advocated the development of effective international institutions for the resolution of disputes between nations, but the absence of world community thwarted such development. If all nations had a stake in preserving order, the United States— as the most powerful and wealthy nation—had additional reasons for preventing the breakdown of the present system. Niebuhr understood the interests of the United States in preserving the present system, but he also saw the instability and injustice of the system. His writing on international politics pressed for reforms in trade policies and international organizations, and for the lessening of international rivalries while, at the same time, preserving the system. His writing did not pretend to an impartial objectivity but represented the demands of a liberal American who was keenly aware of America's interest in the system.[14] He assumed that United States imperialism, in the sense of exercising responsibilities commensurate with power, would give American foreign policy the character of defending the outlines of the status quo[15] against forces which threatened the system with disorder.

The national interest, for Niebuhr, is a term used to express the goals of foreign policy. Each political actor has his individual view regarding the national interest. Argument about what is in the national interest is always in order, and though the administration of a country acts to fulfill the national interest, it may have a mistaken conception of the national interest.

The three revolutions discussed above influenced Niebuhr's understanding of what the United States national interest ought to be. Before everything else the national interest requires the avoidance of nuclear annihilation. This interest is in harmony with the interest of the other competitor of the cold war. The nuclear balance has realized the identity of the human and the imperial interests in the avoidance of nuclear war.[16] The uniting of national interests in mutual interest through nuclear deterrence has been regarded by Niebuhr as the "final revelation of the incongruity of human existence."[17] However, neither the incongruity nor the dread of nuclear war has led Niebuhr to expect significant progress in the dismantling of the deterrent.

Each lacks the capacity or inclination to sacrifice its own interests for the good of mankind, since such a sacrifice would mean capitulation to the adversary. Both lack sufficient mutual trust to engage in a large-scale partnership of peace. But the ideological chasm between them has been bridged by their common sense of responsibility for avoiding nuclear catastrophe. The recently negotiated limited test-ban agreement may be the first step in politically acknowledging this common responsibility.[18]

The second major United States interest is the preservation of open societies that have not succumbed to Communist control. In his most recent writing, Niebuhr has admitted the difficulty of maintaining open societies.[19] He does not think that either the liberal ideology of the West or the Marxist ideology is suitable for the needs of the developing nations. He stressed that each country has its individual needs and urged that dogmatism about developmental patterns be avoided. As the only nation strong enough to resist Communist imperialism, it falls upon the United States to aid in the defense of open societies. His critique of United States policy in Vietnam,[20] for example, was not directed against the general need for United States power to resist Communist expansionism but against many particulars of the policy in Vietnam.

In his retirement, Niebuhr taught a course at Barnard College on the origins of democracy and its relevance to the developing nations. His conclusions about the future of democratic government in the developing nations were not optimistic. However, his plainly expressed preferences were for open societies which presupposed some forms of election of officials, representative institutions, checks on governmental power, and nationalism, as opposed to the pseudo-universalisms of the cold-war ideology. He also expected that some form of socialism was necessary to insure that a large percentage of the gross national product would be invested in machine tools and the infrastructure necessary for industrialization. He regarded nationalism as the chief bulwark against Communism and the need for capital accumulation as a counter to the excesses of liberalism. His survey of the developing nations convinced him that the nations were emerging in a postliberal and post-Marxist age. The major contest would not be between capitalism and Communism, but between various open societies and dogmatisms that did not fit the patterns discovered in history.[21] Niebuhr did not consider it his task to try to articulate the needs of the developing nations. He hoped for open societies, but he saw that the future of democracy was precarious. He assumed that most of the emerging countries would try socialism, but he knew that socialism combined with military leadership would tend toward tyranny. He did not regard it as the responsibility of the United States to promote a particular social-political system around the world. The United States' interest would best be served by countering overt Communist imperialism but allowing the developing nations to evolve their own answers to their needs.[22]

The Concept of Power

There are three basic attitudes toward the concept of power in Niebuhr's political philosophy. Power is, in one sense, morally neutral. It is simply the vitality of human life and is almost synonymous with energy. In this sense Niebuhr uses the balance of power to mean the state of equilibrium which permits the vitalities of social forces to be expressed without annulling any one of the forces.[23] The second use of power regards it as an outgrowth of man's pride and his false attempts to gain security by dominating other men.[24] This use of power equates it with the capacity to impose one's will upon others[25] and has led Niebuhr frequently to equate power with force. The third major use of the term *power* is to treat it as a necessary expression of social organization and cohesion.[26] Given man's nature, an organizing power is needed to prevent social chaos. In this sense, power has a more positive moral connotation than in the first two uses. Depending upon the particular context, power may be regarded by Niebuhr as morally neutral, negative, or positive.

Not only its moral connotations, but the meaning of power varies in Niebuhr's writing with the context. The importance of the term *power* to his political thought, however, requires that the central meaning of the term be understood. Niebuhr characteristically states that "the contest of power . . . is the heart of political life." [27] In this sense, which is fundamental to Niebuhr's political thought, power seems to be the capacity to realize one's purposes, either through authority or force.[28] The struggle which characterizes politics is for control of the institutions and forces which permit one to realize one's goals. It is not always clear in Niebuhr's writing that his definition of power includes the goal factor; often it appears that he is thinking only of the control of the institutions or the forces. But the goal factor, a necessary ingredient for an adequate definition of power, is presupposed in Niebuhr's thought by his doctrine of man, which insists that every political self has certain interests which he is attempting to maximize.

Commentators on Niebuhr's political philosophy have underestimated the subtlety of his understanding of power. Harry R. Davis' dissertation on Niebuhr's political philosophy[29] is an example of a tendency to oversimplify Niebuhr's thought by (1) neglecting the chronological development of his thought and (2) oversystematizing his thought. Davis argued that Niebuhr's political philosophy allowed for three types of social power: military, priestly, and economic. Davis recognized that occasionally Niebuhr hinted there was a fourth type, ideological power, but he pointed to the recurrent listing of the three types[30] as evidence of their basic position in Niebuhr's thought. According to Davis, Niebuhr regarded economic power as the dominant form of power: "It is a major point with Niebuhr the political radical that in the modern period economic power dominates society (an obvious modification from Marx)."[31]

Niebuhr's own writing indicates that, though he may have listed at various times three, four, or five expressions of power as of special importance, his thought emphasizes the limitless combinations of factors which produce power.

> The spiritual and physical faculties of man are able, in their unity and interrelation, to create an endless variety of types and combinations of power, from that of pure reason to that of pure physical force.[32]

Niebuhr's testimony that economic power is not, in the Marxian or any other important sense, the dominant form of power reflects his abandonment of Marxist categories of political philosophy.

> The modern belief that economic power is the most basic form, and that all other forms are derived from it is erroneous.[33]

> The struggle in congress over the tax bill is a harbinger of another new development in modern society. It indicates the gradual ascendency of politics over economics. . . .
> The war has greatly enhanced this supremacy of political over economic society.[34]

Though Davis eliminated some of the subtlety and complexity in his presentation of Niebuhr's understanding of power and mistakenly regarded a passing stage in Niebuhr's development as normative for his thought, he saw the centrality of the struggle for power to Niebuhr's political philosophy. He also recognized the connections between Niebuhr's doctrine of man and his theory of politics.

> In general Niebuhr views activity in the political arena as a collectivized, complicated and grandiose version of the individual's attempt to overcome his insecurity by dominion over his fellows.[35]

All communities are, in Niebuhr's thought, representative of a balance of power. That is, mankind covertly lives in a state of anarchy with each individual pursuing his own interests and trying to achieve a security which he cannot attain.[36] Social peace or the order of any community represents an achievement of order though the peace is never final. The peace achieved is not "the peace of God," but a mere armistice.[37] The armistice is based upon the balance of power, i.e., some adjustment and accommodation of interest have been agreed upon by the major contending forces. The adjustment made is dependent upon the relative power of the contending groups. All such adjustments are regarded as tentative, and "the principle of the balance of power is always pregnant with the possibility of anarchy."[38]

Though the balance of power does not play as significant a role in Niebuhr's thought about American foreign policy as it does in the thought of some other realists,[39] its role is very significant. The balance of power in the domestic sphere represents the achievement of order which is enforced by the authority and force of the dominant group. In the international sphere the balance of power represents an accommodation of interests of nations relative to their power which is sufficient to prevent major wars. The international sphere lacks the organization which can coerce submission and require that the interests of the system be protected. The maintenance of a tolerable degree of order in international relations therefore devolves upon the major countries. They must exercise their responsibilities for the order of the world while attempting to refrain from excessively exploiting their advantaged position.

During World War II, Niebuhr's writing on the reconstruction of the postwar world emphasized the relationship between America's responsible assumption of a position of power and the need to overcome anarchy.

The world must find a way of avoiding complete anarchy in its international life; and America must find a way of using its great power responsibly. These two needs are organically related; for the world problem cannot be solved if America does not accept its full share of responsibility in solving it.[40]

The old balance of power had been destroyed by the two world wars; the choice now was between a new balance or continued anarchy. Throughout the war Niebuhr pleaded with his reading public to accept the responsibilities that the United States' new role gave her.[41] He recognized that to assume the task of shaping a new world order would expose the country to the charge of imperialism. He counseled against both isolationism and imperialism[42] in the postwar period, but he insisted that a new balance of power required active United States involvement. Even while counseling the United States to accept its role as a world power, Niebuhr saw the dangers of pride.

It is intolerable to imagine an America so powerful that we are held responsible for vast historical events in every part of the globe beyond our knowledge or contriving. Nothing is more dangerous to a powerful nation than the temptation to obscure the limits of its power.[43]

In the postwar world, he saw a bipolar balance develop which was secured by the balance of nuclear terror. His primary focus in international politics was how this balance was influenced by events. The balance differed from previous balances in three respects: it was world-wide, it was bipolar, and it was enforced by nuclear terror. The responsibilities of the United States left it no retreat from maintaining this new type of balance; the security of the United States depended upon its maintenance, but there was no final assurance that this new balance of power was stable. The stability of the balance and its bipolar character were challenged in the 1960s by the proliferation of nuclear weapons and the emergence of political and economic strength in various centers in Europe and Asia.

Imperialism: Analysis, Suez, and Vietnam

Niebuhr's style is that of reflecting upon issues of foreign policy in light of the philosophical traditions of the West rather than carefully defining certain political concepts. His discussions of imperialism have consistently focused on contemporary issues of foreign policy. Since his thought includes an understanding of the inevitability of political philosophy being shaped by the political context of the philosopher, it is not a telling point of criticism to indicate that his writing on imperialism has fluctuated over the years. The concept of imperialism has come to bear heavy weight in the political philosophy of the final stage of his career. *The Structure of Nations and Empires* is Niebuhr's most formal work on the theory of international politics. While it does not provide an all-embracing system or a complete model for thinking about international politics, it does analyze the phenomenon of imperialism in its varied expressions. The work argues that there are discernible patterns by which strong nations relate to weak nations. It is the most theoretical of Niebuhr's writing on politics because of his conscious effort to isolate the perennial features of imperialism.[44] The book is not a purely theoretical work, because it intends to relate the perennial features which have been distinguished from historical contingencies to the immediate issues of the struggle between the American and Russian "empires."[45]

Niebuhr has admitted that the connotations of the terms *empire* and *imperialism* make it difficult to use them in describing features of contemporary world politics.[46] The terms are used by Niebuhr to mean all attempts to exercise hegemony over other nations. Imperialism is an intermediate form of political organization between the autonomous nation-state and the dream of world community. *The Structure of Nations and Empires* focused on imperialism as a recurring pattern in history in which "strong nations exercise authority over weaker nations."[47] The forms of contemporary imperialism are different from the imperialism attacked by both liberal and Marxist philosophy, but the tendency for the two postwar superpowers to establish hegemonic relationships over the other nations of their respective alliances was one of the most important features of the international system.

Niebuhr's understanding of imperialism is closely related to his analysis of power. His writing reveals a note of the inevitability of imperialism as well as a fascination with the empirical detail of various imperial ventures. The more vital nations express their vitality through the impingement of their systems upon foreign systems. Niebuhr characteristically emphasizes the mixed motivations under which the strong nations extend their domain. Politicians generally obscure the more self-seeking motivations in their imperialism by reference to universal ideological claims. Such references appear hypocritical to others, but in fact they reflect the conflict and mixture of motives as well as the universal human tendency to hide baser motivations by reference to higher ones.[48] Three motivations, the missionary, the economic, and the political, are assumed to be almost invariably present in imperialism. The missionary motivation is understood to be the promotion of an ideology which the imperial nation regards as exportable if not universalizable. The economic motivation does not imply that an empire necessarily is self-supporting, but only that certain important interests regard it as profitable.[49] The political motivation includes considerations of self-defense, the desire for power, and the seeking of prestige.[50] The parallelism in Niebuhr's thought between the fundamental sources of power[51] and the motivations of imperialism indicates his conviction that national strength inevitably tends toward imperial dominion.

In his writing on imperialism, Niebuhr returns repeatedly to the theme of its moral ambiguity.

> The invariable mixture of the motives gives a certain moral ambiguity to the imperial enterprise, which may be regarded as an accentuated form of the moral ambiguity of the whole political order.[52]

He means to say both (1) that his survey of the historical empires revealed that their claims for the universality of their values were overstated and (2) that the legacy of European imperialism contained harmful as well as beneficial aspects. Each empire must be considered individually, and imperialism itself is not an immoral form of dominion. Though empires were never as beneficial as their ideological supporters imagined, neither were they as evil as nationalist critics contended.

The cold war was characterized by a struggle between Russia and the United States, in Europe and in the third world, to enhance their security, power, and prestige. Both empires possessed power (in the sense of force) sufficient to make the power of previous empires pale in comparison. Though the empires differed in ideology and institutions, they were similar in their rejection of imperialism. The United States rejected imperialism because of its liberal identification with the autonomous nation-state and hopes for world community expressed in the concept of collective security. The Soviet Union rejected imperialism because its loyalty to Marxism forced it to regard imperialism as the final stage of capitalism, and its utopianism contained a promise that all expressions of state power would wither away. Both countries exercised imperial characteristics, but in neither case did the ideology of the country prepare it well for its imperial task.[53]

Rivalry between the two empires was unavoidable, but Niebuhr hoped to provide a perspective on the cold war which would free the American public from fanatically regarding the Soviet Union as a unique, unalloyed evil. The new empires did have unprecedented features, but he believed an emphasis on the "perennial and constant factors" of the rivalry between the two empires would encourage the wisdom needed for a long period of competitive coexistence.[54]

Niebuhr's own attitude toward American imperialism had shifted. Prior to World War II, Niebuhr had seen the development of American imperialism and had warned against it. He had particularly feared that the combination of American military force with American economic influence would create a situation dangerous to world peace. Noting how labor in Britain had been an anti-imperialistic force, he had hoped for the development of an anti-empire force in the United States.[55] During World War II, however, he had adjusted to the reality of the United States exercising a dominant role in the postwar settlement, and he had advocated a rejection of isolationism and a responsible use of its new powers. Throughout the cold war his earlier critiques of empire, derived from liberal or Marxist sources, faded, and imperialism came to mean "the exercise of the responsibilities of power." [56] Niebuhr's definition of imperialism in a neutral or even positive sense as regards United States foreign power did not blind him to the dangers of the exercise of imperial prerogatives. His use of imperialism as a concept of international politics is demonstrated in two cases, the 1956 Suez crisis and the Vietnam war.

The Debate over Suez

The following discussion of the Suez crisis does not attempt to analyze fully the crisis but seeks, by discussing the differences within the Christian realist critique of the administration's handling of the crisis, to show the influence of Niebuhr's conception of imperialism in his understanding of American foreign policy.

Niebuhr anticipated the crisis by writing articles in *Christianity and Crisis* and *The New Leader* in the spring of 1956 on the need for bold initiatives to improve the economy of the region in an attempt to avoid war. The articles held little hope for the prevention of war[57] but in prophetic style called for measures to correct the injustices of the area in order to avoid tragedy. The articles also, incidentally, reaffirmed Niebuhr's strong pro-Israel position.[58]

The rhetoric of the administration emphasized two major goals in the crisis: maintaining peace and strengthening the United Nations. Dulles' speeches were marked by numerous references to legal and moral principles. Statesmen often affirm the desirability of peace, the U.N., international law, and obedience to moral principle; Dulles' unique contribution was his tenacious effort to act in accord with them. Other important values, e.g., the Atlantic alliance, the prestige of allies, maintenance of a Western force in the Middle East, etc., were neglected as Dulles tried to force the invaders to honor the principles of the U.N. Charter. The realist critique of Hans J. Morgenthau,[59] Ernest Lefever,[60] and Kenneth Thompson, as well as Niebuhr, attacked the moralism and legalism of the President and the Secretary of State. Colleagues of Niebuhr (John C. Bennett, M. Searle Bates, and Eduard Heimann) also rejected the moralism, but they disagreed with Thompson's and Niebuhr's attack on the administration. Bennett, Bates, and Heimann were closer to Dulles' anti-colonialism than Niebuhr was, and they lacked the confidence of Morgenthau, Thompson, and Niebuhr in the possibility and desirability of the West exercising decisive responsibility in the third world, particularly if it involved military force. Morgenthau, Thompson, and Niebuhr criticized the administration for its attack upon its strongest ally. They neglected the extent to which opinion in Britain was divided. The British, particularly the Labor Party, exhibited strong revulsion against the Suez campaign. Niebuhr, whose friends had traditionally been in the Labor Party, was found criticizing American policy against Tory policy.

Morgenthau prepared and delivered a devastating indictment of the Dulles-Eisenhower foreign policy[61] in which he argued that the Suez blunders of the United States were not incidental mistakes but were due to the philosophy of foreign policy adopted by Dulles and Eisenhower. He defined the administration's philosophy as that of a new isolationism.[62] Like the old isolationism, it attempted to avoid the responsibilities of the use of power in the international world. This new isolationism contained three central ideas, all of which Professor Morgenthau believed mistaken: (1) a new pacifism, i.e., the refusal to sanction allied or American use of force; (2) a new legalism, i.e., the condemnation of the British and French in the name of the U.N. Charter to the neglect of the national interests involved; and (3) the new internationalism, i.e., the substitution of the U.N. for clearly understood and executed U.S. foreign policy.

Morgenthau regarded the moralism of the American government as absurd and dangerous.

> When we heard spokesmen for the government propound the legal and moral platitudes which had passed for foreign policy in the interwar period, we thought that this was the way in which the government—as all governments must—tried to make the stark facts of foreign policy palatable to the people. They were—so it seemed to us—the tinsel in the show window making the merchandise on the counter attractive to the customer. We were mistaken. Those platitudes *are* the foreign policy of the United States. The counter is bare; that tinsel is all the store has to sell. Hence the alarm, the sadness, and the sorrow.[63]

The same issue of *The New Republic* that carried Morgenthau's article requested, in an unsigned editorial, Dulles' retirement.

Ernest Lefever accused Dulles of misapplying ethics to foreign policy. Lefever's central criticism was that the absence of a strong U.S. policy on the Suez crisis resulted in an abdication of responsibility to the United Nations. Whereas he recognized the legitimacy of executing policy through the U.N., Lefever did not want to attach any special moral significance to policies carried out by the U.N. Criticizing the Secretary's proclamations about the moral force of the United Nations declarations, he wrote: "A two-thirds majority vote of the General Assembly does not change a foolish and irresponsible resolution into a wise and responsible one." [64] Lefever, though not willing to accuse Dulles of being a consistent Wilsonian, saw several similarities between Dulles' and Wilson's idealism. He pointed out that, behind the Wilsonian language, Dulles' decision seemed "to be guided by an unstable combination of abstract 'moral principles,' which are largely irrelevant, and the inexorable pressures of domestic and international politics." [65] This policy of improvisation led to sudden reversals in policy that kept the Atlantic alliance in constant tension until its near rupture in 1956.

Niebuhr joined the critics of the American Suez policy with a polemic against the administration's relaxation of its leadership of the alliance in order to pose as mediator in the East-West struggle. For Niebuhr, Dulles' insistence that we had no interests in the Middle East was surpassed in naïveté only by President Eisenhower's alliance with the U.S.S.R. to thwart British and French interests in the Middle East. Failure to recognize the use of Egyptian force in nationalization preceded our assurance to Egypt that we would not sanction the use of military force to regain European interests in the canal. Consequently, Egyptian resistance to various United States-sponsored solutions stiffened.

Niebuhr criticized the administration for three basic policy failures. First, the United States treated the U.N. as if it were a true vehicle to act authoritatively for the community of nations. In the name of the United Nations, the United States, allied with the U.S.S.R., forced Great Britain and France out of Suez, causing the eventual collapse of the Eden and Mollet governments. It was no moral sanction, but the combined implied and threatened force of the U.S.S.R.-U.S. alliance, that drove the invaders from the Middle East.[66] Furthermore, U.S. moralism in the name of the U.N. caused added resentment in Europe. The U.N. is a channel for international diplomacy, not a world government, Niebuhr insisted. The U.N. has no more power than is delegated to it by the major powers. Second, the response of the United States was primarily pacifistic, Niebuhr claimed. The administration denied the use of military force to American allies with a statement to the effect that any recognition of the settlement of disputes by force would destroy the U.N. Russian use of force in Hungary revealed how mistaken President Eisenhower and Secretary Dulles were about the U.N. and the inability of a nation to use force. Niebuhr's third criticism of United States foreign policy was that it substituted legalistic platitudes for the diplomacy which the Western alliance needed at a time of crisis in the Middle East and eruption in the Soviet empire.

Niebuhr saw in the administration's mistakes typical American mistakes which reflect the liberal-democratic theory of reliance upon collective security. The American tendency toward a consideration of the vague notion of a "community of mankind" leaves little room for diplomacy which recognizes American self-interest and the real sources of power in the world.[67] The resultant error of the liberal theory is to treat the United Nations as a source of foreign policy and to give these U.N-formulated policies special moral sanction. Niebuhr believed that the failure of the administration to recognize the nature of international politics allowed them to condemn the use of force in moralistic terms. Once the decision against allied force had been made on moral grounds, all other relevant factors (U.S. interest, U.S.S.R. penetration of the Middle East, rising Egyptian nationalism) were pushed into the background and not adequately considered in policy formulation.

After a few months' reflection on the Suez crisis, Niebuhr concluded:

> Something has certainly gone wrong with the "moral influence" theory of diplomacy. . . .
> The moral is that idealism in politics is ineffective if it is not implemented in detailed policy. It is particularly dangerous when a great imperial power greater than that of Rome, namely, our own nation, is informed by such vague and fatuous idealism. Perhaps one ought to add that Marcus Aurelius was, in addition to his other virtues, an internationalist who said "as an Antonine my city is Rome but as a man my city is the world," but the world did not profit by the confusion in which he left Rome.[68]

Kenneth Thompson initiated the *Christianity and Crisis* debate on the Suez problem in an article dealing with the crisis which faced the Atlantic alliance early in 1957. He indicated that the United States should have firmly dissociated itself from the action of its allies, but he saw no adequate reason for the U.S. to have taken the lead in opposing the action which its allies believed necessary. Thompson pointed out that a characteristic of American foreign policy was a "sharply rationalistic-legalistic-moralistic approach." This oversimplified view of the moral problems led American statesmen to make sweeping statements about right and wrong and to avoid compromises with moral judgments. The ends of U.S. policy were clearly enunciated and almost absolutized, but the means for attaining the goals were often lost sight of by the Eisenhower administration. "Peace, anti-colonialism and the United Nations currently are invested with absolute ethical value." [69] The absorption of the administration with absolute values had obscured the need for the discriminate moral and political issues which the complexities of the modern political world required.

M. Searle Bates criticized Thompson's article for not recognizing that the values of American foreign policy (i.e., peace, the U.N., and anti-colonialism) required instant repudiation of the Anglo-French invasion. Bates's criticism revealed that he rejected Thompson's political analysis as well as his estimate of the moral situation. Thompson rejected Bates's opinion that Britain and France were enemies of mankind because they invaded Egypt. Bates's criticism of Thompson's article stemmed from his concern for winning the smaller nations' support.

John C. Bennett criticized Thompson's article, of which Niebuhr had approved in substance, for its one-sided view of the Suez crisis. The interests of Egypt and the sympathies of the new Afro-Asian nations deserved much more consideration than they received at Thompson's hands. The legitimate interests of the nonaligned world, and the need for the United States to take an anti-imperialistic stand were supported in following issues of *Christianity and Crisis* by Professors Eduard Heimann and V. E. Devadult. Bennett supported the administration's refusal to allow the British and French to use force in Egypt. His argument against Thompson's position assumed that the invasion was both morally and politically wrong and had to be opposed by the United States. Thompson's reply, in the same issue, to his critics reflected his opinion that the wishes of the Afro-Asian nations were of peripheral importance in Suez and that the U.S.

must rely from case to case upon the dictates of American national interest.[70]

The Thompson paper and the discussion of it exposed the deep divisions Suez had caused among the members of *Christianity and Crisis'* editorial board.[71] Niebuhr and Bennett agreed that Dulles' moralism was quite inappropriate. They disagreed as to the possible military and political success of the Anglo-French invasion. Niebuhr thought the United States should have joined Lester Pearson of Canada in taking a moderate stand against the invasion which would have allowed the Europeans to negotiate with Egypt from a position of strength. Their fundamental difference resided in their divergent views of imperialism. Bennett did not share Niebuhr's dim view of the possibility that the Egyptians would successfully operate the canal, and he shared Heimann's position that the action of the Europeans was inappropriate with the tide running against Western imperialism at mid-twentieth century.

Niebuhr's central concern was that neither Eisenhower nor Dulles understood the responsibility of the West to utilize its power to protect its interests abroad. He listed "seven great errors of U.S. foreign policy": [72] (1) The United States failed to recognize that the European economy required the Middle East's oil. (2) The United States failed to grant the overriding importance of its Atlantic alliance and played to the sympathies of the uncommitted. (3) The United States failed to recognize that the dynamism of the Egyptian dictatorship could only be contained by power. (4) The United States crippled its diplomacy by adopting a policy of "absolute pacifism." (5) The administration entertained illusions about the Soviet Union, shattered only by Hungary. (6) The United States had acted upon a "misconception of United Nations as a super-government." (7) The United States policy toward China was a failure based upon official fictions. The fifth and seventh points are not immediately relevant to Niebuhr's attack upon the administration's Suez policy. The other five points are all related to

Niebuhr's insistence that imperial nations ought to recognize their power and attendant responsibilities and utilize force where necessary to secure the interests of their allies and themselves. The reliance upon the U.N. was mistaken because it failed to account for the more important communal interests of the Western alliance. The conception of the United States as an imperial or superpower did not simply control his thought about Suez. However, his view of American imperialism, when combined with his pro-Israel [73] and Anglophile tendencies, explained his differences with realist colleagues on the *Christianity and Crisis* editorial board.

Vietnam

Niebuhr's willingness to have the United States accept the responsibilities of power in the postwar world was balanced by his argument that the United States should not attempt to arbitrate the fate of the third world.[74] His understanding that the United States' national interest advocated the balancing of Communist power did not imply that the United States should assume total responsibility for stopping all Communist expansionism. His response to the war in Vietnam is consistent with his political philosophy, but his changing response also reflects his concern for a flexible policy which can be altered to meet new evidence. His response to Vietnam indicates the degree to which his approach to international politics is the classical method, drawing evidence from any source: history, empirical evidence, personal experience, and common sense, and examining it by criteria of consistency, coherence, and utility.

In the midst of the civil war in China, he indicated that, though the United States should help to rebuild the war-damaged countries, there were limits beyond which the United States ought not to go. The Nationalist government appeared to Niebuhr to be increasingly corrupt and weak. United States involvement there made it appear as a Western stooge. The problem of China could not be solved by the United States, and he advocated that the United States realize its impotence to accomplish its objectives.

> It is not possible for even the most generous external aid to create health in a nation. If there is residual health there, it is possible to increase it. In China the residual health seems totally lacking.[75]

The criticism of the United States' attempt to support China revealed some themes of his later attack upon United States policy in Vietnam.

He pressed his readers to rediscover the limits of American power. He pointed to a sense of humility as one of the most important contributions of the religious conscience to the dialogue over American foreign policy.

> If there is anything that we can contribute from the standpoint of Christian faith to a nation as powerful as ours, it would be a sense of its impotence and lack of majesty before the Supreme Majesty which governs the nations. . . . It is intolerable to imagine an America so powerful that we are held responsible for vast historical events in every part of the globe beyond our knowledge or contriving. Nothing is more dangerous to a powerful nation than the temptation to obscure the limits of its power. It will be our undoing if we imagine ourselves the masters of contemporary history.[76]

Though he did not share the passion of many American liberals for decolonization, Niebuhr regarded the French effort to hold Indochina against the rising forces of nationalism as ill conceived. The French war, according to Niebuhr's analysis, revealed the impossibility of the West to hold positions in Asia with military power after the disappearance of moral prestige.[77]

The American position in Vietnam in 1955 led Niebuhr to write an essay condemning the tendency of the United States to rely too heavily on military force in Asia. The poverty of the American cause in Vietnam was exposed by the resentment of the West, the disunity within the country, the inefficiency of the government, and the opposition to Bao Dai. An article on "The Limits of Military Power" contained one major note of equivocation. Niebuhr criticized the United States for being overly preoccupied with its "defense perimeter" in Asia to the extent of ignoring the political complexities of the continent.[78] Later in the same article he emphasized the disinterested quality of the American involvement in Vietnam.

> We are certainly more disinterested than the French in desiring only the health of the new nation, and its sufficient strength to ward off the Communist peril from the north. Perhaps we have done well enough to give us a better reputation in Asia as a political, rather than a military, power.[79]

Niebuhr's view of the United States' involvement in Vietnam in 1955 was one of vague uneasiness. While conscious of the dangers of America's prideful use of power, he did not regard Vietnam as a primary threat to United States interests.

In 1962, while the United States' role was publicly limited to advice and support for the government and army of South Vietnam, Niebuhr questioned the wisdom of committing American prestige to the defense of President Ngo Dinh Diem. He did not urge an abandonment of United States policy in Vietnam, but he regarded the policy as very precarious. He admitted that sometimes, for strategic reasons, United States policy had to support dubious leaders. He quoted President Roosevelt as saying that undesirable allies "may be bastards but are at least our bastards." [80] However, Diem's regime was so unjust and unpopular that the United States was suffering a loss in prestige for its continued support.

His criticism of United States policy deepened, though he did not see how the United States could have remained free of involvement in Vietnam.[81] His hopes for possible settlement of the conflict altered as various suggestions were made public. He came to distrust administration announcements as to the facts about the war, and he attacked the administration's pretense of virtue in the conflict.[82] As late as January 1965, he entertained hopes that the administration was serving wise interests of the United States which it could not make public.[83] His public strictures against the administration were moderated by his awareness of not having access to the information which policy makers were utilizing. He attacked the administration for its lack of candor and for its failure to present a convincing case for the policy in Vietnam. He became convinced during 1966 that it was highly unlikely that President Johnson's administration would be able to extricate itself from its policy of escalation. He did not believe a military victory was possible except at an unacceptable cost. His criticism was largely directed at the administration's justification of its policy. Lacking the information that the policy makers had, he did not attempt to map out an alternative policy, but he had sufficient information, in his opinion, to expose the shallowness of administration arguments. He hoped for an alternative to the administration for the 1968 election, but his analysis of both major parties provided him with little comfort that a way out of the "quagmire" [84] of Vietnam could be found.

Niebuhr attacked the idea that either the principle of self-determination or democracy was being defended in Vietnam. He rejected the concept that the security of the United States rested to an important degree upon a war in Vietnam.[85] Niebuhr acknowledged that there were certain imperial interests which might have been forwarded by a defense of South Vietnam. However, these imperial interests, which apparently included harbors, forward bases in anticipation of a war with China, and a military presence on the mainland to increase the security of the "non-Communist nations on the fringes of Asia," were not admitted by the administration to be the reasons for the American involvement.[86] In a published interview, Niebuhr implied that in his estimation such interests were not worth the price being paid to maintain them and that the war failed to meet the test of proportionality.[87]

Niebuhr did not advocate, and could not advocate without contradicting major motifs in his political thought, an admission of defeat at the hands of the Viet Cong or an immediate withdrawal. His essays have emphasized the need for a downgrading of the importance of the ideological issues in the war, for a compromise settlement which protects the imperial interests of Russia, China, and the United States, and for a settlement which minimizes the loss to the United States of the chief interest in the war, imperial prestige.

The Perspective on Morality and United States Foreign Policy

Niebuhr wrote about the morality of international politics from the context of Western experience and, more particularly, from an American perspective. Most of his later writing about the morality of United States foreign policy was as a defender of Western culture, first from Nazism and then from Communism. His theory was not an attempt to encompass all international politics, but to reflect upon the conduct of United States foreign policy. His writing on the moral conduct of nations included observations about other nations, but his focus was upon the United States. Any studies of the morality of other nations were undertaken either to illumine American experience or to investigate how that country's foreign policy related to the United States. His most far-reaching study of the conduct of nations, *The Structure of Nations and Empires,* was undertaken to illumine concrete problems that the United States faced in the cold war.[88] This tendency to confine his discussions about the morality of international politics to the United States does not reflect provincialism; rather, it is an integral part of his understanding of the relationship of morality to international politics. The hazards of making moral judgments about politics are increased when the country in question is not one's own. His judgments about the morality of American foreign policy often were indebted to citizens of foreign countries with whom he maintained contact. Reference to wise foreign opinion served in his thought as a corrective against the narrow pursuit of national interest. The transcendent reference from which Niebuhr judged American conduct was that of

Christian faith, not that of the community of nations or international public opinion.

Niebuhr's earlier writing on the morality of international politics had been largely that of the exposure of the hypocritical use of morality as ideology.[89] The final period of his career saw a significant change. The difference is due partially to a shift in his thought, but also to his opponent in each case. In *Moral Man and Immoral Society,* he had attacked liberal illusions about the degree to which politics could be conducted morally. In *Man's Nature and His Communities,* he leveled criticisms at realists, including some of his own followers, who too easily dismissed the influence of morality. In both volumes, however, he was attempting to unite the perspectives of the moralist and the realist.

The basic limiting factor upon the role of morality in international politics is the anarchic situation. Each nation lacking security must pursue its own security by increasing wherever possible the power of the nation. In this condition, morality is more often used as an ideological ally in the quest of power than it is to limit the nation's pursuit of power.

The nation-state's natural and necessary pursuit of self-interest in the midst of international anarchy is increased by the interests of its citizens. The nation-state receives the loyalties of its citizens and combines their various hopes for glory, power, and prestige in a political process which acts on the international scene to further those hopes. This function of fulfilling the role of an alter ego for millions of citizens also reduces the role of moral limitations in international politics.

A third force which tends to relegate moral judgments to the realm of ideology is the various self-interested drives of particular individuals and groups. Though imperialism may not have paid for the United Kingdom economically, it did make many powerful men wealthy. Though particular policies might be regarded as contrary to a sensitive moral estimate of the national interest, they could be serving institutional interest within the government or the careers of particular statesmen.

A fourth factor in making morality less relevant to international politics than to personal life is the absence of other sanctions which function in the realm of personal relations. The forces of law, custom, and religion do not exert the same degree of control over international politics that they do over interpersonal relations.

Niebuhr's writing about the morality of United States foreign policy was characterized by an acute sense for hypocrisy.

> Since nations constitute an extreme case of the sinful pride of groups, perhaps the best that can be expected of them is that they should justify their hypocrisies by a slight measure of real international achievement, and learn how to do justice to wider interests than their own, while they pursue their own.[20]

Basic to his theology was the conviction that men could be expected to hide their self-interested motivations behind a veil of moral-sounding justifications. He probed behind the moral protestations of statesmen for the real interest they were pursuing whether it be power, prestige, security, or economic gain. This expectation of hypocrisy led him to expose it and to insist that the proper role of morality in regard to foreign policy could only be understood when its limitations were observed.

Another reason for Niebuhr's modesty in claiming a role for morality in foreign policy was his fear of ideological crusades. In the postwar period he advocated that the United States accept worldwide responsibilities, but he urged that such responsibilities be accepted humbly and in full acknowledgment of the self-interested character of the role of the United States. Niebuhr's critique of President Johnson's treatment of the war in Vietnam included the charge that American foreign policy was suffering from undue reverence for the principle of self-determination of nations. The policy in Vietnam reflected the hypocritical use of moral language to obscure hegemonial interests. The ideological commitment led to a crusade beyond the rationally calculable national interest. Idealism or too simple an affirmation of morality in international politics led to confusion and hypocrisy.

> Our engagement in Vietnam has consequently forced the Administration to create a series of obvious fictions or myths calculated to obscure the hiatus between our idealism and our hegemonial responsibilities. . . .
> Unfortunately, these myths and pretensions of our foreign policy are not sufficiently credible to obscure our real hegemonial purposes.[91]

The role of morality in guiding foreign policy was severely limited in Niebuhr's early thought about international politics because he thought of morality as finally subject to the ethic of Jesus. The absolute ethic of Jesus was the final vision of what moral discourse ought to be, and this had no tolerance for considerations of power or concessions to pride. Later, Niebuhr developed a model of social ethical thinking relying upon secular as well as Christian principles of morality. But his insistence upon the moral ambiguity of the realm of politics depended in part upon its contrast with an ethic of love.

In his early writing, Niebuhr had developed the outlines of a metaphysic which depended upon the two poles of the ideal and the real.[92] The influence of this metaphysic over his thought faded, but the model of the powerless ideal standing in sharp contrast to the concerns of power-seeking politics was retained. The contrast between the ideal and the real is seen both in his Christology and in his political philosophy. Christ remains the symbol of the expression of the ideal in human life, which necessarily renounced power.[93] Political philosophy is divisible into two camps, the idealists and the realists, though a number of political philosophers reflect a mixture of the two motifs.[94]

Politics remains, for Niebuhr, the realm in which the interests of power-seeking men and groups interact with the realm of conscience. Niebuhr develops discriminate standards of justice and he criticizes Augustine for refusing to do so. Niebuhr regards such standards for political life as ambiguous and contingent because of his respect for the absolute ethic of Jesus and the degree to which history proves all principles of social morality relative.

The historical relativity of the principles of social morality, the peculiar problems involved in relating morality and international politics, and the hypocritical use of morality by statesmen did not drive Niebuhr to cynicism. His thought bordered on cynicism and made use of cynicism, but his aim was to discover a way to make moral claims relevant to international politics. The moral pretensions of certain British statesmen and imperial spokesmen were intolerable, but the moral cynicism which characterized the German attempt to build an empire was far more dangerous.[95]

The bulk of Niebuhr's formal writing on the morality of sovereign states is a record of the hypocritical pretensions of the state and the limitations of morality in international politics. However, he has not hesitated in his occasional writings to judge nations, particularly the United States, for violating moral standards. The positive statements which he makes about the relationship of morality to international politics reveal the foundations of his moral philosophy. The pursuit of one's own interest must be harmonized with the interests of others to be moral. Recognition of the equal claims of others is the beginning of moral reflection. Niebuhr does not demand the impossible, that a nation sacrifice its own interests. The beginning of a moral and a wise foreign policy, however, is recognition of and consideration for the interests of other nations.

The force of "alter-egoism" is, however, so strong on the national level that it is almost universally recognized that a nation cannot simply espouse a more universal value at the expense of its interests. The highest morality possible for nations seems to be, not a sacrifice of its interests, but a prudent self-interest, which knows how to find the point of concurrence between its interests and the more universal interest.[96]

Niebuhr's concern is to avoid the errors of either overly consistent realism or idealism. He does not want to obscure the latent capacity for moral action on the part of either self-regarding men or nations. Neither does he want to exaggerate the factors which prompt men and nations to act for the good of the whole community. A sense of justice does qualify the pursuit of national self-interest, and it often works to broaden the definition of national interest. Such a sense of justice is derived from religious and moral sources as well as from a vague respect for the opinion of other nations based, for example, on United Nations resolutions or public opinion polls. The wise and moral statesman will seek ways to accommodate conflicting interests and to define his own national interest humbly so as to allow for accommodation. Competition is inevitable in an anarchic world beset by rival ideologies, none of which is adequate for organizing the whole, but it need not be violent and can be limited if it is violent. Finally the relevance of morality to the struggle for power and peace depends upon the prudence of the actors. The moral act in foreign policy is the wise act which considers the interests of those affected by the act. The "good" in international politics is, in Santayana's phrase, "the harmony of the whole which does not destroy the vitality of the parts." [97]

Niebuhr has regarded Morgenthau's work on international politics as very similar to his own. The two realists have often found themselves allied in political controversy and academic debate. Niebuhr helped to introduce Morgenthau to scholars of international politics who had avoided him because of a suspicion of Machiavellian tendencies in his thought. Their relationship has been one of mutual dependence and friendship. On the question of the relationship of morality to politics, however, there are several differences. A consideration of these differences sharpens the outlines of Niebuhr's thought on morality and foreign policy. The differences between the two realists are apparent in their views of the gap between Christian ethics and politics, in their doctrines of man, and in their evaluation of the inevitable tendency of nations to pursue their own interests.

In his desire to discriminate between the requirements of ethics and political success, Morgenthau has often stated the Christian ethic in extreme terms. For example, at the Reinhold Niebuhr Colloquium, Morgenthau argues, "It is impossible, if I may put it in somewhat extreme and striking terms, to be a successful politician and a good Christian." [98] Niebuhr's earlier writing contains statements almost as extreme, but by emphasizing the Christian social teaching on justice and responsibility for order, his thought has reduced the impossibility to a tension-filled possibility. The church's norms of social justice and social order are more relevant to political problems than the perfectionist tendencies of Jesus. Niebuhr thought that Morgenthau's statement of the dichotomy conceded too much to the Christian perfectionists. [99] Morgenthau's emphasis on the gap between "the moral ideal and the facts of political life" moderated the temptation to pretense and hypocrisy. He was aware of a realm of moral ideals which reveal the moral failure of the states. He requested

> . . . cosmic humility with regard to the moral evaluation of the actions of states. To know that states are subject to the moral law is one thing; to pretend to know what is morally required of states in a particular situation is quite another. [100]

In political life, morality functions as a judgment but only infrequently as a goal, for Morgenthau. Formally stated, Morgenthau's morality is deontological and not teleological. The teleological elements of his prescriptions for foreign policy are stated in terms of the national interest which Morgenthau would not want to regard as a moral concept. In his concern to distinguish political realism from legalistic-moralistic approaches to international politics, he has insisted upon the autonomy of the political sphere. [101] Students of Morgenthau's thought find a degree of ambivalence in his relationship of interest and principle.[102] The overall impact of Morgenthau's writing is to maintain a separation of the political sphere and the moral sphere, though judgments are made about the immorality of politics. These moral judgments are sometimes relevant to policy, but Morgenthau provides few criteria for deciding whether they are or not. Niebuhr insists that moral considerations are relevant to every stage of the policy-making process, and his theory is less consistently realistic than Morgenthau's. He cannot grant to any realm the relative autonomy from morality than Morgenthau claims for politics. To the extent that there is a gap between a realistic political analysis and moral concerns, Niebuhr wants to bridge it. "In a sense, the bridging of this chasm by putting political realism into the service of justice, however defined, remains one of the paramount problems of an adequate political ethic." [103]

Niebuhr agrees with Morgenthau that the pursuit of national interest is the dominant motive of foreign policy, but he thinks that in his concern to isolate the dominant motive Morgenthau has obscured the degree to which statesmen act out of loyalty to higher values. He maintains that Morgenthau's description of the human situation also obscures the influence of morality upon social life. Niebuhr argues against Morgenthau that power and love are not opposite responses of the self. The pursuit of power is a corruption of the love impulse. The will to power in statesmen is not a substitute for love, according to Niebuhr, but a corruption of his desire to serve the community.[104] Niebuhr emphasizes both man's creative and destructive tendencies, whereas Morgenthau's doctrine of man is almost consistently pessimistic. For example, he writes:

> There can be no actual denial of lust for power without denying the very conditions of human existence in this world. . . . There is no escape from the evil of power, regardless of what one does. Whenever we act with reference to our fellow men we must sin.[105]

This is a tragic description of man and his political action. Divorced from the transcendent ethic by his sinfulness, man's political life is doomed to produce evil. Niebuhr insists upon the mixture of evil and good and finds politics, like man, morally ambiguous rather than evil.

A final point of difference between the two realists is their degree of commitment to the pursuit of national interest. Niebuhr accepts as adequately descriptive the statement that nations pursue their national interests defined in terms of power. Morgenthau accepts the statement both descriptively and prescriptively. He insists not only that they do but that they should pursue their national interest on both moral and political grounds. Addressing the Truman administration he wrote:

And above all, remember always that it is not only a political necessity but also a moral duty for a nation to follow in its dealings with other nations but one guiding star, one standard for thought, one rule for action: the National Interest.[106]

Niebuhr will not admit that what may be descriptive of a nation's foreign policy should be prescriptive. He urges that the understanding of the national interest be continually broadened. The egoism of the state can be expected, but it cannot be accepted as normative; it is the recognition of norms beyond the national interest which helps to qualify the nation's egoism and to assist it in achieving what may at least be regarded as enlightened self-interest. Against certain extreme statements by Morgenthau, Niebuhr argues that norms are not derived from political practice but from moral and ultimately religious sources. A narrowly conceived pursuit of the national interest is poor politics, in Niebuhr's analysis, as well as immoral. A nation which is overly concerned about its own interests will tend to define those interests narrowly. It will fail to realize the degree to which its well-being is connected to the well-being of other nations. Against Morgenthau he argues, "Nations as well as individuals stand under the law: 'Whosoever seeketh to gain his life will lose it.' "[107]

Niebuhr's criticism of Morgenthau[108] indicates a move within the realist school to look again at the possibilities as well as the limitations of morality for international politics. Morgenthau's attack upon the Johnson administration has revealed more clearly than his formal writing on the subject his own willingness to allow moral arguments to bear a significant weight in international politics. Realism has moderated its stance, and it is no longer inclined, as it once was, to place itself in a polar position to idealism. Niebuhr now is inclined to regard both realism and idealism as inadequate and to claim the middle ground of a "moderate realism."

The Democratic Experience on the World Scene

Niebuhr continued in his retirement [109] to reflect upon the problems which had exercised him in his teaching career, and in 1969 he published another book on politics. At Harvard in 1962, he taught a course jointly with P. E. Sigmund, analyzing democracy as a theory and system of government and discussing its future in the developing nations of the world. He gave the same course himself at Barnard in 1963, and these class notes have yielded the book, *The Democratic Experience: Past and Prospects*.[110] The genesis of the book was in the early 1960s during the bloom of the promises of the Kennedy era. It was conceived and planned before the intractability of the race problem was conceived as clearly as it was in the late 1960s. The malaise caused by the Vietnam war had not yet spread to rust away the confidence of the citizens of the United States in her purposes. Paul Sigmund, working with Niebuhr's outline and general concepts, completed the book when Niebuhr's health prohibited him from finishing it. Sigmund's influence and style are more noticeable in Part II, on the developing nations, than in Part I, democracy in the West. Sigmund's contributions made it possible to reflect on the specifics of the recent developments in the developing nations of Asia,

Latin America, and Africa. The discussion of the particulars of the origins of the book is relevant as it explains some of the weaknesses of the book when it is examined in the context of the year of its publication. The consideration of the date of the lectures also makes it necessary to consider *Man's Nature and His Communities* published in 1965 as representing his reflection at a later point than that of *The Democratic Experience,* published in 1969.

The book brings together many themes of Niebuhr's earlier thought on democratic politics. Its purpose is both to support the concept of democracy for those countries which possess its prerequisites and to argue that democracy cannot be superimposed on societies which lack the conditions of democracy. The authors described their position as a "pessimistic faith in the democratic idea." [111] They admitted the dangers and problems of democratic government to be sizeable, but they found alternative forms of government less attractive. Communist utopians and democratic utopians both were judged to be productive of illusions which threatened man's ability to regulate his common life. The exposure of utopian illusions and the attempts to understand the inevitable tensions between the individual man and his communities are similar to the thrust of his other volume on democratic theory, *The Children of Light and the Children of Darkness.*

Niebuhr treats the claims of Marxists and democrats alike when they speak of freedom from fear or absolute egalitarianism. He trusts that democrats will be wiser and safer for avoiding political slogans while seeing the dangers of Marxist utopianism. The title of his first chapter, "Democracy and Communism: Two Utopian Ideologies," overstates his case. There are large elements of sober political thought in both systems. Marx had some utopian notions, and Niebuhr has some eschatological ones, but neither Marx nor Niebuhr can be dismissed as utopian or otherworldly. Men live by visions as well as by systems of production, and both Marx and Niebuhr knew it when they were not polemicizing against the illusions of others. Niebuhr is correct that both Franklin D. Roosevelt and Karl Marx had some utopian elements in their perspectives, but to obscure their respective pragmatic and empirical elements is to attack straw men. The analyst of democracy must certainly subject the government to the most sober and realistic analysis possible. Niebuhr recognized the element of vision as a perennial feature of American life, and he could have reflected longer on why this was so. Is it true that most societies have some utopian expressions which give, to greater or lesser degrees, some legitimation to the reality which exists? Is the role of a utopian vision as a mythological support for social change or revolution always a negative element? He noted that: "Some deep current in the American tradition must undoubtedly account for the persistence of this note in our national life." [112] The observation raises the possibility of the necessity for a political system to have mythological support. The issue may not be the need to destroy utopian illusions but to analyze them for their usefulness in promoting desired values.

Democracy is a term with many possible meanings, and the authors of the volume do not pin it down to any precise definition. They use it to cover various forms of the republican organization of government, constitutional monarchies, and to encompass the governments of France, the United Kingdom, Japan, India, the United States, Mexico, et al. It is often used synonymously with their term "free government" which one can define at least functionally. A "free government" is one outside the Communist orbit which presupposes national unity, protects individual rights, has independent institutions, competitive elections, and enough political equilibrium to begin to meet issues of social justice.[113] The book is written against a cold-war background which contrasts democracy and communism as if they were polar concepts, the one incarnated in the United States and the other in the Soviet Union.[114] The utilization of the same term for so many different governments gives the term an equivocal character. The equivocation is necessary if the term is to be used to trace the emergence of present patterns of government from the contingencies of European history. In the modern world the term is not being used by the authors equivocally as much as analogously. There are analogies between the contemporary forms of government discussed which justify the use of a common term at a very general level of discussion. The equivocation occurs when the same term is applied to all the governmental experience of Britain, France, and the United States, 1800-1969.

The authors discuss the contribution of predemocratic Europe to the conditions necessary for the emergence of democracy. Three factors were thought to be necessary prerequisites for democracy: (1) a unity of the nation which would hold despite conflicting subnational group interests; (2) humanism expressed in terms of individual rights and values; and (3) a balance of power which permitted the development of a tolerable level of social justice.[115]

Their analysis of the situations in the world led them to a mixed prognosis for the future of democracy. Democracy was expected to remain more of an ideal than a reality. Authoritarianism seemed destined to continue to hold sway in Communist states. Though they expected democratic leaders and particular historical contingencies to allow for democratic growth in some of the developing nations, a more common phenomenon would be, they predicted, cycles of alternating democracies and dictatorships.[116] They were not pessimistic about democracy in Western Europe and North America, but its future in the rest of the world was an embattled one.

The book had three major weaknesses. They were the weaknesses of omission of the problems that racism, imperialism, and militarism created for the United States. As the problem of racism has been referred to before,[117] the criticism here is reserved to the interrelated issues of imperialism and militarism.

The authors spoke of an impending crisis in Latin America,

but their hopes that it could be avoided were clear.[118] Their hopes were based upon political parties like Chile's Christian Democrats, events in Venezuela and Colombia, and the cooperation-support of the United States for democracy in Latin America. The authors' support for the Alliance for Progress and their rejection of Castroite solutions distinguishes them from the left which would regard the United States as "the principle obstacle to the establishment of meaningful democracy in Latin America." [119]

It is possible to agree with the authors that a judgment on the influence of the United States on Latin American democracy is a mixed one[120] and still deplore the pattern of U.S. exploitation in Latin America. The dangers of revolutions in Latin America may have hidden the dangers of imperialism from these scholars. The alternatives of democracy and communism which provide the polar concepts for the book disguise the problems confronting Latin America. Democracy has been in many countries, as the authors recognize, imposed upon a feudal system blended with laissez-faire economic structures. Social change may have to come through revolutionary movements with Marxist overtones and the possibilities of how to evolve just social patterns out of such a catastrophe is more relevant than speculating how exploitative American capitalism can produce a democratic system in Latin America. The World Council of Churches has wisely used the term "the responsible society" instead of democracy as a goal for social development in the third world. The term with its connotations of state direction, pluralism, civil liberties, and resistance to foreign exploitation may be a better goal for Latin America than democracy. Dom Camara, the head of the Roman Catholic Archdiocese of Olinda and Recife in northeastern Brazil, has pointed out the dangers of anti-Communism in Latin America.

All around me—in my diocese, in my country, in the whole of Latin America—I see millions of people who are ill and underfed, who live in miserable shacks and who have no opportunity to improve their lot. They

208

suffer the consequences of an extremism—a massive, hysterical anticommunism which reaches such a point of blindness and hate that, in some instances at least, it seems to be (and may God forgive me if I pass judgment) a new form of industry. Any new idea or any suggestion aimed at improving the condition of the poor is instantly and efficiently labeled "communism." This attitude leads to deadlocks that in turn lead to repression, despair and terrorism.[121]

Brazil is as good an example as any in Latin America to point out that the United States' influence is retrogressive, even though the case is not as extreme as in Guatemala, the Dominican Republic, Haiti, and Cuba. The United States has not hesitated to express its desire for changes in the government of Brazil. In 1964, U.S. displeasure with the leftist-leaning President Goulard was a precipitating factor in the right-wing military coup d'état which drove him from office. The United States responded to the changes in the governing structure of Brazil with a four-hundred-million-dollar loan beyond the funds previously programmed for the Alliance for Progress.

Soon after assuming office President Castelo Branco was pressured by the U.S. Ambassador Lincoln Gordon and John J. McCloy of Hanna Mining interests to expedite the Hanna Mining interests in Brazil which were under litigation in Brazil's Federal Court of Appeals. Various warnings from U.S. officials like Thomas Mann encouraged the government to conclude that U.S. help was not unconnected with the rulings on the Hanna interests. Leftist gains in the elections of October 1965 were annulled by decree and the Supreme Court was packed. In less than a year the new Supreme Court ruled in favor of the United States' mining interests.[122]

The evidence of the merging of United States economic interests and political pressures in Brazil points to the need for a more complex model of political life in Brazil than the authors provided. The political future of Brazil is inseparable from its relations with the colossus of the North, and more attention to the economic imperialism of the United States must be given in studies of the prospects for democratic government in Latin America.

The second criticism of the volume, that it failed to wrestle with the danger to American society of the increasing militarism, is based upon both the general omission of the problem and the specific disavowal of the problem. "The result of this subordination of military power to civil authority was to eliminate the military oligarchy as an important part of the power structure in free societies." [123] The neglect of the growing military influence on American institutions was due partially to the fact that in 1961, when the course was first given, or even in 1963, when the course was last given, the problem was not so apparent as it was by 1969, when the book finally appeared. This interpretation is partially supported by statements about the danger of the military that Niebuhr made elsewhere. For example, in an interview published in 1969 he responded to a question regarding the realistic possibility of stopping the military and industry from building the anti-ballistic missile system then under debate in the Senate with a far-reaching skepticism about the military:

> Well, I don't know. I'm not enough of an expert on all the details. I think that the dominance of the military, whether in the ABM system or in Viet Nam War, is nearly overwhelming. I think that Ike was quite right at the end of his term when he warned against what he called the military-industrial complex. After all, we've got a budget of which 50 percent goes to the military, and military expenses account for many of the high production rates that reduce unemployment and so forth.
>
> So these are fantastic problems that American technological society faces. . . . The question is, "What will the President do in relationship to the Joint Chiefs of Staff?" [124]

Further evidence that Niebuhr too was becoming increasingly alarmed over the expansion of the military is his response to my criticism of his book on this problem. He wrote: "You are right; in the light of Viet Nam my confidence in the subjection of military to political authority is too simple." [125]

Niebuhr's political philosophy is not endangered by the evidence that the offices of the Pentagon had come to dominate "the largest network of submanagement and industrial resources in the world." [126] The threat to the continuation of democracy as he understands it is increased, however, by the escalation of military influence.

The combined problems of racism, imperialism, and militarism force a less sanguine picture of the prospects of democracy than the volume provided. Niebuhr's preference for democracy is not invalidated; his faith in it was after all a pessimistic faith which found it less objectionable than other forms of government. The measures necessary to keep democracy in the United States and to free the rest of the world to strive for their own patterns of responsible society are, it would seem, more radical than the tactics suggested in *The Democratic Experience*.

Conclusion

The Contribution of Reinhold Niebuhr to American Thought on International Politics

An evaluation of Niebuhr's contribution to American thought on international politics must distinguish between his contribution to Protestant political philosophy, the theory of international politics, and an understanding of American foreign policy. His contribution to Protestant political philosophy is the most obvious. He is the most important American contributor to Protestant political thought of this century.[127] All studies of Protestant philosophy must take account of his work, and occasionally a study of contemporary Protestant political thought turns out to be basically a study of his work and influence.[128]

His thought, publications, and polemics suppressed the tendency in American Protestantism toward utopianism. He furnished the critique of the Social Gospel's ideas while the events of history were refuting its program. The symbol of the kingdom of God was transmuted through his critique; in his thought it became eschatological fulfillment, rather than the historical product of the evolution of democracy. There are contemporary signs of the revival of the symbol of the kingdom of God, but any revival must bear the marks of Niebuhr's polemics. A return to the optimism of the Social Gospel by the mainstream of American Protestantism is highly improbable.

His activities and writing contributed to the preparation of American Protestants for the involvement and rigor of World War II and the cold war. He provided an ideological justification for both struggles and strengthened fellow churchmen for the terrors of the twentieth century.

His extreme criticism of liberal culture during his Marxist period and during the period when he was identified as a neoorthodox spokesman made it difficult for his thought to be used as a practical guide to American politics. His later thought, which has been typed in this study as pragmatic-liberal, permitted him to participate as a Protestant theologian in the mainstream of the debate over American policy. In his total career he gave Protestantism a more concrete grasp of its own strengths but also opened it to a pluralist culture. In Protestant social ethics he laid a secure ground for the utilization of secular political wisdom by the Christian moralist and made it more possible for the Christian moralist to enter into the debate over the goals for a pluralistic society.

His deep debt to Troeltsch and his own skepticism about the pretensions of the Christian churches prevented him from emphasizing the role of the churches as institutions in social change. D. B. Robertson has convincingly answered Niebuhr's critics who imply that he neglected the church, by editing a 343-page volume of Niebuhr's writing on the church.[129] Students who took Niebuhr's courses on the history of Christian ethics knew his concern for the ethical integrity of the church. However, it may still be asserted that the sociology of religious institutions and the rallying of the religious forces to a full consciousness of what they might accomplish through church action were not his primary concerns. Comments on Niebuhr's lack of a doctrine of the church[130] reveal as much about the perspective of the critic as they do about Niebuhr's thought. Students of Niebuhr's thought who possess a high doctrine of the church or a passion for what the church can accomplish in society are destined to remain unsatisfied with Niebuhr's formulations.

Reinhold Niebuhr has not attempted to construct a theory of international politics. His writing has been directed more toward the nation's educated public, its churchmen, and its makers of policy than toward its academics. He has entered into the discussion of the theory of international politics, but he has remained skeptical of theoretical systems that would attempt to explain all international politics. Part of the function of the theorist of international politics is to keep the discussion open and to prevent any premature closing of the debate over theory. Niebuhr has done this by continually attacking the grand designers of international politics, whether they were the Buchmanites, the Marxists, or the World Federalists. The debate over the theory of international politics is far from finished. The present is the time for the gathering of the pieces of insight, theory, and fact which may eventually be part of an adequate theory. The insights of the realists[131] will be part of a future, refined theory. Niebuhr's contribution is made through his influence on the realist school and by his own analysis of the doctrine of man and the role of normative theory in the study of international politics. A further contribution is his own disavowal of single-factor approaches or any inclination to regard politics as a game which follows certain rules. His writings have stressed the need for understanding material factors, the character of the political actors, the role of illusion and myth in foreign policies, the history of international politics, the tools of foreign policy, the nature of the societies under consideration, and the character of international competition and cooperation.

Niebuhr's contributions to American foreign policy have been numerous. His influence has been exposed through the contributions of Americans for Democratic Action, the realist school,[132] and the social action work of the churches in international affairs. His influence cannot, of course, be measured. Among his most important contributions, however, have been his polemics against American moralisms and their offspring: isolationism and globalism. Through his writing on American history he has given many interpretations of American character which are relevant to an understanding of American national interests. He has, through hundreds of articles and editorials, contributed to urging a policy of enlightened national interest which attempts to maximize the degree of mutual interests between nations while defending American interests, culture, and political institutions. His moderate realism has permitted him to be particularly wise during the crises of the confrontations with Nazism and Communism. He has counseled stiff resistance while keeping open the possibility of adjusting one's policy to new developments and has insisted on the priority of political considerations over military factors.

Beyond Reinhold Niebuhr

The study has been largely analytic and expository, though points of critique of Niebuhr's thought have been included within the analysis. The following five points are suggestions for further development of Protestant thought about international politics. The points are all related to certain deficiencies in Niebuhr's own thought. Protestant thought ought not to ignore Niebuhr's thought or to return to alternatives which he destroyed during his career. The best direction for Protestant thought about American foreign policy is to continue to refine and develop the position which Niebuhr hammered out for more than a half century.

1) There is a need for a closer relationship between morals and politics than Niebuhr has been able to achieve. The note of perfectionism in his thought has freed him to expose the moral shortcomings of political life. He has, to a large degree, freed his thought from its earlier perspective on love as fundamentally sacrificial love. The need is to shift the focus of Protestant thought from the gap between politics and the pinnacles of morality to the dependence of politics upon prescriptive and goal-oriented considerations. The need is to develop the implications of power understood as the capacity to realize certain goals in relationship to other selves in particular circumstances. Such an understanding of power, which some of Niebuhr's writing reflects, emphasizes the goal orientation of power and de-emphasizes the factor of coercion. Power is more closely related to value than Niebuhr sometimes realized. One meaning of the moral ambiguity of politics is that it involves both the fulfillment of community purposes and competition for self-interest. Niebuhr has countered idealists by emphasizing the competition for self-interest. With Niebuhr's corrective in mind, future Protestant thought about politics can stress the close relationship between political power and community purposes.

2) Several of Niebuhr's central concepts (national interest, power, imperialism, liberalism, conservatism, idealism, and realism) reveal equivocal usage. His critics have often misunderstood Niebuhr's point because of his reluctance to define rigorously and to adhere to the definition. Though the moralist or the political philosopher may have more important tasks than the careful definition of terms and analysis of concepts, such analysis is their first responsibility.

3) There is a deficiency in Niebuhr's writing on international politics which reflects a general failure of the major realist theoreticians. More case studies of how foreign policy is actually made and executed are needed. The development of case studies might enable the outside commentator to have a

clearer idea of when decisions are in flux, how decisions are made, and what sorts of pressure will affect policy decisions. Niebuhr's writing also reveals very little awareness of how various governmental agencies shape policy. Writers on American foreign policy cannot be experts on each institution that affects American foreign policy, but more attention to the characteristics of the major United States' governmental institutions and their rivalries would strengthen their analyses. Many of the most significant influences on policy may not be obvious to the commentator who concentrates on the normal study of international politics. Some of the important decisions are being made or significantly influenced by "decisions in the wings," for example in the scientific laboratories. Analysis of American foreign policy would be strengthened by further development than Niebuhr has given to case studies of the decision-making process, institutional analysis, and consideration of "outside factors."

4) Niebuhr has not given sufficient attention to the manner of ending the cold war. His thought has emphasized the rigidity and dangers of Communism rather than the plurality of its forms. He, of course, has taken account of the proliferation of Communism into nationalist movements, but his tendency has been to be generally pessimistic about the possibilities of détente. He has strengthened Americans for the struggle and assured them that it was worthwhile. The most creative statemanship, however, seeks to resolve issues that are resolvable. Niebuhr has seen more clearly the real conflicts of interest than he has the mutual interests of the antagonists. He has, in the words of his famous prayer, looked for patience to endure when he could have been seeking courage to change the course of the conflict. It is not naïvely optimistic to argue that the United States ought to saturate China and the Soviet Union with proposals which would promote our common interest. Some of the issues in the cold war may obsolesce with time, others will have to be negotiated, some may have to remain unsettled for the time in

which policy can be planned. Granted that some points are beyond immediate settlement, there are many areas of common interest, the exploitation of which might significantly improve the position of the United States and increase overall security. The development of a body of theory about the use of unilateral initiatives to increase security by promoting mutual interests is needed.

5) Niebuhr's polemics against the illusions of world government often obscured his hopes for the United Nations and the work of its specialized agencies, particularly UNESCO. Further work in international politics by those approaching the subject from a moral perspective will involve reflection upon the development of international community. Niebuhr's point that world law presupposes world community seems correct in broad outline. More emphasis is needed upon how international institutions and American foreign policy can realistically build international community. The sort of international community that could serve as a society for world government is probably generations removed, but the national governments which rule man's destiny now have occupied only a small period in the total story of man's history. They are in flux now, and their future evolution is not at all clear. International community is a desirable goal regardless of the desirability of world government, and the articulation of the theoretical issues for its attainment has begun even though the leading political realists have contributed little to the effort.

VII. THE RELEVANCE OF FAITH

The Critique of Religion and the Life of Faith

Man is, for Reinhold Niebuhr, a religious animal. He does not claim that no one can escape religion. But he believes that very few men have really forsaken all religion. Religion is such a constant in human existence that no culture has been able to shake off all forms of religious expression. An examination of the history of mankind and of projections of possibly relevant models for the future reveals that man is nearly inevitably religious.

Religion has different connotations for Niebuhr as he uses it in different contexts. In a foreword to a volume of essays on religion in 1968 he defined religious faith: "Religious faith is essentially the projection of a mysterious source of order and meaning transcending all the disorders and ills of nature and history." [1] This use of the term *religion* is the primary one for Niebuhr, and it characterizes his early writings as well as his late works. One note in this 1968 foreword that was not emphasized earlier was his reference to religious faith as a *projection* of meaning. The use of projection was due, it seems, to a greater appreciation of the work of his Stockbridge neighbor, Erik Erikson. His appreciation of Erikson's psychology had been noted in his 1965 volume, *Man's Nature and His Communities*, but the 1968 foreword carried the analysis further.

For Niebuhr, man's existence is a study in incongruity as man participates in both history and nature but cannot be secure in either one. Religion, which for Niebuhr is a human phenomenon, is the multifaceted way that man tries through symbol, ritual, and dogma to express both this incongruity and his relationship to the mystery of the unknowable. Niebuhr does not believe that the acceptance of religion as a product of human need and imagination lessens its value. The study of religion, like the study of politics, requires a process of demythologization. As politics met human needs even after the historical contingencies of man's existence were seen, so religion meets human needs after assertions that a literal God has ordained the requirements of man's religious life are abandoned.

Can man admit that God is a symbol of his religious imagination and still be nurtured by that symbol? Niebuhr can; in the same foreword in which he speaks of "projection" he emphasizes that the faith is in the God who is related as *Alpha* and *Omega* or as the creator and redeemer of mankind. Religion is believed poetry for Niebuhr. Though the poetry can be analyzed with many human disciplines, it still can be believed and made the basis for what is, in Niebuhr's estimation, the fullest human life.

All religions make use of symbols, metaphors, and myths to point to sources of meaning beyond the flux of the phenomenal world. Leaders of contemporary religions have to be helped to avoid becoming literalistic about their faith. They must also be cautioned against becoming ashamed of the metaphors which protect reverence for mystery and majesty beyond the competency of empirical studies.[2]

The Weakness of American Religion

Niebuhr has deplored the lack of vitality in American religious life. Most of his critiques of American religious communities have been directed at his own Protestantism. As his attitudes toward the church have been consistently Protestant, much of what he wrote about Roman Catholicism has been critical. His criticism of Roman Catholicism has mellowed since the 1930s when Roman Catholicism found itself in some tragic political alliances in Europe. He has welcomed the reforming spirit of the second Vatican Council, but he was not surprised when the curia delayed the implementation of reforms. Recently[3] he has noted particular signs of vitality in Dutch Roman Catholicism and urged American Catholics and Protestants to take note. His treatment of Judaism has in large part been deliberately uncritical, and most of his references to Judaism emphasize its rigorous response to problems of social justice. Protestantism, however, which is clearly his inspiration, he has attacked.

He has confided that on Christmas Day in New York, when he was freed from the responsibility of preaching, he liked to attend the Cathedral of St. John the Divine a few blocks from his home.[4] The liturgical services preserved the drama of the high holidays of the Christian year better than most preaching. He had modified his own services in Detroit after visiting some of the nonconformist churches in Europe in 1924. His tendencies toward improving the rather casual worship of his own Protestantism were deepened by his marriage to Ursula Kempel-Compton. The marriage ceremony itself in Winchester Cathedral may have prefigured a gradual drift toward deeper appreciation of well-done liturgical services.

He, himself, has recorded the engaging dialogue between his Anglican wife and himself over the relative merits of Protestant preaching services and Anglican liturgical services. The short essay, "Sunday Morning Debate," is among the more charming pieces Niebuhr has written. It is a beautiful example of how two Christians can intelligently and rigorously disagree over the forms of the service in a way which handles the immediate issues seriously while admitting the contingent and relative aspects of one's own position. The reader of the dialogue is left to his own devices to choose whether the stronger case was made by the Anglican or the Protestant. On this sort of question, Ursula usually had the edge because of her background and greater interest in art and culture. Also her interest in religion was more radically involved in acts of devotion than was Reinhold's activist Protestantism. An essay of hers, "The Testing of Our Calling," [5] which reveals deep faith and rigorous scholarship demands that religion's strength must be evaluated by its own intrinsic value. Certainly this is true and Reinhold would agree, but she shows a tendency to dismiss the pragmatic criteria much more quickly than he would.

The evangelism of the frontier had a spiritual vitality. The ebbing of the vitality, combined with the protest against liturgy, left American Protestantism burdened with rather banal religious services. Long before the recent revival in liturgical renewal he was attacking the sentimentality and awkwardness of the prevailing patterns of worship. He enumerated some of his charges:

1. The pastoral prayer is both too long and too formless. . . .

2. Without the discipline of traditional and historic prayers there is a tendency to neglect some of the necessary and perennial themes of prayer. . . .

3. The language of the prayers of common worship is either too common, too sentimental, or too extravagant. . . .

4. The use of Biblical ideas in prayer is necessary not merely to purify the expressions but to correct the thought. . . .

5. The free worship tends to be too personal in every respect. . . .

6. The reading of the Scripture in Protestant worship leaves much to be desired. . . .

7. The participation of the congregation in the worship service is too minimal.

8. Choir music in the nonliturgical churches and in some liturgical ones is still affected by the sentimentality which began to corrupt religious music in the latter part of the last century. . . .[6]

Niebuhr often criticized American Protestantism for its disunity. He labored hard in the ecumenical movement, but he could take little pride in the fact that the Protestant churches were finally seeking unity. They had delayed too long. As early as 1924 he criticized those who boasted of the churches moving together.

The church has lost the chance of becoming the unifying element in our American society. It is not anticipating any facts. It is merely catching up very slowly to the new social facts created by economic and other forces. The American melting pot is doing its work. The churches merely represent various European cultures lost in the amalgam of American life and maintaining a separate existence only in religion.[7]

The major reason he wanted more unity among the churches was so that each sect or denomination could borrow from others the elements of the fullness of the Christian tradition which respective groups had preserved. The spectacle of competition among the denominations was a scandal, and it had to end. He rejected, however, arguments for unity based upon notions of a united front against Catholicism or of more power and prestige. His work for the cooperation among Protestant denominations involved him at the local level in Detroit, at the national level while in New York, and in two world councils, at Oxford in 1937 and Amsterdam in 1948.

The third important failing of the American churches for which he criticized them was their lack of providing moral leadership. Moral leadership required spiritual vigor and social intelligence both of which were in meager supply in American Protestantism. Men needed to be confronted with the ethic of love so that the essential selfishness and poverty of American life could be exposed. The church did not have to become a political agency. However the greater danger to the church was its failure to involve itself in the contentious issues of American common life. In his attitude toward the church taking a prophetic and educational role concerning the ills of American society, Reinhold Niebuhr revealed himself as a true son of the Social Gospel movement. He spent his life trying to find ways to articulate the relevance of the gospel and the love ethic to American social problems. In his writings on the churches' need for an adequate social ethic his dual attitude of love for and critique of the church is most obvious. He was a Protestant clergyman with his whole heart, but that did not interfere with delivering scathing criticisms of the church's failure to fulfill its ethical tasks. His book *Man's Nature and His Communities* leveled its strongest criticism of religion at the self-righteousness which religious communities encouraged. Religious self-righteousness and strictly legalistic moral codes sealed off the gates of grace and vital ethical concerns. The ideal of humility was obscured by the tendency of religious self-righteousness to reinforce community mores. Whereas vital religion should reveal the need for repentance for all commonly accepted standards of the life of church, race, or nation, in fact, American religion blessed the status quo in the country. Instead of becoming a constant source of community renewal, religion had served to obscure the need for renewal in corporate life.

The Life of Faith

Niebuhr's magnum opus, *The Nature and Destiny of Man*, traces through 621 pages the meaning of Christian faith to modern man and a refutation of alternative schemes of meaning. It is a bold book which makes far-reaching claims for the truth of the Christian life. A contemporary reader of the book, however, needs to preface it by reading two of Niebuhr's essays[8] on the role of myth and symbol in religious language. The essays make clear the roles of the disciplined religious imagination and the poet writing theological prose in the construction of this work in Christian anthropology.

Faith does not mean belief for Niebuhr. It involves belief, but essentially it is much more a state of trust that there is meaning in human existence and in one's own existence. The content of that meaning is perceived for Niebuhr through the symbol of Christ. There is no existential security for Niebuhr other than the security of a trust that one is forgiven and affirmed by the source of one's being. The contradictions of man's life which are dependent upon his standing simultaneously in nature and history but refusing to be at home in either cannot be overcome. However, they can be accepted and man can live in trust.

The trust, however, for Niebuhr who stands in immense debt to Luther, is never secure in this life. He has faith and yet he does not securely possess it. Whenever he thinks he has control of his situation through faith he falls again into pride—spiritual pride.

Niebuhr lived since his illness in 1952 with an awareness of the radical contingency of his own life. For the last decade his life and comfort depended upon the sacrifice and love of his wife, whose constant ministering to his needs and defense of his health witnessed to what human love at its best means. Minor strokes reminded him regularly of the closeness of death. He talked with friends about his approaching death without fear while revealing impatience about his inability to contribute more to various struggles for justice.

His inaugural address at Union in 1930 on the spiritual life of modern man[9] emphasized the incompleteness of modern man and his confused social life. Man's Promethian technology contained within itself possibilities of evil as well as good, and to regard it as essentially self-correcting and beneficent was naïve. Modern man's anxieties and illusions prepared him poorly for the crises of his communal life. Niebuhr believed man needed faith in the essential purposefulness of his life and in the forgiveness of his failures. The faith could not be in outworn creeds which were unbelievable but would depend upon an adequate restatement of the symbolic affirmations of Christian faith.

An adequate restatement of Christian faith for Niebuhr combined poetry and moral insight. Both have to be united. Our moral efforts depend upon our convictions that they are not irrelevant to the deeper purposes of life. Expressions of the purposes of life beyond the empirical evidence are assertions which can be expressed philosophically, but are usually better expressed in either poetry or biblical metaphors. Philosophy, for Niebuhr, has its place and needs to be combined with the imagination of the poets and prophets to discipline their insights.[10] Vital religion is dependent upon its ethical rigor, and religion properly interpreted furnishes a basis of hope for moral heroism.

Religious faith, which means in Niebuhr's life a critically appropriated Protestantism, frees men to accept the finiteness of their lives, but still to live with a sense of basic trust. It promotes a sense of concern for the well-being of the neighbor which, when defined in terms of love, has no arbitrary limits. It provides in its more theologically developed insights a pattern for thinking about man and society. In all these areas it risks the judgment that the incomplete meanings perceived in faith are related to the ultimate structure of reality. Faith when it knows what it is about knows that it is incomplete and cannot in history claim to possess that sureness of life and meaning which is beyond history. Finally the life of faith cannot be validated; it can only be lived. It is the witness of the quality of the life which is the ultimate test, but no Christian can claim righteousness for himself without becoming self-righteous. Close to the center of the life of faith is a humility which, of course, cannot by its nature be claimed as evidence for the truth of the faith. One of this country's most careful New Testament scholars, who is known for the cautious, circumspect nature of his judgments, remarked to a former student of his and to a Roman Catholic scholar: "If I had the power to canonize only one Christian, I would make Reinhold Niebuhr a saint! He is a grace-filled man." [11]

God as the Symbol of Ultimate Mystery and Meaning

It is not easy to think or write clearly about God in the twentieth century. It has never been easy, but perhaps it is more difficult in the twentieth century than before. Niebuhr uses the term *God* often in his writing, but beyond asserting that God is the creator, redeemer, and judge who is known most clearly through Jesus Christ, he does not often present precisely what he means by the term. His concerns were with the nature of man and his political and ethical life, but even so the infrequency of the rigorous discussions of God in his hundreds of articles and over a score of books is striking. Similarly, though there are hundreds of essays, several books, and more than a score of dissertations on his thought, there is no adequate discussion of his thought on God. The editors of the most important critical volume on his thought did not even include an essay on his doctrine of God among the twenty subjects they chose to discuss.[12]

The paucity of analysis reflects Niebuhr's own refusal to equate God with some rational structures of thought. His tendency to emphasize the freedom and person of God encouraged him not to develop a doctrine of God. Similarly, his preference for historical studies and a leaning toward empiricism meant that thorough investigation of the problems about the doctrine of God was outside his usual frame of reference.

Niebuhr's attack upon the death of God theologians in 1966 reveals the essential meaning of God to him.[13] He objected to the death of God theologians' failure to suggest viable alternative schemes of meaning for the symbols they were asserting had died. He suspected that the death of God theologians were attacking literal readings of symbolic assertions. Such attacks were beside the point. Their use of Tillich or, in Niebuhr's opinion, their misuse of Tillich said more clearly that Tillich had died than that God had. Niebuhr pointed out that the Tillich to whom Thomas J. Altizer and William Hamilton had dedicated their book[14] had insisted that all propositions, either affirmative or negative, about God's existence were irrelevant. God was not subject to the categories of existence.[15]

In his attack upon the death of God theologians he asserted that there was a realm of mystery which secularism was defective in expressing. Also there was, as men of faith knew instinctively, a universe with an order and a purpose. The concept of God expressed better than any alternative way of speaking both the mystery and the meaning. He wrote:

> The very word *God* represents both the unknowable "X" of mystery and the fullness of meaning—perhaps the "God the Father Almighty, Maker of heaven and earth" of the Christian creed and the "King of the world" of Jewish faith. . . .[16]

Niebuhr has throughout his career returned to Alfred N. Whitehead's model of God as the principle of creation as a way of speaking about God's creative role. In his 1928 book, *Does Civilization Need Religion?* in *Faith and History* of 1949, and again in his 1966 essay against the death of God theologians he regarded Whitehead as stating metaphysically what the man of faith knew intuitively about the dependence of the world upon God. Unfortunately he did not enter into the metaphysical subtleties of the issue. For his purposes it was enough to have a metaphysician point toward the unity of mystery and meaning in the emergency of particular entities. Niebuhr's interests were not in metaphysical arguments. However, his tangential references to metaphysicians and his critique of other metaphysical theologians (e.g., Paul Tillich) are inadequate without more rigorous development of his own ideas. His interests were in human problems, but inasmuch as the problem of man's thoughts and illusions about the gods are very important human problems, scholars interested in Niebuhr will puzzle over this deficiency.

God for Niebuhr remains the hidden God. "He is *Deus Absconditus*."[17] He cannot be reduced to the categories of a particular philosophy or to the understanding and doctrine of a particular church. God is radically different from all man's expectations and interpretations. Yet he does not develop a negative theology; he understands Judaism and Christianity as religions of revelation in which God has taken the initiative to reveal himself. The covenants, laws, prophets, the songs of the psalmists, and ultimately Christ do indicate God's graciousness and purposes for man.

Niebuhr uses the word *God* in many different ways in his preaching and teaching. His tendency was not to define the word rigorously, but to use it as a symbol rather loosely. Like both the Old and New Testaments, he did not ordinarily analyze language about God but related his faith in God to perplexing issues of human justice, meaning in history, and the suffering of men. The three motifs of God's action which were most meaningful to Niebuhr were creation, judgment, and redemption.

The role of God as creator has been alluded to in this chapter and is important for Niebuhr as man is ultimately dependent upon God. Man's analysis of his human condition drives him to recognize this dependence. Man cannot complete himself and all of man's experience contains an overtone of the dependence upon God. Here Niebuhr reveals his continuity with Schleiermacher, and he understands this experience of man as being that which Schleiermacher named the experience of "unqualified dependence" (*schlechthinnige Abhängigkeit*).[18]

God as redeemer was discussed above in Chapter II in his Christology and also in Chapter IV with his doctrine of man. The pointing to the redemptive work of God in human life was the primary task of the church. An address prepared for the World Council of Churches' assembly in Evanston, Illinois in 1954 emphasized this responsibility.

It is in the light of this overwhelming testimony in history to this truth, first discerned by the prophets and then conclusively proved in Christ's revelation, that we insist that the church's duty is to point to God, our creator, judge and redeemer, as the source of our peace, rather than to any human virtue or power.[19]

Before God can be understood as redeemer, however, he must be known as judge. Niebuhr holds that men generally have an experience of being judged from beyond themselves. Analysis of the experience of judgment, he argues, leads man beyond his own communities and culture to a sense of a more ultimate judgment. The presuppositions of a biblical faith allow the interpretation that the sense of judgment is dependent upon a transcendent God. The role of God as the standard of universal judgment beyond any particular human understanding of moral law is of exceeding importance to the thought of Niebuhr. There is a standard beyond human standards. The sense of moral rigor in Niebuhr's thought is so strong because he firmly believes that human morality is an approximation of God's will. Finally, moral standards are rooted in a sense of ultimate concern. God is not only the one upon whom men depend but also the troubler of their consciences.

There are intimations of God as creator, judge, and redeemer in human experience. The filling out of these intimations is, for Niebuhr, done in terms of particular qualities of biblical neo-reformation theology. His own confidence in God was seldom if ever shaken. His quoting of Professor John Baillie on the reality of God seems to apply biographically to his own life:

"No matter how far back I go, no matter by what effort of memory I attempt to reach the virgin soil of childish innocence, I cannot get back to an atheistic mentality. As little can I reach a day when I was conscious of myself but not of God as I can reach a day when I was conscious of myself but not of other human beings." *Our Knowledge of God,* p. 4.[20]

God is a hypothesis without which Niebuhr's analysis of the human condition is inadequate. God is the symbol of unity, purpose, moral seriousness, and graciousness as being constitutive of reality itself. Finally only in God are the ideal and the real united. From a sense of the presence of God came Niebuhr's freedom to analyze man's situation in the world so powerfully.

The Relevance of the Social Ethic

Reinhold Niebuhr's thought and action have affected American life significantly in the areas of religion and politics. Scholars in both disciplines take his thought seriously, and many active in both realms have admitted the impact of his life upon their work. Still, the relationship of his Christian faith to his practical politics has remained a puzzle to some. The most direct connection between faith and politics for him is social ethics. Social ethics for Niebuhr is an interdisciplinary field of research and teaching which relates theology to the disciplines of the social sciences and religion to the problems of community life.

Social ethics depends upon theology for its sense of meaningfulness in history and for its conception of the deeper dimensions of man. It relates these theological insights to the questions raised by political science or sociology. When pushed as to the exact connection between his faith and his political philosophy, he indicated first that it was a broad question with many different levels of response, but then replied:

> I would say that man's collective life is related to his stature as a human being. This stature is best grasped by the spirit of true humanism, which in the phrase of my friend Jacques Maritain means a humanism in which the human spirit transcends nature and history. In that sense a religious viewpoint is relevant to all the moral problems of the individual and of society.[21]

If religion relates to politics primarily through the way it informs man about dimensions of his life and illumines his moral dilemmas, it is important to ask: "How relevant is Niebuhr's social ethic to contemporary life?" Niebuhr himself regarded *relevance* in the sense of adequacy to inform and to fortify man about contemporary problems as a test of any social philosophy or theology. The consensus of scholarly writing on Niebuhr would uphold the relevance of his thought to the problems of the 1930s, 1940s, and 1950s. Even a historian as critical of Niebuhr as Walter LaFeber admits his influence:

> Not since Jonathan Edwards' day of the 1740's had an American theologian so affected his society and, like Edwards, Niebuhr emphasized the role of sin and sinful power in that society.[22]

During the 1960s he fulfilled the role of revered and wise counselor to students, faculty, and statesmen and was honored by the Presidential Medal of Freedom in 1964 and a banquet at which the Vice President paid honor to Niebuhr as the most influential preacher of his time. The historian may be excused for refusing so soon to enter into the question of the relative influence of particular social philosophers in the turbulent 1960s. However, the pressure to provide an evaluation of his social ethic as was done in Chapter VI with his thought on international politics and to suggest the degree of its relevance to the 1970s cannot be avoided by the ethicist. The following discussion suggests that, though Protestant social ethics cannot remain content with all of Niebuhr's answers, he quite consistently asked the right questions. The decade ahead presents problems with which Niebuhr did not wrestle. The ecological crisis, for example, presents a challenge and an opportunity of wider scope than the problems with which he dealt. The theology of hope and the militancy of some church leaders will suggest new modes of social thought and action. A new world is emerging, for which Niebuhr could not have prepared anyone. But there is wisdom in Niebuhr's thought about ethics, faith, and society which is neglected at the twin perils of falling either into despair or into sentimental illusions.

Love and Justice

The key to understanding Niebuhr's ethic is the dialectical relationship between love and justice. Love for Niebuhr is the way men would live together if they were not selfish and if they consistently sought to fulfill the greatest good for their neighbor. Love is an outgoing acceptance of the other and a seeking of his good. The model of love for man is the ethic of Jesus. Man lives under two commandments: to love God and to love his neighbor. The Greek word *agape* is used in both commandments and is translated *love*. The love for God, however, is more an act of adoration and trust, while the love for man is understood in a decision to treat him as one would have oneself treated. Love for Niebuhr describes both the motive for social action and the

231

greatest possible state of mutuality between two people or among those of a group.

Justice in the sense of God's justice or the perfect state of justice would not differ greatly from love. However, justice as Niebuhr usually uses it refers to a state of harmony among men in which the values of freedom and equality are fulfilled to the degree possible under the given conditions. Justice depends upon the interests and the capacity of various individuals and groups in a community to agree on a tolerable solution to their inevitable conflicts. Justice refers both to the agreed-upon rules for settling conflicts and to the more ideal standards which men in their transcendence over the status quo of their communities continually express.

Love refers to the possibilities for human mutuality that are always relevant to any social situation as inspiration and critique. Justice refers to the degree of love that can be achieved under the pressures of conflicting interests among men who pursue their own advantage at the cost of the greater social good. Love motivates the search for justice, and in history love reaches further than justice. Love cannot be substituted for justice in society, for men need rules for classes of decisions to maintain their community life. Justice at its best utilizes power to enforce its judgments for the social welfare of men; love at its best, for Niebuhr, is willing to sacrifice the self for the other.

Niebuhr is concerned to mine the philosophical traditions of Western thought so that principles of social wisdom can be reformulated for contemporary life. The notion that there are laws of any kind which can be relied upon to furnish universal-eternal ideals for human society is rejected by Niebuhr. Scripture, reason, and nature do not provide universally valid concepts of justice for all time. Man in his freedom changes his communities and himself. The double love commandment presupposes this freedom, but particular formulations of principles of justice reveal the particular historical contingencies of the formulators and must be revised in each new era. Of course, there is wisdom in the various expressions of the natural law traditions. Man does continue to transform his present societies by reference to new standards beyond his present societies. However, man is not free to escape his historical contingencies by reference to an eternal natural law. What was claimed as natural law by Thomas or eighteenth-century philosophers reveals that these laws were fully human-historical products as were the positive laws of those periods.

Man's search and struggle for justice is endless as is his quest for truth. As with truth, he both has it and cannot grasp it. If justice is the harmony which preserves the vitalities of the participants or the approximation of full human community under the conditions of sin, it is a transforming process which ought not be halted. Man from time to time possesses a tolerable degree of justice, but as he refers to his understanding of principles of justice he criticizes the tolerable settlement and moves toward a fuller community.

Because justice implies a balance or a harmony, it is not found without order in society. An order may be unjust if it maximizes force to gain consent to its existence. Most orders imply some approximation of justice; justice implies order. In the society Niebuhr usually comments on, Western democratic society, the principles relevant to a just order are primarily liberty, equality, and tolerance.[23] The three principles can in certain expressions be in tension; in Niebuhr's understanding they complement one another.

The understanding of justice not only as an ideal but finally as a harmony reinforced by a balance of power relates Niebuhr's ethic directly to politics. In a society in which the important decisions are made via political action, to pursue justice means to engage in politics. The struggle for justice is the struggle for power, in part. Justice without power is a vague ideal; power without justice is either chaos or tyranny, depending upon how it is organized. Given Niebuhr's understanding, politics is not strange ground for a Protestant social moralist; rather, it is his proper field of study.

Since his acceptance of the New Deal, Niebuhr's social ethic has been articulated in terms relevant to the American political process. He has not advocated a displacement of that system, though he has often severely criticized it. He has regarded most revolutionary rhetoric as irrelevant to the hard choices confronting the American public. There is nothing in his social ethic itself which eliminates the possibility of sanctioning revolution. He has not opposed revolutionary movements throughout the world, and some contemporary theologians of revolution have testified that they found Niebuhr's thought helpful in difficult situations in Latin America.[24] Politics, and neither revolution nor evolution, has been the most effective instrument of obtaining justice in the United States, and so he has remained a political man making hard and often unpleasant choices between lesser evils.

His ethic is controlled by love, and that has a sobering effect in one sense. Concrete human needs and lives take priority over conceptual schemes for a new society or over dreams which may comfort one but produce no results in political action.

The expression of the social ethics of Protestantism with which he identifies his own thought most consistently is revolutionary Calvinism. He has again and again emphasized that seventeenth-century Calvinism, particularly when mixed with sectarian radicalism, produced the greatest social fruits of Protestantism's history. His words unequivocally indicate his own identification with militant Protestantism:

Perhaps the most impressive social ethic of the churches of the Reformation was that which developed in seventeenth-century Calvinism. This form of Calvinism revealed itself in the struggles with Catholic princes in Scotland and Holland and in the Cromwellian revolution in England. It laid the foundations for a free society and for toleration in the religious sphere, without which a modern pluralistic national community would not be possible. . . . It is the only form of Protestant social ethic which I find congenial to present perplexities.[25]

Love is expressed socially through justice. The particular ways of achieving justice are evaluated in terms of pragmatic calculation. The ethic itself has a bias toward thorough change, as no situation perfectly embodies justice and men are continually reaching for better communities. However, the reaching for fuller justice is resisted. The choice of tactics for achieving justice where justice is resisted is a pragmatic or prudential affair which grounds its politics but not its goals on what is possible.

Hope and Social Ethics

The question of whether Niebuhr was overly pessimistic arose afresh in the late 1960s with the emergence of the theology of hope. Drawing upon the work of the Marxist philosopher, Ernst Bloch, Christian theologians emphasized hope as a major motif of Christian thought. Jürgen Moltmann wants to move beyond the militant optimism of Bloch's *Das Prinzip Hoffnung* to argue that there is hope even beyond the powers of men. There is, within Moltmann's writing, a radical trust in the Easter faith. God can create a new future out of the abyss. Moltmann hangs his theology upon the resurrection and upon eschatology.[26]

Rubem A. Alves adds a Brazilian note to the chorus of theologians of hope. He hints that the problem with Niebuhr's thought is that it is too anthropological and that it does not trust enough in the "messianic thrust of God's activity." [27] Alves does not develop his critique, but further development of his argument can be anticipated.

Harvey Cox's *The Secular City* and his *Feast of Fools*[28] both glorify optimism, and the latter argues for the projecting of models of utopian thought while the former was an example of utopian writing itself.

The tendency of the theologians of hope to move from theological symbols to secular hopes has tremendous methodological problems. These problems are more obvious in Moltmann than in Alves and Cox.

In a symposium on Christian realism held in 1968, those most eager to move beyond Niebuhr to new forms of political imagination and more hopeful attitude toward man's social life included Tom Driver, Richard Shaull, and Harvey Cox. There were significant differences between them, but all felt that realist analysis promoted despair or at least defeatism. Ironically, in 1968, Niebuhr as an old man kept fighting for what he believed to be the best political choice available to the country long after some of the more youthful hopeful theologians had despaired. Committed to Eugene McCarthy early in the campaign, he could still after the Chicago convention support his old liberal ally, Hubert Humphrey. Many of the younger liberal theologians could not distinguish sufficiently between Richard Nixon and Hubert Humphrey to continue to participate actively in the political process. It is too early to pretend to mediate a debate between Reinhold Niebuhr and the theologians of hope. The questions, however, do cause a renewed interest in what Niebuhr said about the possibilities of renewal of human community. A picture of Niebuhr's reflections on hope within man's social life can be seen in an early 1930s debate with his brother, the text of *The Nature and Destiny of Man,* and his commitment to social action.

Niebuhr's major hope was in a fulfillment beyond history. Human history by definition would remain fragmentary and incomplete. The problem of the hopefulness of history became an issue between Reinhold and his brother H. Richard, and they debated the issue in public in the pages of *The Christian Century.*[29] In 1932 Reinhold was more inclined to urge the United States to an activist role vis-à-vis Japan's aggression than was H. Richard. Beneath their political disagreements were several theological issues. The Niebuhr brothers were sometimes unable to interpret accurately each other's thought, and the exchange in *The Christian Century* reveals several misunderstandings. H. Richard's criticism of Reinhold's view of history as tragic was, however, justified. Reinhold had written: "To say all this is really to confess that the history of mankind is a perennial tragedy; . . ." [30] H. Richard replied:

> History is not a perennial tragedy but a road to fulfillment and that fulfillment requires the tragic outcome of every self-assertion, for it is a fulfillment which can only be designated as love. . . .
>
> For my brother God is outside the historical processes. . . . But God, I believe, is always in history.[31]

He understood his brother's position as being more idealistic and, consequently, regarding the reality of history as being tragic. He understood himself to be a "bit pantheistic" with more of a hope in the divine creative process and a better future emerging out of the present.

Reinhold Niebuhr's view of history mellowed with time; the categories of irony were substituted for the emphasis upon tragedy. Both Niebuhr brothers had hope. Reinhold's hope, however, was more inclined to be a hope for fulfillment beyond history. In his address prepared for the World Council of Churches at Evanston he returned again and again to hope. The hope is not in the divine creative process, or the newly emerging order, or man's involvement in shaping his destiny. The hope is in God's triumph at the end of history. He wrote:

> Therefore we are saved, not by what we can do, but by the hope that the Lord of history will bring this mysterious drama to a conclusion, that the suffering Christ will in the end be the triumphant Lord.[32]

Reinhold Niebuhr had his ultimate hopes as well as did H. Richard, but H. Richard was more open to the transformation of man and society within history. Reinhold, though, labored with tremendous strength and determination for numerous political and social causes. In part his motivation rested upon his understanding of Christian ethics as a love ethic. If H. Richard had greater hope for society, still Reinhold labored more realistically within the given political alternatives to improve society. Reinhold was motivated by a sense of grace and forgiveness to labor to fulfill an ethic of obedience. Love rather than hope was the major motivation of his action.

The first examination of *The Nature and Destiny of Man* confirms the impression that hope for Niebuhr is a term used more often with ultimate references than in regard to the social struggles of contemporary history. More careful research, however, turns up several passages which suggest that the claims of the theologians of hope do not add much substance to Niebuhr's model. Rewriting the second volume during the second world war, he wrote:

> The new world must be built by resolute men who "when hope is dead will hope by faith"; who will neither seek premature escape from the guilt of history, nor yet call the evil, which taints all their achievements, good. . . . History moves towards the realization of the Kingdom but yet the judgment of God is upon every new realization.[33]

The central purpose of the philosophy of history he presented was to unite Renaissance insights with Reformation. He regarded the Reformation pessimism about historical possibilities as extreme. Reformation pessimism needed to be corrected with valid insights of Renaissance optimism like the following:

> Life in history must be recognized as filled with indeterminate possibilities. There is no individual or interior spiritual situation, no cultural or scientific task, and no social or political problem in which men do not face new possibilities of the good and the obligation to realize them.[34]

On the other hand, the Reformation understanding that history did not complete itself also needed to be protected.

His attack was leveled against a rather sentimental optimism of a relatively untroubled bourgeois culture. The attack strikes readers sobered by events as well as by his critique of optimism as polemically realistic. Faithfulness to his writings forces interpreters of Niebuhr to note passages like the following:

> There is no limit to either sanctification in individual life, or social perfection in collective life, or to the discovery of truth in cultural life; except

of course the one limit, that there will be some corruption, as well as deficiency, of virtue and truth on the new level of achievement.[35]

The very structure of the first volume of *The Nature and Destiny of Man* suggests a point of criticism on this issue. In a theological understanding of man the concept of original righteousness is as important as the concept of original sin. Only a dialectical relationship of the two concepts can adequately express the dynamic of the Christian view of man if either symbol is used. The first thing a theologian should say about man concerns his original righteousness. Niebuhr reversed the order, speaking in chapter nine of his original sin and only in chapter ten of his righteousness. The three chapters in the volume on the doctrine of sin have received most attention. Given Niebuhr's assumptions about too easy a conscience of the contemporary man he was addressing, the emphasis and perhaps even the order of the chapters made sense. Thirty years later a guilt-ridden and despairing generation finds an overemphasis upon man's sin and needs the dialectic changed by a prior emphasis upon man's creative possibilities.

Niebuhr's work was dedicated to helping Protestant Christians and others engage in action for a more just society. His participation in and commitment to the process of social action imply, as his writings confirm, that society could be meaningfully improved. There were no a priori limits of what man could accomplish except the insight that within history men would not eliminate their creative and corrupting egoistic drives. Social action requires hope and, though Niebuhr occasionally flirted with the idea that illusions might produce more action, he resisted the articulation of illusory hopes. Between illusion and despair was a hope-filled reading of events which in each new situation found a task in which to engage oneself. The discipline of social ethics implies hope, though it does not commit one to the boundless optimism of the Social Gospel. Social ethics assumes that it is meaningful to talk about the way things ought to be as opposed to the way society is structured. The movement from the way things are to the way they ought to be implies hope and action. Niebuhr refuses to close the future; just as there are successes in building a better future so there are continued ambiguities in the future. No utopian schemes or concretizations can seal man off from continuing both to realize and to violate his dreams for human brotherhood and justice.

The Prospects for Niebuhr's Social Ethic

The contemporary debates in Protestant social ethics are dominated by former students of either H. Richard or Reinhold Niebuhr. The future prospects of Reinhold's influence are necessarily unclear at this time. There is a vitiating tendency in contemporary Protestant scholarship to rush one's cocktail-hour views into the hot paperback-theology market. Fads blow across the theological landscape, soon to disappear. In the midst of the tempest over ethics, the best starting place for the serious student of social ethics is Reinhold Niebuhr's thought. His historical and biblical interests will drive them back to the roots of their tradition. His political and social philosophy will bring them into the contemporary debates at a relevant point. The dialectic of his life between active involvement and reflection can provide a model for the life of the social ethicist. Exclusive attention to his work and interests would be antithetical to his message, of course.

There is a sense in which Reinhold Niebuhr cannot be bypassed by students of American Christian social thought. His critique of the Social Gospel, theological liberalism, pragmatism, Lutheranism, and American political structures and values, while incorporating aspects of all of them, makes his work a watershed for social ethics in this country. The problems of social ethics have been redefined by Reinhold Niebuhr, and an inquiry into his thought reveals how the redefinition occurred.

Resting in his answers would seem strange to one who never failed to have the courage to change his emphases or conclusions with new situations and/or new data. Failing to wrestle seriously with his mind may only leave the future of social ethics the weaker.

It is a bit irrelevant to criticize one who has covered so many subjects for not writing more on one's own special interests. Also, when one has as many followers as Reinhold Niebuhr has, one cannot responsibly hold Niebuhr guilty for all the mistakes his followers make. Critics of Niebuhr have often engaged in both errors. Some have criticized him because others have supported, in his name, aspects of the Vietnam war and neglected that he has for years opposed the administration on the war. Others have criticized him for not adequately providing an ethic suitable for a cybernetic age, or revolutions in the third world, or international economic systems. There is much to be done, and men must get on with it rather than either repeating Niebuhr or criticizing him for not solving all their problems.

Throughout this book points of criticism have been leveled at Niebuhr's work. In evaluating his social ethic three general points of critique are emphasized. (1) His use of labels and terms is not very consistent. *Liberalism* is an example of a term used without due care. His social ethics needed to be subjected to the cold-cleansing showers of contemporary developments in linguistic philosophy. (2) Passionate movements of social protest have developed in Niebuhr's mature years. Early work of his, like *Moral Man and Immoral Society,* is often more relevant to today's issues than some later writing. His thought needed the influence of being brought closer to the passionate fires of revolution in the third world. Ill health prevented his traveling to and living in the third world since 1952, and American social thought is poorer because of this historical contingency. (3) Niebuhr's break with Marxism was in large part a break with its Stalinist expressions. History forced him into an anti-Communist posture which was relevant to the founding of Americans for Democratic Action and the early days of the very real cold war. There was greater vitality in Marxism than some of his polemics recognized. Contemporary writing about Marxism must consider the liberal Marxists of the Czechoslovakian regime of 1968 as well as the Russian leadership which crushed them. Anti-Communism is a cancer on the soul of America which must be transcended if the country is ever to have the realistic policies Niebuhr advocated.

His primary emphases in ethics remain sound, with love as the motive of social ethics, principles of justice as the norms for social ethics, and democratic politics broadly conceived as the primary method for social change in the United States.

Conclusion

Faith as Niebuhr understands it is credible, a real option for the cultured critic of religion today. His major interests were not in theological problems per se, but rather in the social and ethical functions of religion. He deals with the symbols of theology as they affect the formulation of an adequate doctrine of man on the development of political thought. He believed so deeply in the social relevance of religion that he did not hesitate to demythologize and reformulate the Christian tradition to meet human problems of the modern world. His utilization of symbols combines a loyalty to the tradition with a concern for the ethical and pedagogical integrity of the tradition. Concerned with the function of religious language, his method moves beyond analysis to the reformulation of traditional symbols to promote the integrity of the church in its confession and social action.

A contrast which appears throughout his work is the relationship of the ideal to the real. The relationship of man's hopes for community to the real communities in which he lives is the central problem in political philosophy for Niebuhr.

Throughout his career, he has wrestled with the contradictory drives within himself toward political cynicism and Christian perfectionism. Neither pole prevailed, and his writing emphasizes the greatness of man in his freedom and the selfishness of man in his anxiety more dramatically than that of alternative political philosophers. The ideal of the love of Christ and the reality of Machiavellian politics are the poles within which he discusses man's social hopes and political strategies. Niebuhr's use of the dialectic denies neither altruism nor egoism, but shows how most of man's social life is a product of both self-giving and self-seeking impulses.

Reflection on two of Niebuhr's last essays prompted the title for this book. In "The Presidency and the Irony of American History," he attacked American policy in Vietnam and raised searching questions about the adequacy of the structure of American government to the contemporary crisis in foreign policy. However, it was not only a structural problem he exposed. American pride and self-righteousness and overconfidence had led the country into the tragic situation of Vietnam. Ironically our strength had led us into a burden too heavy to bear which had taken on the proportions of tragedy.[36]

A slightly earlier essay, "The King's Chapel and the King's Court," [37] attacked the President for perverting the critical stance of religion by bringing ecclesiastics in as court chaplains to conduct White House chapel services. He criticized President and clergy for promoting court piety which had lost its prophetic voice. The White House chapel encouraged the preachers and priests to become priests promoting complacency and pride. Against such a travesty of religion he argued in the name of Amos, quoting the text Martin Luther King, Jr. used to rally the black revolution:

> I hate, I despise your feasts, and I take no delight in your solemn assemblies. . . . Take away from me the noise of your songs; to the melody of your harps I will not listen. But let justice roll down like waters, and righteousness like an everflowing stream. (Amos 5:21, 23-24.)

Niebuhr was most at home attacking, as had Amos, politicians and clergy who misused religion for the sake of complacency and their own security.

Death on June 1, 1971, finally stilled his prophetic voice. Shortly before he died he wrote a note[38] indicating that his chief regret about his declining strength was that it prevented him from being more active in turning the nation away from mistaken paths. Even in his last letter to me he humbly indicated where some of his thought needed correcting. He was cheered to learn that some students, going to prison in Washington, D.C., because of legal protest against the war in Asia, were trying to take volumes of his theology and social analysis into jail with them. He expressed how grateful he was that his thought was considered relevant, and, noting that the country was losing the illusions of its era of national innocence, he hoped that we were coming into an age of social maturity.

Notes

Preface

1. Reinhold Niebuhr, *Man's Nature and His Communities* (New York: Charles Scribner's Sons, 1965), p. 15.
2. Niebuhr once defined his work as about evenly divided between theology and international relations. "While I am not an expert in the field of international relations, you probably know that I spend as much time in that field as in the field of theology, since the days that I was on the Advisory Committee of the Policy Planning Staff of the State Department." Letter to Gilbert A. Harrison, January 11, 1956. Reinhold Niebuhr Papers (MSS in the Library of Congress, Washington, D.C.), Container 6.
3. Harold R. Landon, ed., *Reinhold Niebuhr: A Prophetic Voice in Our Time* (Greenwich, Conn.: The Seabury Press, 1962), p. 109.
4. Hubert H. Humphrey, "Address by Honorable Hubert Humphrey Vice President of the United States at a Banquet Honoring the 25th Anniversary of *Christianity and Crisis*," New York, February 25, 1966, p. 2. The structure of the vice president's tribute is notably similar to that of Arthur Schlesinger, Jr., "No man has had as much influence as a preacher in this generation; no preacher has had as much influence in the secular world." Charles W. Kegley and Robert W. Bretall, eds., *Reinhold Niebuhr: His Religious, Social, and Political Thought* (New York: The Macmillan Company, 1956), p. 149.
5. June Bingham, *The Courage to Change* (New York: Charles Scribner's Sons, 1961), p. 368.
6. Statement by Reinhold Niebuhr, personal interview, November 19, 1966.
7. Reinhold Niebuhr, *Does Civilization Need Religion?* (New York: The Macmillan Company, 1927), chapters VIII and IX.
8. Reinhold Niebuhr, "The Nation's Crime Against the Individual," *Atlantic Monthly*, CXVIII (November, 1916), 609-14.

Chapter I. The Early Years

1. The Evangelical Synod, a Lutheran sect transplanted from Germany to the United States, merged with a Calvinist group in 1934 to form the Evangelical and Reformed Church. In 1956, another merger with the Congregational Church produced The United Church of Christ, of which Reinhold Niebuhr was a member.
2. Hulda died in 1959; among her books are *Greatness Passing By* (New York: Charles Scribner's Sons, 1931); *Ventures in Dramatics* (New York: Charles Scribner's Sons, 1935); *The One Story* (Philadelphia: Westminster Press, 1949).
3. Helmut Richard died in 1962. Among his more important writings are *The Social Sources of Denominationalism* (New York: Henry Holt and Co., 1929); *The Kingdom of God in America* (Chicago: Willett Clark and Co., 1937); *The Meaning of Revelation* (New York: The Macmillan Company, 1941); *Christ and Culture* (New York: Harper and Bros., 1951); *Radical Monotheism and Western Culture* (New York: Harper and Bros., 1960); and *The Responsible Self: An Essay in Christian Moral Philosophy* (New York: Harper & Row, 1963).

4. Several incidents from the boyhood years of Reinhold Niebuhr are interestingly recorded in the major biography to date: Bingham, *Courage to Change*, pp. 49-65.

5. During H. Richard Niebuhr's presidency of Elmhurst College (1924-1927) it received full accreditation.

6. The letters from Reinhold Niebuhr to Samuel Press are in the June Bingham Correspondence (MSS in the Library of Congress, Washington, D.C.), Container 25.

7. Kegley and Bretall, eds., *Reinhold Niebuhr;* pp. 3-4.

8. Letter to Samuel Press in the June Bingham Correspondence (MSS in the Library of Congress, Washington, D.C.), Container 25.

9. Inquiries at the Council on Religion and International Affairs, the successor to the Church Peace Union, about the existence of the manuscript provided no clues as to its location.

10. The debate is recorded in Reinhold Niebuhr's essay, "The Truth in Myths," which was published in a volume of essays honoring Douglas C. Macintosh, J. S. Bixler, ed., *The Nature of Religious Experience* (New York: Harper and Bros., 1937), pp. 117-35. D. C. Macintosh replied in an article, "Is Theology Reducible to Mythology?" *Review of Religion,* IV (January, 1940), 140-58.

11. Reinhold Niebuhr, "The Contribution of Christianity to the Doctrine of Immortality" (unpublished Master's Thesis, Yale University, New Haven, 1915).

12. *Ibid.,* p. 7.

13. Allan Nevins, *Ford: Expansion and Challenge 1915-1933* (New York: Charles Scribner's Sons, 1957), p. 3.

14. *Ibid.,* p. 7.

15. Reinhold Niebuhr, *Leaves from the Notebook of a Tamed Cynic* (New York: Meridian Books, 1957), pp. 200-201.

16. Bingham, *Courage to Change,* pp. 101-2.

17. Niebuhr, *Leaves,* p. 56.

18. *Ibid.,* p. 57.

19. *Ibid.,* pp. 59-60.

20. Reinhold Niebuhr has reflected upon his years 1915-1928 in Detroit in the short "Intellectual Autobiography" in Kegley and Bretall, eds., *Reinhold Niebuhr,* pp. 4-7. Another, more important, source for his thoughts about the Detroit years is "The Reminiscences of Reinhold Niebuhr" (Oral History Research Office of Columbia University, 1957). As these remarks, taken on a tape recorder and transcribed onto a 95-page manuscript, are closed to the public, no direct quotes from the manuscript are included in this book.

21. Reinhold Niebuhr, "How Philanthropic Is Henry Ford?" *The Christian Century,* XLIII (December 9, 1926), 1517.

22. Samuel S. Marquis, *Henry Ford: An Interpretation* (Boston: Little, Brown and Company, 1923).

23. Niebuhr, "How Philanthropic Is Henry Ford?" p. 1516.

24. *Ibid.,* p. 1517.

25. Reinhold Niebuhr, "Lessons of the Detroit Experience," *The Christian Century,* LXXXII (April 21, 1965), 488.

26. *Report of the Mayor's Committee on Race Relations* (Detroit, 1926), p. 4.

27. Reinhold Niebuhr, *The Children of Light and the Children of Darkness* (New York: Charles Scribner's Sons, 1944), p. 141.

28. The committee did not use the terms *black* or *racism* which have meanings in 1971 which would have been unknown to the committee in 1926.

29. *Report of the Mayor's Committee,* p. 15.
30. *Ibid.,* p. 13.
31. *Ibid.,* p. 14.

Chapter II. The Disillusioning of a Liberal

1. Kenneth Cauthen, *The Impact of American Religious Liberalism* (New York: Harper & Row, 1962), p. 6.
2. *Ibid.,* pp. 215-20.
3. John Plamenatz, *Readings from Liberal Writers* (London: George Allen and Unwin, 1965), p. 13.
4. Niebuhr, *Leaves,* p. 13.
5. "Professor Williams thinks my characterizations of 'liberalism' and 'liberal Christianity' are too sweeping and inexact and he is right; . . ." Kegley and Bretall, eds., *Reinhold Niebuhr,* p. 441.
6. Niebuhr, *Civilization,* pp. 9-10.
7. Reinhold Niebuhr, "Liberalism: Illusions and Realities," *The New Republic,* CXXXIII (July 4, 1955), 12.
8. Reinhold Niebuhr, "The Blindness of Liberalism," *Radical Religion,* I (Autumn, 1936), 4.
9. *Ibid.,* pp. 4-5.
10. Niebuhr, "The Nation's Crime Against the Individual," pp. 609-14.
11. Reinhold Niebuhr, "Failure of German-Americanism," *Atlantic Monthly,* CXVIII (July, 1916), 13-18.
12. In 1916 Reinhold Niebuhr shared the Social Gospel movement's enthusiasm for prohibition. "The prohibition movement has come to express the most enlightened conscience of the American people. It has the practically unanimous support of the churches and is being championed with increasing vigor by the press. It is natural that opposition to a movement that has the support of the intelligent public opinion of our country should cause resentment, . . . In this attitude, as well as in his attitude upon other issues, the indifference and hostility of the German-American to our ideals is a betrayal of the ideals of his own people." *Ibid.,* p. 17.
13. Niebuhr, *Leaves,* p. 32.
14. *Ibid.,* p. 40.
15. *Ibid.,* p. 61.
16. Reinhold Niebuhr, "The Youth Movement of Germany," *The Christian Century,* XL (November 1, 1923), 1396-97.
17. Donald B. Meyer, *The Protestant Search for Political Realism, 1919-1941* (Berkeley: University of California Press, 1961), p. 9.
18. See the concluding note in his 1928 diary: "Modern industry, particularly American industry, is not Christian. The economic forces which move it are hardly qualified at a single point by real ethical considerations." Niebuhr, *Leaves,* p. 224.
19. The following year his deep disillusionment with liberalism is stated in "The Confession of a Tired Radical," *The Christian Century,* XLV (August 30, 1928), 1046-47.
20. Religion is left undefined in *Does Civilization Need Religion?* and its meaning changes slightly in various contexts. In 1927, Niebuhr usually means by the

term the institutions, life patterns, and ideas identified with Western Christianity.

21. Metaphysical dualism is attributable to ethical dualism, according to Niebuhr. "The real difference between naturalistic monism and dualistic supernaturalism is derived from ethical feeling. If it is recognized or believed that the moral imagination conceives ideals for life which history in any immediate or even in any conceivable form is unable to realize a dualistic world-view will emerge. Thus classical religion with its various types of dualism grows out of the conflict of spirit and impulse in human life." Reinhold Niebuhr, *Reflections on the End of an Era* (New York: Charles Scribner's Sons, 1934), p. 198.
22. Niebuhr, *Civilization*, p. 200.
23. *Ibid.*, p. 212.
24. *Ibid.*, p. 198.
25. Kegley and Bretall, eds., *Reinhold Niebuhr*, p. 439.
26. "Christology is the leitmotive of Reinhold Niebuhr's theology. . . . Plainly, if unobtrusively, Niebuhr's account of Jesus Christ is the presupposition of his anthropology. . . . Christology is *pivotal*, not *peripheral*, in Niebuhr's theology." *Ibid.*, pp. 253-55.
27. *Ibid.*, p. 277.
28. Niebuhr, *Civilization*, p. 198.
29. *Ibid.*, pp. 199-200.
30. Niebuhr, *Leaves*, pp. 106-7.
31. Kegley and Bretall, eds., *Reinhold Niebuhr*, p. 279.
32. Reinhold Niebuhr, "What the War Did to My Mind," *The Christian Century*, XLV (September 27, 1928), 1161.
33. Niebuhr, "The Nation's Crime Against the Individual," pp. 609-14.
34. *Ibid.*, p. 612.
35. *Ibid.*
36. Reinhold Niebuhr, "Can Christianity Survive?" *Atlantic Monthly*, CXXXV (January, 1925), 87.
37. Reinhold Niebuhr, "Our Secularized Civilization," *The Christian Century*, XLIII (April 22, 1926), 508.
38. Reinhold Niebuhr, "Missions and World Peace," *The World Tomorrow*, X (April, 1927), 171.
39. Niebuhr, "Confession of a Tired Radical."
40. Niebuhr, *Civilization*, p. 153.
41. *Ibid.*, p. 158.
42. Niebuhr, "Confession of a Tired Radical," p. 1046.
43. Reinhold Niebuhr, "The German Klan," *The Christian Century*, XLI (October 6, 1924), 1330-31.
44. Niebuhr, "Our Secularized Civilization," p. 509.

Chapter III. The Rise and Fall of the Socialist Alternative

1. Douglas Clyde Macintosh, *Social Religion* (New York: Charles Scribner's Sons, 1939), p. 239.
2. Charles D. Williams, *The Christian Ministry and Social Problems* (New York: The Macmillan Company, 1917).
3. A later comment reveals Niebuhr's encounter with socialism at Union Theological Seminary: "I remember that, at one of the first table conversations in

which I participated, the remark was made: 'All we have to do is to put the sanction of the Gospel behind a collectivist conception of society.'" "A Third of a Century at Union Seminary," Reinhold Niebuhr Papers (MSS in the Library of Congress, Washington, D.C.), Container 17.

4. Reinhold Niebuhr, "Political Action and Social Change," *The World Tomorrow,* XII (December, 1929), 491-93.

5. Reinhold Niebuhr, "Property and the Ethical Life," *The World Tomorrow,* XIV (January, 1931), 19.

6. Reinhold Niebuhr, "Is Peace or Justice the Goal?" *The World Tomorrow,* XV (September, 1932), 276.

7. Rauschenbusch's thought was not as devoid of the idea of class struggle as Niebuhr suggested. Rauschenbusch's idea of the class struggle was different from Marx's, but so was Niebuhr's. The concluding chapter of *Christianity and the Social Crisis* is filled with references to the class struggle. Rauschenbusch wrote, for example, "The class struggle is bound to be transferred to the field of politics in our country in some form. It would be folly if the working class failed to use the leverage which their political power gives them. . . . This is a war of conflicting interests which is not likely to be fought out in love and tenderness. The possessing class will make concessions not in brotherly love but in fear, because it has to. The working class will force its demands, not merely because they are just, but because it feels it cannot do without them, and because it is strong enough to coerce." Walter Rauschenbusch, *Christianity and the Social Crisis* (New York: The Macmillan Company, 1916), pp. 410-11.

8. Niebuhr, "Is Peace or Justice the Goal?" p. 276.

9. Reinhold Niebuhr, "Radicalism and Religion," *The World Tomorrow,* XIV (October, 1931), 324-27.

10. Statement by Reinhold Niebuhr, personal interview, December 16, 1966.

11. Reinhold Niebuhr, "George Lansbury," *Radical Religion,* I (Spring, 1936), 10.

12. Reinhold Niebuhr, "Radicalism in British Christianity," *Radical Religion,* I (Autumn, 1936), 6-7.

13. Statement by Reinhold Niebuhr, personal interview, March 3, 1967.

14. Meyer, *The Protestant Search,* pp. 233-34.

15. Reinhold Niebuhr, *Moral Man and Immoral Society* (New York: Charles Scribner's Sons, 1960), p. 165.

16. *Ibid.,* p. 163.

17. Reinhold Niebuhr, "Radical Religion," *Radical Religion,* I (Autumn, 1935), 3-5.

18. Reinhold Niebuhr, "Russia and Karl Marx," *The Nation,* CXLVI (May 7, 1938), 530.

19. Statement by Reinhold Niebuhr, personal interview, March 10, 1967.

20. Niebuhr, "Russia and Karl Marx," pp. 530-31.

21. Reinhold Niebuhr, *Christian Realism and Political Problems* (New York: Charles Scribner's Sons, 1953), p. 36.

22. Reinhold Niebuhr's tendency to overestimate the rigidity of Communist dogma is represented by the following quotation made in 1953. "Significantly the hope inside and outside the party that Communist inflexibility would be modified, for instance, by the western traditions of Czechoslovakia or the Confucian traditions of China, proved to be mistaken. Communism has been consistently totalitarian in every political and historical environment. Nothing modifies its evil display of tyranny." *Ibid.,* p. 41.

23. Reinhold Niebuhr, "Introduction," *Karl Marx and Friedrich Engels on Religion* (New York: Schocken Books, 1957), p. xi.
24. Kegley and Bretall, eds., *Reinhold Niebuhr*, p. 72.
25. Reinhold Niebuhr, "The Religion of Communism" *Atlantic Monthly*, CXLVII (April, 1931), 462.
26. *Ibid.*, p. 465.
27. *Ibid.*, p. 468.
28. H. Richard Niebuhr, *Christ and Culture* (New York: Harper and Bros., 1956), p. 15.
29. Niebuhr, "The Religion of Communism," p. 467.
30. *Ibid.*, p. 468.
31. Niebuhr, *Christian Realism*, p. 38.
32. Niebuhr, "Political Action and Social Change," p. 491.
33. Reinhold Niebuhr, "Making Radicalism Effective," *The World Tomorrow*, XVI (December, 1933), 682.
34. *Ibid.*
35. *Ibid.*, p. 684.
36. See Donald B. Meyer's analysis of the socialists' relationship to labor and other groups. *The Protestant Search*, p. 236.
37. Kegley and Bretall, eds., *Reinhold Niebuhr*, pp. 72, 146.
38. Reinhold Niebuhr, "The Coming Presidential Election," *Radical Religion*, IV (Fall, 1939), 3.
39. *Ibid.*, p. 4.
40. Reinhold Niebuhr, "The Socialist Campaign," *Christianity and Society*, V (Summer, 1940), 4.
41. "With the ADA, in the postwar years, he accepted the established two-party system, never to resume his nearly twenty years of agitation on the fringe." Meyer, *The Protestant Search*, pp. 236-37.
42. The Liberal Party of New York State is a coalition including the International Ladies Garment Workers Union, intellectuals from Morningside Heights in New York City, and others. Its origins are in the domination of the American Labor Party in 1944 by the Amalgamated Clothing Workers of America. The Amalgamated was open to political cooperation with Communists as the ILGWU and Niebuhr and his friends were not. The defectors from the American Labor Party in 1944 formed the Liberal Party, and Niebuhr was elected a vice president. The Liberal Party supports the national ticket of the Democratic Party and exercises independence in choosing candidates for state and local offices. In the 1966 election, the Conservative Party received more votes than the Liberal Party, thereby reducing the Liberal Party to the role of the fourth party in the state.
43. Reinhold Niebuhr, in an address at Union Theological Seminary, January 11, 1967. The statement was, of course, intended humorously and it received a response of laughter from the student assembly. It did, however, reflect his continued position of practically supporting the Democrats since 1940. His support, however, has been qualified by his criticism of Democratic administrations and his continued support of the Liberal Party of New York.
44. Niebuhr, "The Religion of Communism," pp. 462-63.
45. Morton White criticizes Niebuhr for his somewhat careless examination of the facts of history and his doctrine of historical inevitability. There is considerable evidence that the "doctrine of historical inevitability" is most apparent where Niebuhr has deliberately hung a mythological interpretation upon a few facts.

See Morton White, *Social Thought in America* (Boston: Beacon Press, 1957), pp. 247-67, 277-79.

46. Niebuhr, *Reflections*, pp. 146-47, 148, 161, 239. Italics mine.

47. *Ibid.*, p. 135.

48. *Ibid.*, pp. 53, 59.

49. While arguing that pacifism does not adequately account for the need to balance power with power to attain an approximation of justice, he paid tribute to Gandhi's tactics and predicted that the Negro advance in the United States would best be served by nonviolent coercive tactics. Niebuhr, *Moral Man*, pp. 251-54. His support of Martin Luther King in 1964 emphasized the distinction between absolute pacifism and nonviolent resistance. "The second concern is about Dr. King's position on nonviolent resistance to evil. Many of the journals and the public have confused his position with absolute pacifism, which they reject. I think, as a rather dedicated anti-pacifist, that Dr. King's conception of the nonviolent resistance to evil is a real contribution to our civil, moral and political life." Reinhold Niebuhr, "A Foreword," *Martin Luther King et al. Speak on the War in Vietnam* (New York: Clergy and Laymen Concerned about Vietnam, 1967), p. 3.

50. Reinhold Niebuhr, "Why I Leave the F.O.R.," *The Christian Century*, LI (January 3, 1934), 18.

51. Reinhold Niebuhr, "George Lansbury: Christian and Socialist," *Radical Religion*, I (Autumn, 1935), 9.

52. Reinhold Niebuhr, *An Interpretation of Christian Ethics* (New York: Meridian Books, 1960), p. 170.

53. *Ibid.*, p. 174.

54. Reinhold Niebuhr, *Why the Church Is Not Pacifist* (London: Student Christian Movement Press, 1940).

55. Reinhold Niebuhr, "Christian Politics and Communist Religion," in John Lewis, Karl Polanyi, and Donald B. Kitchin (eds.), *Christianity and the Social Revolution* (New York: Charles Scribner's Sons, 1936), p. 457.

56. Reinhold Niebuhr, "An Open Letter to Richard Roberts," *Christianity and Society*, V (Summer, 1940), 30.

57. A. J. Muste, *Pacifism and Perfectionism* (New York: [n.n.], 1951); G. H. C. Macgregor, *The New Testament Basis of Pacifism and the Relevance of an Impossible Ideal* (Nyack, N.Y.: Fellowship Publications, 1960); John H. Yoder, *Reinhold Niebuhr and Christian Pacifism* (Washington, D.C.: The Church Peace Mission, 1966).

58. Macgregor, *The New Testament Basis of Pacifism*, p. 144.

59. Yoder, *Reinhold Niebuhr and Christian Pacifism*, p. 7.

60. Niebuhr, *Moral Man*, p. 233.

61. Niebuhr, *Interpretation of Christian Ethics*, p. 18.

62. Niebuhr, *Moral Man*, p. 270.

63. Niebuhr, *Interpretation of Christian Ethics*, p. 147.

64. *Ibid.*, p. 149.

65. Niebuhr, *Moral Man*, p. 273.

66. Reinhold Niebuhr, "Economic Perils to World Peace," *The World Tomorrow*, XIV (May, 1931), 154.

67. See Niebuhr, "The German Klan," pp. 1330-31.

68. Reinhold Niebuhr, "Religion and the New Germany," *The Christian Century*, L (June 28, 1933), 845.

69. Reinhold Niebuhr, "Germany Must Be Told!" *The Christian Century*, L (August 9, 1933), 1014.

70. Reinhold Niebuhr, "Perils of American Power," *Atlantic Monthly*, CXLIX (January, 1932), 90.

71. Reinhold Niebuhr, "Shall We Seek World Peace or the Peace of America?" *The World Tomorrow*, XVII (March, 1934), 132-33.

72. *Ibid.*

73. Reinhold Niebuhr, "Pacifism and Sanctions," *Radical Religion*, I (Winter, 1935), 29.

74. Reinhold Niebuhr, "On the International Situation," *Radical Religion*, III (Spring, 1938), 4-5.

75. "The billion dollar defense budget of the Roosevelt administration cries to heaven as the worst piece of militarism in modern history. All the reactionary forces which have been crying for a balanced budget raise not a word of protest against this supplementary budget for which no taxation provisions are made. Our nation like England is drifting into the worst possible foreign policy. We refuse to use the non-military pressure which we have to stop the fascist nations and then build up huge armaments to fight them when they have grown strong enough to throw down the gauntlet." Reinhold Niebuhr, "Brief Notes," *Radical Religion*, III (Spring, 1938), 7.

76. Reinhold Niebuhr, "The International Situation," *Radical Religion*, V (Winter, 1940), 3.

77. Reinhold Niebuhr, "American Neutrality," *Radical Religion*, V (Summer, 1940), 6.

78. The interventionist side of Niebuhr's thought is seen most clearly in his editorship of *Christianity and Crisis* in 1941 which is discussed in the next chapter. *Infra*, pp. 108-11.

79. Reinhold Niebuhr, "Union for Democratic Action," *Radical Religion*, VI (Summer, 1941), 6.

80. Reinhold Niebuhr, "History (God) Has Overtaken Us," *Radical Religion*, VII (Winter, 1941), 3.

81. For an interpretation of the connections with the German underground, see Bingham, *Courage to Change*, pp. 168-71.

Chapter IV. The Exposition of Christian Realism

1. Niebuhr, *Christian Realism*, p. 119.

2. "I have not sought to elaborate the religious and theological convictions upon which the political philosophy of the following pages rests. It will be apparent, however, that they are informed by the belief that a Christian view of human nature is more adequate for the development of a democratic society than either the optimism with which democracy has become historically associated or the moral cynicism which inclines human communities to tyrannical political strategies." Niebuhr, *The Children of Light*, pp. xiv-xv.

3. Theodore Alexander Gill, *Recent Protestant Political Theory* (Zürich: University of Zürich, 1948), p. 145. The term *Christian sociology* is an unfortunate one for Niebuhr's reflections as a Christian upon social theory, but Gill's assertion that this is his central concern and that as such it influences his method is valid.

4. Niebuhr, *Man's Nature*, p. 24.

5. Niebuhr, *Reflections*, pp. 261-62.

6. Reinhold Niebuhr, *The Nature and Destiny of Man,* I (New York: Charles Scribner's Sons, 1941), 121.

7. *Ibid.,* p. 181.

8. *Ibid.,* p. 192.

9. Niebuhr, *Interpretation of Christian Ethics,* pp. 203-4.

10. John C. Bennett, "The Contribution of Reinhold Niebuhr," *Religion in Life,* VI (Spring, 1937), 280-82.

11. William J. Wolf has suggested that "Niebuhr's phrase 'the equality of sin and the inequality of guilt' seems to raise more questions than it solves." Kegley and Bretall, eds., *Reinhold Niebuhr,* p. 240. Replying to Wolf, on page 437 of the same volume, Niebuhr admitted that he had long been dissatisfied with the quantitative implications of the doctrine, and that he had finally abandoned it. "I remain baffled in my search for an adequate description of the situation which will allow for discriminate judgments between good and evil on the one hand, and which will, on the other, preserve the Biblical affirmation that all men fall short before God's judgment."

12. Niebuhr, *Nature and Destiny,* I, 16.

13. "The problem of meaning, which is the basic problem of religion, transcends the ordinary rational problem of tracing the relation of things to each other as the freedom of man's spirit transcends his rational faculties." *Ibid.,* p. 164.

14. Reinhold Niebuhr, *The Self and the Dramas of History* (New York: Charles Scribner's Sons, 1955), pp. 114-15.

15. Niebuhr, *Christian Realism,* pp. 3-4.

16. *Ibid.,* p. 10.

17. The footnotes to *The Nature and Destiny of Man* demonstrate that Niebuhr was no longer relying upon secondary sources for his grasp of Augustine's thought. The references to Augustine in *The Nature and Destiny of Man* and *Faith and History* do not reveal the full dependence of Niebuhr on Augustine. Many arguments in the former work are taken from or adapted from *The City of God. Faith and History* is not misunderstood as an attempt to do for the Christian view of time and history in the modern world what *De Civitate Dei* did for it at the end of the classical world.

18. Reinhold Niebuhr, *Faith and History* (New York: Charles Scribner's Sons, 1949), p. 3.

19. *Ibid.,* p. 65.

20. *Ibid.,* p. 69.

21. *Ibid.,* p. 136.

22. Kegley and Bretall, eds., *Reinhold Niebuhr,* pp. 293-94.

23. Reinhold Niebuhr, "The Christian Faith and the World Crisis," *Christianity and Crisis,* I (February 10, 1941), 4-6.

24. *Ibid.,* p. 3.

25. Reinhold Niebuhr, "Repeal the Neutrality Act," *Christianity and Crisis,* I (October 20, 1941), 1.

26. Reinhold Niebuhr, "Plans for World Reorganization," *Christianity and Crisis,* II (October 19, 1942), 3-6.

27. Reinhold Niebuhr Papers (MSS in the Library of Congress, Washington, D.C.), Container 22.

28. Reinhold Niebuhr, "Toward a Christian Approach to International Issues," *Christianity and Crisis,* VI (December 9, 1946), 1-2.

29. Niebuhr, *Children of Light,* p. 5.

30. *Ibid.,* p. xiii.

31. Reinhold Niebuhr, *Christianity and Power Politics* (New York: Charles Scribner's Sons, 1940), pp. 65-66.
32. *Ibid.*, p. 69.
33. *Ibid.*, p. 63.
34. *Ibid.*, p. 108.
35. Niebuhr, "The International Situation," p. 3.
36. Reinhold Niebuhr, "The Spiritual Problem of the Coming Decades," *Christianity and Society*, X (Summer, 1945), 7.
37. Reinhold Niebuhr, "Is This 'Peace in Our Time'?" *The Nation*, CLX (April 7, 1945), 383.
38. The staff was formally created on May 5, 1947, with George Kennan as director. It had the broadest of mandates to formulate and develop long-term, foreign policy programs and to recommend their adoption to the appropriate officials of the State Department. George F. Kennan, *Memoirs 1925-1950* (Boston: Little, Brown and Company, 1967), p. 327.
39. Niebuhr, *Christian Realism*, p. 17.
40. Niebuhr, *Children of Light*, pp. 153-90.
41. Reinhold Niebuhr, "Anglo-Saxon Destiny and Responsibility," *Christianity and Crisis*, III (October 4, 1943), 2.
42. *Ibid.*, p. 4.
43. Reinhold Niebuhr, "American Power and World Responsibility," *Christianity and Crisis*, III (April 5, 1943), 2-4.
44. *Ibid.*, p. 4.
45. Reinhold Niebuhr, "We Are in Peril," *Christianity and Crisis*, III (October 18, 1943), 2-3.
46. Reinhold Niebuhr, "The Death of the President," *Christianity and Crisis*, V (April 30, 1945), 5.
47. Emil Brunner, *Der Mensch im Widerspruch* (Berlin: Furche Verlag, 1937).
48. Kegley and Bretall, eds., *Reinhold Niebuhr*, p. 431. Brunner had protested that he could find "no mention" of the influence his work *Man in Revolt* had exerted upon *The Nature and Destiny of Man* (*Ibid.*, p. 32). Niebuhr assumed Brunner was correct that he had completely failed to mention Brunner's work. In fact there were footnote references to Brunner's *Man in Revolt* on pp. 237, 272 of *The Nature and Destiny of Man*, I. In summary Brunner's criticism was over-drawn and reflected careless reading on his own part.
49. Charles C. West, *Communism and the Theologians* (Philadelphia: The Westminster Press, 1958), p. 14.
50. John C. Bennett, "Review of *Communism and the Theologians* by Charles C. West," *Union Seminary Quarterly Review*, XIV (January, 1959), 65.
51. Collected in D. B. Robertson, ed., *Essays in Applied Christianity* (New York: Meridian Books, 1959), pp. 141-96.
52. *Ibid.*, p. 146.
53. *Ibid.*, p. 148.
54. *Ibid.*, p. 151.
55. *Ibid.*, p. 156.
56. *Ibid.*, p. 166.
57. *Ibid.*, p. 172.
58. *Ibid.*, p. 187.
59. *Ibid.*, pp. 188, 189.
60. *Ibid.*, p. 190.

61. Eduard Heimann, "Niebuhr's Pragmatic Conservatism," *Union Seminary Quarterly Review*, XI (May, 1956), 7.
62. Kegley and Bretall, eds., *Reinhold Niebuhr*, pp. 76-77.
63. Heimann, "Niebuhr's Pragmatic Conservatism," p. 7.
64. *Ibid.*, p. 8.
65. Will Herberg, "Christian Apologist to the Secular World," *Union Seminary Quarterly Review*, XI (May, 1956), 15.
66. *Ibid.*
67. Gordon Harland, *The Thought of Reinhold Niebuhr* (New York: Oxford University Press, 1960), p. 186.
68. An example of Niebuhr's critique of Churchill reveals the deep differences between the two even on the foreign policy of the allied democracies. "Churchill's great achievements as leader of an embattled nation cannot hide the fact that the Indian policy has been a blind spot for years in his career. He has been consistently wrong about India; . . ." Reinhold Niebuhr, "Common Counsel for United Nations," *Christianity and Crisis*, II (October 5, 1942), 1.
69. Niebuhr, *Christian Realism*, p. 71.
70. *Ibid.*, p. 72.

Chapter V. A Pragmatic-Liberal Synthesis in Christian Political Philosophy

1. Kegley and Bretall, eds., *Reinhold Niebuhr*, p. 149.
2. H. Richard Niebuhr, "Reinhold Niebuhr's Interpretation of History," Reinhold Niebuhr Papers (MSS in the Library of Congress, Washington, D.C.), Container 17.
3. Niebuhr, *Man's Nature*, p. 15.
4. *Ibid.*, p. 24.
5. *Ibid.*
6. Kegley and Bretall, eds., *Reinhold Niebuhr*, p. 435.
7. Landon, ed., *Reinhold Niebuhr: A Prophetic Voice*, pp. 34-35.
8. *Ibid.*, p. 120.
9. E.g., Niebuhr, *Man's Nature*, p. 106.
10. *Ibid.*, p. 111.
11. *Ibid.*, p. 125.
12. Reinhold Niebuhr, *The Irony of American History* (New York: Charles Scribner's Sons, 1952), pp. viii-ix.
13. Henry F. May, "A Meditation on an Unfashionable Book," *Christianity and Crisis*, XXVIII (May 27, 1968), 120. Henry F. May is Margaret Byrne Professor of History at the University of California, Berkeley.
14. "Christianity's view of history is tragic insofar as it recognizes evil as an inevitable concomitant of even the highest spiritual enterprises." Reinhold Niebuhr, *Beyond Tragedy* (New York: Charles Scribner's Sons, 1937), pp. x-xi.
15. Kegley and Bretall, eds., *Reinhold Niebuhr*, p. 303.
16. Niebuhr, *Reflections*, p. 94. Quoted by Robert E. Fitch in Kegley and Bretall, eds., *Reinhold Niebuhr*, p. 303.
17. "Pathos is that element in an historic situation which elicits pity, but neither deserves admiration nor warrants contrition." Niebuhr, *Irony of History*, p. vii.
18. *Infra*, p. 141.

19. Kegley and Bretall, eds., *Reinhold Niebuhr*, p. 303.
20. Niebuhr, *Irony of History*, p. viii.
21. *Ibid.*
22. *Ibid.*
23. *Ibid.*, p. 155.
24. *Ibid.*, p. 157.
25. *Supra*, p. 44.
26. Niebuhr, *Irony of History*, p. 167.
27. *Ibid.*, p. 169.
28. Reinhold Niebuhr, *Pious and Secular America* (New York: Charles Scribner's Sons, 1958), published in England under the title *The Godly and the Ungodly* (London: Faber and Faber, 1958).
29. Reinhold Niebuhr and Alan Heimert, *A Nation So Conceived* (New York: Charles Scribner's Sons, 1963).
30. Reinhold Niebuhr and Paul E. Sigmund, *The Democratic Experience Past and Prospects* (New York: Frederick A. Praeger, 1969). Although the volume was published in 1969 and reveals the thought as well as the editing of its coauthor, the bulk of the book was presented at Barnard College in the lectures Niebuhr gave there in 1963.
31. Niebuhr, *Irony of History*, p. 2.
32. *Ibid.*
33. *Ibid.*, p. 3.
34. *Ibid.*
35. *Ibid.*, p. 63.
36. Niebuhr and Heimert, *A Nation So Conceived*, p. 4.
37. Niebuhr and Sigmund, *Democratic Experience*, p. vi.
38. Reinhold Niebuhr, "The Negro Minority and Its Fate in a Self-righteous Nation," *Social Action/Social Progress*, XXXV/LVIV (October, 1968), 53-64. As Chapter I indicates, Niebuhr had been engaged in the struggle for racial justice since his ministry in Detroit, and he had written articles and chapters on the problem decades before it was recognized publicly as a major issue in the country. The above article is a particularly good example of the type of writing to which Niebuhr subjected other American social problems. The publication of the essay in a book of essays would restore a balance to his writing on American history which may be needed.
39. In a letter to Samuel Press in 1914, he mentioned that he had found William James's *The Varieties of Religious Experience* and *The Will to Believe* "very good." Bingham, *Courage to Change*, p. 85.
40. Robertson, ed., *Applied Christianity*, p. 186.
41. Quoted in Bingham, *Courage to Change*, p. 224.
42. Harry R. Davis and Robert C. Good, eds., *Reinhold Niebuhr on Politics* (New York: Charles Scribner's Sons, 1960), p. 200.
43. Kegley and Bretall, eds., *Reinhold Niebuhr*, p. 36.
44. *Discerning the Signs of the Times* (New York: Charles Scribner's Sons, 1946); *Christian Realism and Political Problems* (New York: Charles Scribner's Sons, 1953); and *Pious and Secular America* (New York: Charles Scribner's Sons, 1958).
45. Niebuhr, *Pious and Secular America*, p. 7.
46. Niebuhr, *Christian Realism*, p. 176.
47. Niebuhr's trust in the coherence of the world and man's ability to create models adequate to portray these coherences is most applicable in the natural sciences,

in the human sciences dependent upon biology and chemistry, and in the areas of social sciences amenable to statistics and predictions of probability. The emphasis upon coherence is radically qualified, and the mystery of man's existence is emphasized in the tradition of Pascal to provide a basis for dealing with unique events, necessary rational contradictions, the failure to provide one scheme of meaning for all the structures of human life, and human freedom. Cf. *ibid.*, pp. 176-79.

48. *Ibid.*, p. 175.
49. *Ibid.*, pp. 175-76.
50. William James, *Pragmatism, A New Name for Some Old Ways of Thinking* (New York: Longmans, Green and Co., 1907), p. 218.
51. Statement by Reinhold Niebuhr, personal interview, March 24, 1967.
52. William James, *The Will to Believe* (New York: Longmans, Green and Co., 1896), p. 17.
53. *Ibid.*, pp. 188-89.
54. James, *Pragmatism*, p. 73.
55. Niebuhr, *Pious and Secular America*, p. 142.
56. Niebuhr, *Nature and Destiny*, II, 149.
57. Niebuhr, *Moral Man*, p. 53.
58. Niebuhr, *Irony of History*, p. 168.
59. James, *Pragmatism*, p. 20.
60. Niebuhr, *Moral Man*, pp. xiii, 35, 212; Niebuhr, *Interpretation of Christian Ethics*, pp. 207-8; Niebuhr, *Nature and Destiny*, I, 110-14; Niebuhr, *Children of Light*, p. 129; Niebuhr, *Faith and History*, pp. 67, 68, 83, 95, 156.
61. E.g., Sidney Hook, "Social Change and Original Sin: Answer to Niebuhr," *The New Leader*, XXIV (November 8, 1941), 5-7; Sidney Hook, "The New Failure of Nerve," *Partisan Review*, X (January-February, 1943), 2-17; George A. Coe and Reinhold Niebuhr, "Coe vs. Niebuhr," *The Christian Century*, L (March 15, 1933), 362-64; White, *Social Thought in America*, pp. 247-67, 277-79.
62. See Roger L. Shinn, "Some Notes on Reinhold Niebuhr's Use of Philosophy" (unpublished paper for The Society for Theological Discussion, [n.d.]), p. 2.
63. E.g., John Dewey was chairman and Reinhold Niebuhr was on the executive committee of the League for Independent Political Action founded in 1929.
64. Reinhold Niebuhr, "A Footnote on Religion," *The Nation*, CXXXIX (September 26, 1934), 358-59.
65. *Supra*, pp. 102-4.
66. Niebuhr, *Nature and Destiny*, I, 110.
67. Kegley and Bretall, eds., *Reinhold Niebuhr*, p. 141.
68. Reinhold Niebuhr, "The Pathos of Liberalism," *The Nation*, CXLI (September 11, 1935), 303-4.
69. White, *Social Thought in America*, p. 255.
70. John Dewey, *Human Nature and Conduct* (New York: The Modern Library, 1930), p. 13.
71. Dewey guarded himself against charges of optimism by admitting the difficulties of applying intelligence to social problems but advocating the attempt in the face of no acceptable alternative. "There is no need to dwell upon the enormous obstacles that stand in the way of extending from its limited field to larger field of human relations the control of organized intelligence, operating through the release of individual powers and capabilities. There is the weight of past history on the side of those who are pessimistic about the possibility of achieving this humanly desirable and humanly necessary task. I do not predict that the

extension will ever be effectively actualized. . . . The failure of other methods and the desperateness of the present situation will be a spur to some to do their best to make the extension actual." John Dewey, "Authority and Resistance to Social Change," *School and Society*, XLIV (October 10, 1936), 466.

72. John Dewey, "Foreword," in Charles Clayton Morrison, *The Outlawry of War* (Chicago: Willet, Clark and Colby, 1927), pp. vii-xxv.

73. Niebuhr, *Moral Man*, pp. 212-15.

74. Daniel J. Boorstein, *The Genius of American Politics* (Chicago: The University of Chicago Press, 1943), p. 159.

75. Reinhold Niebuhr, "Theology and Political Thought in the Western World," *The Ecumenical Review*, IX (April, 1957), 253-62.

76. Marvin Halverson, ed., *A Handbook of Christian Theology* (New York: The World Publishing Company, 1958), p. 141.

77. Niebuhr, "The Death of the President," p. 4.

78. *Ibid.*, p. 5.

79. Statement by Reinhold Niebuhr, personal interview, January 6, 1967.

80. Reinhold Niebuhr, "Draft of Americans for Democratic Action Statement on Foreign Policy," November 30, 1955. Reinhold Niebuhr Papers (MSS in the Library of Congress, Washington, D.C.), Container 1.

81. Personal letter to Mr. David C. Williams, Reinhold Niebuhr Papers (MSS in the Library of Congress, Washington, D.C.), Container 1.

82. Reinhold Niebuhr, "Greeting Message for Tenth Anniversary Convention Journal of ADA," Reinhold Niebuhr Papers (MSS in the Library of Congress, Washington, D.C.), Container 1.

83. *Supra*, pp. 37-40.

84. Kegley and Bretall, eds., *Reinhold Niebuhr*, p. 197.

85. *Ibid.*, p. 441.

86. Niebuhr's volume on democratic political theory suffers from his exaggeration of the historic dependence of democratic theory on optimistic estimates of man. Niebuhr's judgment that "the excessively optimistic estimates of human nature and of human history with which the democratic credo has been historically associated are a source of peril to a democratic society; . . ." is supported in *The Children of Light and the Children of Darkness* by reference to the history of political ideas. However, the volume ignores the contributions to democratic theory of Harrington, Montesquieu, and Madison. One may agree with Niebuhr's conclusion that a high degree of optimism is dangerous to democracy without agreeing that American democracy has historically been dependent upon such optimism. Niebuhr, *Children of Light*, p. xii.

87. Louis Hartz, *The Liberal Tradition in America* (New York: Harcourt, Brace and Company, 1955), p. 49.

88. *Ibid.*, p. 41.

89. Plamenatz, *Readings from Liberal Writers*, p. 14.

90. The claim that political theorists may be identified as liberal does not imply that such theorists are only liberals. "No liberal is only a liberal; for even in his public life, there are other sides to him which sometimes conflict with his liberalism." *Ibid.*, p. 37. The assertion that Niebuhr is a liberal is accurate given the understanding of liberal discussed here. However, the factors of his pragmatism, his particular version of Christian theology, his history of political activity, and his particular political context are needed to describe his political philosophy.

91. Niebuhr, *Man's Nature*, p. 21.

92. The relationship of Hans Morgenthau's thought to Reinhold Niebuhr's is discussed in Chapter VI.
93. Niebuhr, *Christian Realism*, p. 146. Italics mine.
94. Niebuhr, *Man's Nature*, p. 46. Italics mine.
95. *Ibid.*, p. 66.

Chapter VI. The United States' Role in International Politics Since World War II

1. See Kenneth W. Thompson, *Political Realism and the Crisis of World Politics* (Princeton: Princeton University Press, 1960), p. 23.
2. Quoted in Bingham, *Courage to Change*, p. 368.
3. John C. Bennett, *Christian Realism* (New York: Charles Scribner's Sons, 1941), p. 48.
4. Thompson, *Political Realism*, pp. 50-61.
5. Theodore R. Weber, "Dissentiment dans la Maison Niebuhr: la crise des normes au sein du réalisme politique chretien," trad. Ch. Junker, *Christianisme Social*, LXXI (Septembre-Décembre, 1963), 747-67.
6. *Ibid.*, p. 754.
7. Raymond Aron, *Peace and War* (Garden City: Doubleday and Company, 1966), p. 599.
8. Thompson, *Political Realism*, p. 50.
9. *Supra*, pp. 118-20.
10. Reinhold Niebuhr, "Plans for World Reorganization," *Christianity and Crisis*, II (October 19, 1942), 3-6.
11. John H. Herz has argued the case that the development of weaponry deserves to be regarded as a revolutionary change in international politics. "It will be the main thesis of this study that some of the factors which underlay the 'modern state system' as it emerged about three hundred years ago . . . have now, in our century and even within the lifetime of many of us, undergone such fundamental changes that the structure of international relations itself is different, or in the process of becoming different, and can no longer be interpreted exclusively in traditional terms." John H. Herz, *International Politics in the Atomic Age* (New York: Columbia University Press, 1962), p. 11.
12. J. Robert Oppenheimer, "Atomic Weapons and American Policy," *Foreign Affairs*, XXXI (1952-1953), 529.
13. *Supra*, pp. 119-20.
14. *Supra*, pp. 156-58.
15. Niebuhr's recognition of the role of the United States as both an imperialist and a status quo nation contrasts with Hans J. Morgenthau's division of a nation's foreign policies into one category or the other. "A nation whose foreign policy tends toward keeping power and not toward changing the distribution of power in its favor pursues a policy of the status quo. A nation whose foreign policy aims at acquiring more power than it actually has, through a reversal of existing power relations . . . pursues a policy of imperialism." Hans J. Morgenthau, *Politics Among Nations, The Struggle for Power and Peace* (New York: Alfred A. Knopf, 1962), p. 39. The difference between the two lies in the definition of imperialism, and they both agree that the United States is committed to preserving the present system while favoring adjustments within the system.

16. Niebuhr, *Man's Nature*, p. 82.
17. *Ibid.*, p. 83.
18. *Ibid.*, p. 82.
19. Reinhold Niebuhr, "The Social Myths in the 'Cold War,'" *Journal of International Affairs*, XXI (1967), 53.
20. *Infra*, pp. 189-93.
21. Reinhold Niebuhr, Lecture at Barnard College, New York City, April 15, 1963.
22. *Ibid.*
23. Niebuhr, *Nature and Destiny*, II, 257-58, 265.
24. Niebuhr, *Nature and Destiny*, I, 192.
25. Niebuhr, *Nature and Destiny*, II, 258; *Power Politics*, p. 156; *Moral Man*, pp. 6, 16.
26. E.g., Niebuhr, *Power Politics*, p. 123.
27. Reinhold Niebuhr, "Leaves from the Notebook of a War-Bound American," *The Christian Century*, LVI (November 15, 1939), 1405.
28. "Political power deserves to be placed in a special category, because it rests upon the ability to use and manipulate other forms of social power for the particular purpose of organizing and dominating the community." Niebuhr, *Nature and Destiny*, II, 263.
29. Harry Rex Davis, "The Political Philosophy of Reinhold Niebuhr" (unpublished Ph.D. dissertation, University of Chicago, 1951).
30. Niebuhr, *Moral Man*, pp. 7-8, 237; Niebuhr, *Children of Light*, pp. 62-63; Niebuhr, *Reflections*, p. 151.
31. Davis, "The Political Philosophy of Reinhold Niebuhr," p. 61.
32. Niebuhr, *Nature and Destiny*, II, 260.
33. *Ibid.*, p. 261.
34. Reinhold Niebuhr, "Politics and Economics," *Christianity and Society*, VII (Autumn, 1942), 7-8.
35. Davis, "The Political Philosophy of Reinhold Niebuhr," p. 56.
36. Niebuhr, *Moral Man*, p. 19.
37. Niebuhr, *Discerning the Signs of the Times*, p. 187.
38. Niebuhr, *Nature and Destiny*, II, 258.
39. Cf. Morgenthau, *Politics among Nations*, pp. 161-218.
40. Niebuhr, "American Power and World Responsibility," *Christianity and Crisis*, III (April 5, 1943), 2.
41. "The real contribution of Christian faith to problems of world organization lies not in imitating the utopianism of secular rationalists, adding only pious phrases to their dreams, but in encouraging men and nations to assume the responsibilities which inhere in the possession of power with as little pride as possible." Reinhold Niebuhr, "Power and Justice," *Christianity and Society*, VIII (Winter, 1942), 10.
42. *Ibid.*
43. Reinhold Niebuhr, "The Limits of American Power," *Christianity and Society*, XVII (Autumn, 1952), 5.
44. *The Structure of Nations and Empires*, published in 1958, was not available to the writers of early studies of Niebuhr. The otherwise quite solid research done by Robert C. Good at Yale in 1956 and Harry R. Davis at Chicago in 1951 in their dissertations suffers from having been written before Niebuhr's political philosophy was fully developed.
45. Reinhold Niebuhr, *The Structure of Nations and Empires* (New York: Charles Scribner's Sons, 1959), p. 1.

46. *Ibid.*, p. 2.

47. *Ibid.*, p. 3.

48. *Ibid.*, p. 206.

49. Niebuhr has repeatedly attacked the theory that capitalism is the cause of imperialism. Niebuhr, *Structure of Nations*, p. 23; *Christian Realism*, p. 57.

50. Niebuhr, *Structure of Nations*, pp. 202-3.

51. *Supra*, pp. 174-77.

52. Niebuhr, *Structure of Nations*, p. 215. See also pp. 25, 216, 293, and 298.

53. *Ibid.*, pp. 10-32.

54. *Ibid.*, p. 11.

55. Niebuhr, "Perils of American Power," pp. 90-96.

56. Niebuhr, *Structure of Nations*, p. 15.

57. Niebuhr's judgment as to the gravity of the situation in May, 1956, was prophetic, but his estimate in September, 1956, was mistaken. He then wrote, "It is quite apparent, however, that the Suez crisis will not lead to war and that Nasser will not seriously challenge the international stakes in the waterway." Reinhold Niebuhr, "The Crisis in the Suez Canal," *Christianity and Crisis*, XVI (September 17, 1956), 113.

58. "For the state of Israel is, whatever its limitations, a heartening adventure in nationhood. . . . Whatever our political or religious positions may be, it is not possible to withhold admiration, sympathy and respect for such an achievement." Reinhold Niebuhr, "New Hopes for Peace in the Middle East," *Christianity and Crisis*, XVI (May 28, 1956), 65. The other article urged the easing of restrictions on arms to Israel and utilized the metaphor of David and Goliath in describing Israel's relationship to its Arab opponents, a metaphor which was to recur in Niebuhr's writing on the Middle East. Reinhold Niebuhr, "Mideast Impasse: Is There a Way Out," *The New Leader*, XXXIX (June 4, 1956), 9-10.

59. Hans J. Morgenthau, "The Decline and Fall of American Foreign Policy," *The New Republic*, CXXXV (December 10, 1956), 11-16.

60. Ernest Lefever, *Ethics and United States Foreign Policy* (New York: Meridian Books, 1957), p. 109.

61. Morgenthau, "The Decline and Fall of American Foreign Policy," pp. 11-16.

62. "In one word, it is the philosophy of isolationism, adapted to the conditions of the mid-Twentieth Century." *Ibid.*, p. 11.

63. *Ibid.*, p. 12.

64. Lefever, *Ethics and United States Foreign Policy*, p.109.

65. Ernest Lefever, "Correspondence," *Christianity and Crisis*, XVII (February 18, 1957), 15.

66. Niebuhr, *Structure of Nations*, p. 15.

67. *Ibid.*

68. Reinhold Niebuhr, "The Situation in the Middle East," *Christianity and Crisis*, XVII (April 15, 1957), 43.

69. Kenneth Thompson, "Europe's Crisis and America's Dilemma," *Christianity and Crisis*, XVI (January 7, 1957), 184.

70. *Ibid.*, p. 188.

71. The editors referred to the dispute in an editorial note. "Foreign policy issues today, especially in relation to the Middle East, divide those who usually agree on social questions. . . . Usually we can predict what our friends will think about an issue if we know their general point of view—but not in the present situation. The Editorial Board of this journal finds itself in surprising disagreements." *Christianity and crisis*, XVI (January 7, 1957), 181.

72. Reinhold Niebuhr, "Seven Great Errors of U.S. Foreign Policy," *The New Leader*, XXXIX (December 24-31, 1956), 3-5.

73. There is also a tendency toward a rejection of Arab culture, seen in references to "the moribund cultures of the Islamic world." *Ibid.*, p. 4.

74. *Supra*, pp. 173-74.

75. Reinhold Niebuhr, "The Dilemma in China," *The Messenger*, XIV (January 4, 1949), 7.

76. Niebuhr, "The Limits of American Power," p. 5.

77. Reinhold Niebuhr, "Our Relations to Asia," *The Messenger*, XIX (June 1, 1954), 7.

78. Reinhold Niebuhr, "The Limits of Military Power," *The New Leader*, XXXVIII (May 30, 1955), 16-17.

79. *Ibid.*, p. 17.

80. Reinhold Niebuhr, "Can Democracy Work?" *The New Leader*, XLV (May 28, 1962), 9.

81. Reinhold Niebuhr, "Pretense and Power," *The New Leader*, XLVIII (March 1, 1965), 6-7.

82. *Ibid.*, p. 6.

83. Reinhold Niebuhr, "The Fateful Triangle," *The New Leader*, XLVIII (January 4, 1965), 18-20.

84. This term became characteristic of Niebuhr's talk about Vietnam in a manner similar to the role *sin, irony,* and *paradox* had played in his rhetoric.

85. Reinhold Niebuhr and Hans J. Morgenthau, "The Ethics of War and Peace in the Nuclear Age," *War/Peace Report*, VII (February, 1967), 3-7.

86. Niebuhr, "The Social Myths in the 'Cold War,'" p. 55.

87. Niebuhr and Morgenthau, "Ethics of War and Peace," pp. 4-5.

88. "This study of the perennial patterns, recurring problems, and varied but similar structures of the political order was undertaken with an eye on our present perplexities." Niebuhr, *Structure of Nations*, p. ix.

89. E.g., "Perhaps the most significant moral characteristic of a nation is its hypocrisy." Niebuhr, *Moral Man*, p. 95.

90. *Ibid.*, p. 108.

91. Niebuhr, "The Social Myths in the 'Cold War,'" pp. 54-55.

92. *Supra*, pp. 45-49.

93. This understanding of Niebuhr's Christology allows recognition of the insight of several of Niebuhr's critics, i.e., Christology does not control his politics or his Christology is in one sense "abstract." It leaves open the question whether it is possible or desirable to develop a consistently christological political ethic. J. L. Hromádka, for example, has written that he regards the differences between himself and Niebuhr on the international situation and contemporary history as due to their differences in Christology. He criticized Niebuhr's Christology: "I think, however, that Niebuhr's weak point (even in his political thought) was his excessively abstract, almost artificially created Christology." J. L. Hromádka, "America 1966," *Religion in Communist Dominated Areas*, VI (August 15/31, 1967), 125. Hromádka failed, however, to show the connections between their differences in Christology and their differences in politics. Hromádka apparently did not recognize the vast differences in their understandings of the process of politics which, for Niebuhr, would have been independent of christological concerns. From a continental perspective Niebuhr's Christology may have been deficient, but the very deficiency to which Hromádka points makes it impossible to ascribe to his Christology a controlling influence over his political thought.

94. Niebuhr, *Man's Nature*, pp. 30-83.

95. Davis and Good, eds., *Reinhold Niebuhr on Politics*, p. 330.

96. *Ibid.*, p. 328.

97. *Ibid.*, p. 327.

98. Landon, ed., *Reinhold Niebuhr: A Prophetic Voice*, p. 102.

99. *Ibid.*, p. 121.

100. Hans J. Morgenthau, "Another Great Debate," *The American Political Science Review*, XLVI (December, 1952), 984.

101. Morgenthau, *Politics Among Nations*, p. 11.

102. "Contrast, for example, his frequent assertion that 'politics is interest defined in terms of power' and a less quoted statement in which he says that 'political action can be defined as an attempt to realize moral values through the medium of politics, that is, power.' [Morgenthau, 'Another Great Debate,' *The American Political Science Review*, XLVI (December, 1952), 987]." Robert C. Good, "The National Interest and Political Realism: Niebuhr's 'Debate' with Morgenthau and Kennan," *The Journal of Politics*, XXII (1960), 613.

103. Niebuhr, *Structure of Nations*, p. 144.

104. Niebuhr, *Man's Nature*, p. 75.

105. Hans J. Morgenthau, *Scientific Man vs. Power Politics* (Chicago: The University of Chicago Press, 1946), p. 207.

106. Hans J. Morgenthau, *In Defense of the National Interest* (New York: Alfred A. Knopf, 1951), p. 242.

107. Davis and Good, eds., *Reinhold Niebuhr on Politics*, p. 333.

108. Isolating the differences between Reinhold Niebuhr and Hans J. Morgenthau should not obscure their basic agreement. Niebuhr has said recently, "I wouldn't say that the views of Morgenthau and myself are 'somewhat different.' We basically have common ideas with certain peripheral differences." Niebuhr, "The Ethics of War and Peace," p. 3.

109. He retired from Union in 1960 at the required retirement age of 68, he offered one course at Union in 1961, moved on to teach at Harvard in 1962, and back to Morningside Heights to Barnard College in 1963. From 1964-1968 he returned to Union to offer a seminar in social ethics, first at the Seminary and then in his apartment on Riverside Drive overlooking the Hudson River.

110. Niebuhr and Sigmund, *Democratic Experience*.

111. *Ibid.*, p. vi.

112. *Ibid.*, p. 9.

113. *Ibid.*, p. 92.

114. *Ibid.*, p. 3.

115. *Ibid.*, p. 73.

116. *Ibid.*, p. 184.

117. *Supra*, p. 144.

118. Niebuhr and Sigmund, *Democratic Experience*, pp. 151-52.

119. *Ibid.*, p. 146.

120. *Ibid.*, p. 148.

121. Helder Camara, "From Dichotomy to Integration," *The Christian Century*, LXXXVI (December 10, 1969), p. 1574.

122. Carl Oglesby and Richard Shaull, *Containment and Change* (New York: The Macmillan Company, 1967), pp. 83-97.

123. Niebuhr and Sigmund, *Democratic Experience*, p. 85.

124. Ronald H. Stone, "An Interview with Reinhold Niebuhr," *Christianity and Crisis,* XXIX (March 17, 1969), p. 51.
125. Letter to Ronald H. Stone (May 27, 1969).
126. Seymour Melman, "How to Cut the Military Budget by $54 Billion," *Commonweal,* XCI (November 28, 1969), p. 274. Cf. Seymour Melman, *Our Depleted Society* (New York: Dell Publishing Company, 1965).
127. The evidence of his influence abroad is hard to estimate. It appears to be greatest in the English-speaking world and in the Netherlands, though his books have been translated into Spanish, Portuguese, Japanese, and other languages. Several of his major works have been translated into German, but his influence in Germany has not compared with that of the German and Swiss theologians. Dietz Lange has written in his study of Niebuhr "[dass] Reinhold Niebuhr ausserhalb Amerikas und Englands immer noch wenig bekannt ist." *Christlicher Glaube und soziale Probleme* (Gütersloh: Gütersloher Verlagshaus Gerd Mohn, 1964), p. 11.
128. E.g., Meyer, *The Protestant Search.*
129. Robertson, ed., *Applied Christianity.*
130. E.g., William J. Wolf in Kegley and Bretall, eds., *Reinhold Niebuhr,* pp. 248-49.
131. *Supra,* pp. 167-69.
132. *Supra,* pp. 167-69.

Chapter VII. The Relevance of Faith

1. Reinhold Niebuhr, "Foreword," in Donald P. Cutler, ed., *The Religious Situation: 1968* (Boston: Beacon Press, 1968), p. xi.
2. Ronald H. Stone, ed., *Faith and Politics* (New York: George Braziller, 1968), pp. 12-13.
3. Reinhold Niebuhr, "Toward New Intra-Christian Endeavors," *The Christian Century,* LXXXVI (December 31, 1969), 1662-67.
4. Robertson, ed., *Applied Christianity,* p. 29.
5. Ursula M. Niebuhr, "The Testing of Our Calling," in Martin Caldwell, ed., *Lift Up Your Hearts* (New York: Morehouse-Gorham Company, 1956), pp. 35-53.
6. Robertson, ed., *Applied Christianity,* pp. 57-63.
7. Niebuhr, *Leaves,* p. 90.
8. "Faith as the Sense of Meaning in Human Existence" and "The Truth in Myths," in Stone, ed., *Faith and Politics,* pp. 3-31.
9. *Ibid.,* pp. 67-76.
10. *Ibid.,* p. 73.
11. W. D. Davies, a remark made at the Pittsburgh Festival of the Gospels, April 10, 1970.
12. Kegley and Bretall, eds., *Reinhold Niebuhr.*
13. Stone, ed., *Faith and Politics,* pp. 3-13.
14. Thomas J. Altizer and William Hamilton, *Radical Theology and the Death of God* (New York: Bobbs-Merrill, 1966).
15. Stone, ed., *Faith and Politics,* p. 4.
16. *Ibid.,* p. 5.
17. Niebuhr, *Faith and History,* p. 103.
18. Niebuhr, *Nature and Destiny,* I, 128.

19. Reinhold Niebuhr, "Our Dependence Is on God," *The Christian Century*, LXXI (September 1, 1954), 1034.
20. Quoted in Niebuhr, *Nature and Destiny*, I, 127.
21. Stone, "An Interview," p. 52.
22. Walter LaFeber, *America, Russia, and the Cold War, 1945-1966* (New York: John Wiley and Sons, 1967), p. 40.
23. Niebuhr usually writes of two regulative principles including only liberty and equality. This is true because during much of his career it seemed as if the struggle for tolerance had been won. The writing in *Nature and Destiny*, II, 220-43, places tolerance in the center of his thought and reinforces the view that it deserves a place with liberty and equality as a regulative principle.
24. E.g., "Niebuhr's writings made such a profound impression on me and proved so valuable in my work in Latin America." Richard Shaull, "Christian Realism: A Symposium," *Christianity and Crisis*, XXVIII (August 5, 1968), 177.
25. Reinhold Niebuhr, "The Problem of a Protestant Social Ethic," *Union Seminary Quarterly Review*, XV (November, 1959), 5.
26. Jürgen Moltmann, *Theology of Hope* (New York: Harper & Row, 1967), and *Religion, Revolution and the Future* (New York: Charles Scribner's Sons, 1969).
27. Rubem A. Alves, *A Theology of Human Hope* (Washington: Corpus Books, 1969), p. 181.
28. Harvey Cox, *The Secular City* (New York: The Macmillan Company, 1965), and *The Feast of Fools* (Cambridge: Harvard University Press, 1969).
29. II. Richard Niebuhr, "The Grace of Doing Nothing," *The Christian Century*, XLIX (March 23, 1932), 378-80; Reinhold Niebuhr, "Must We Do Nothing?" *The Christian Century*, XLIX (March 30, 1932), 415-17; H. Richard Niebuhr, "The Only Way into the Kingdom of God," *The Christian Century*, XLIX (April 6, 1932), 447.
30. *Ibid.*, p. 417.
31. *Ibid.*, p. 447.
32. Niebuhr, "Our Dependence Is on God," p. 1037.
33. Niebuhr, *Nature and Destiny*, II, 285-86.
34. *Ibid.*, p. 207.
35. *Ibid.*, p. 156.
36. Reinhold Niebuhr, "The Presidency and the Irony of American History," *Christianity and Crisis*, XXX (April 13, 1970), 72.
37. Reinhold Niebuhr, "The King's Chapel and the King's Court," *Christianity and Crisis*, XXIX (August 4, 1969).
38. Letter to Ronald H. Stone (April 27, 1971).

INDEX